THE FACE
OF
WAR

THE FACE

OF

WAR

Reflections on
Men and Combat

by
Jean Larteguy

translated by
Beth de Bilio

The Bobbs-Merrill Company, Inc.
Indianapolis • New York

La Guerre Nue by Jean Lartéguy, copyright © 1976, Editions
 Stock
English-language translation © 1979, The Bobbs-Merrill Company,
 Inc.
All rights reserved, including the right of reproduction in whole
 or in part in any form
Published by The Bobbs-Merrill Company, Inc.
Indianapolis   New York

Designed by Lou Keach
Manufactured in the United States of America

First printing

Library of Congress Cataloging in Publication Data
Lartéguy, Jean, 1920–
  The face of war.

  Translation of La guerre nue.

  1. Lartéguy, Jean, 1920– —Biography. 2. War—History—
20th century. 3. Authors, French—20th century—Biography. I.
Title.
PQ2672.A73Z46413   843'.9'14 [B]   79-2049
ISBN 0-672-52350-7

CONTENTS

"Neither revolution nor war exists to please itself."
ANDRÉ MALRAUX

INTRODUCTION

I wrote in the preface of one of my first books: "Now an unarmed civilian, I have been through the wars. More or less well equipped, I served as a soldier in some of them. Later, as a journalist, I described a certain number of them—whether they were classical, whether they were subversive or revolutionary, in what ways they were considered just by some or detestable by others. I, too, should be allowed, then, to speak of war. . . ."

In 1940 I personally experienced our collapse. A little chocolate soldier, I retreated from the Loire to the Garonne without ever "letting fall my rifle on the field of honor." My rifle! It was as ridiculously long as a fishing rod and caused a great deal of laughter among the German Panzer units. They passed me on the road to Bordeaux. I was all alone, and they didn't even take me prisoner! Provoked, I decided then to go on with the war in whatever way I could, this decision leading me first to the nine months I spent in Spanish prisons—my time of gestation.

Then there followed the hard school of the commandos, of the reconquest of France, of the occupation of Germany. Afterwards I tried and failed to become a mercenary in Iran, then went to Korea, where I was injured.

I became a journalist, that privileged spectator of war, and lived for twenty-five years in its shadow. In Indochina, in the Maghreb, in black Africa, in Latin America, in Israel, in Libya, and in all the Middle East. Only yesterday I witnessed the fall of Saigon.

I would like to speak of war without deception, a difficult thing to do. I haven't the least desire to write a learned piece of work crammed with facts, with figures, and with references; even less with philosophical or political considerations, which permit one to condemn war while at the same time assert that it is inevitable, if not necessary. I want only to relate a series of anecdotes, to share some reflections which came to me as I thought about war, as I took part in it, as I observed it.

I engaged in war because of the force of circumstances, because of the accidental fortunes of life, and because I detested the sound of German boots on the streets of our city. Afterwards I made my living from war: with my articles, then my books, in which I've described war without finding any particular satisfaction. One really should read them again in order to judge them.

I have been called the bard of war because of my expressions of affection for those who suffered or died in war. But such expressions don't mean I like war.

As with all those who are war correspondents for a long period of time, I always naïvely hoped I could discover the remedy, the magic herb that could rid us of war. We correspondents become like those doctors who, after having seen all their research fail, continue to haunt the cancer wards, always hoping that some accident, some overturned test tube—who knows what else?—will hand them the secret of the disease.

Can one accuse the doctor who persists against all reason in studying an incurable disease of loving that disease? Of being its bard?

I've not discovered the miracle potion. It doesn't exist.

For Gaston Bouthoul, "great patron" of war, in the clinical sense of the term, war isn't a sickness; rather, it is a curse. First, when people were polytheistic, war was the earthly reflection of the gigantic contest between the gods. Then, when civilizations were preponderantly monotheistic, war became the judgment of God. Finally, when the one God, in his turn, died in agony, war was transformed into "the instrument of destiny charged with accomplishing the mysterious designs or revelations of history." Thus we arrived at the Marxist conception of war, which bears the same stamp of religiosity and fetishism that the preceding conceptions did. And the only way ever to combat war was to try to avert it. That isn't easy.

War isn't without imagination. She is capable of altering herself, of tearing away one mask and replacing it with another for the benefit of the pacifists, who for centuries have confined themselves to their repetition of Christ's words: "Thou shalt not kill." War knows how to veil her face when she must move contrary to that injunction.

With cruel humor, war sometimes delights in forcing these same pacifists into employing her jargon and her methods—when, for instance, they organize themselves as "champions of peace," but are ready, in order to make peace prevail, to use war's weapons to eliminate all who want war.

At the time of Jaurès, the political left was pacifist and antimilitarist. The right wing dreamed of revenge, fixed their eyes on the blue lines of the Vosges, and applauded the lines of our poor soldiers—our soldiers, not missing a single button from their leggings, only their machine guns, which might have saved their lives. Both the left and the right, plus the English, the French, the Germans, and the Bulgarians, *all* went to replenish by the millions one of the largest charnel houses in history.

In 1938 there was Munich. Those who wanted peace at any price were discovered too late to be the real fomenters of war.

The Soviet Union, which for the most part sets the tone for pacifist movements, has the largest army in the world. By the use of her armed forces she has hewn for herself an immense empire, and when one of her European "colonies" wants to free itself of her protection, the red army sets that colony on the right track, that of subjection. Pacifists are flattered and decorated so long as they protest against the American intervention in Southeast Asia, but if they are Russian and protest the intervention of Russian tanks in Prague, they find themselves in detention camps or psychiatric asylums. Truth on one side of the iron curtain, error on the other.

What does that man say to us who is considered by most of the left wing to be at the extreme left, Mao Tse-tung?

"There is only one way to abolish war: oppose war with war; oppose revolutionary war with counter-revolutionary war; oppose a national revolution with a counternational revolution; oppose a class revolution with a counterclass revolution. . . . All the wars of history can be divided into two categories: just wars and unjust wars. We are for just wars against unjust wars. . . ."

It couldn't be clearer.

Our old Europe behaved before the war as before death. She veiled her face and kept saying: "Don't speak of it to me. It's too horrible." Clinging to her last remaining privileges, she no longer even envisaged fighting for her liberties. And the pacifists were like oxen being led to the slaughter. Resigned to disappearing and so prepared by her subjection, Europe didn't do even the little the Romans did before their fall—try to remain alive by paying mercenaries to defend them.

I simply record. Nothing more. But I can't refrain from trembling before the wink of the eye war directs at me. It seems to me I hear her say:

"You poor ignoramus, you've seen how I have won them over again. I reign throughout the world now. With impunity and at will I can change camps and flags. No one notices and no one protests. I am the good war of the left, after having been the holy war of the right. Excellent operation! My troops of the right have already worn themselves down and believe in nothing any longer. Tomorrow I will have all the Third World behind me as well."

This book—rather, let us say this rambling conversation—I would like to be a settling of accounts with war. But with myself as well, who sometimes served war and who has taken such a long time to fully understand what has lain beneath all its various disguises.

I was born with a taste for victory—it's simply an affair of the chromosomes. But I haven't been corrupted. I've defended those ramparts that were toppling, helped where I could, though I was powerless and sickened, during the fall of rotten cities, of despairing countries. In my nostrils was always the odor of the end of civilization: a mixture of burning wood, of decaying flesh, of rape, and of excrement, all, still today, the odors of war for me.

For the first time I am not writing this down. I am speaking into a dictaphone, something I haven't tried before. Priests of religions that no longer really exist or of those religions that still survive for a little while chant their prayers in high voices to exorcise evil. I am therefore going to do as they do. I want so much to exorcise war.

I commence.

THE FACE
OF
WAR

PART ONE

WAR
I WAS TOLD ABOUT

I belong, as you know, to those families of poor mountain peasants whose names are found inscribed on war memorials, but not in history books.

I was ten years old, perhaps eleven, when I discovered war.

I was raised by my grandmother, Marie Osty, whom I always called Mamé. She lived in an old house in the Baraquette section of Aumont-Aubrac in Upper Lozère. She knew neither how to read nor how to write and signed her name with a cross. From morning till night she sang old ballads, ditties, and especially hymns.

As she aged, her voice became harsh, trembling, and pathetic, a voice that sounded like an old wax phonograph record, badly scratched and worn from having been played so often. I remember her voice better than I do her face. And I remember her hands, which were gnarled, deformed by rheumatism and the hard work of the land. She had not had an easy life.

When she was still a child she'd been hired out as a shepherdess, and one day she'd had to fight off a wolf with no weapon other than her staff to protect her flock.

More often than not she spoke to me in patois, which I still love. It was forbidden in school and in church.

Very pious, Mamé made her sister Julie, who was as lazy as a dormouse, go with her to first Mass every morning. Each morning, even in winter, I was awakened about six o'clock by this dialogue:

"Get up, Julie!"

"Oh, Marie, it's too cold!"

And you could have said that again! The water would be frozen solid in the washbasin in my room, and the windows would be covered with frost. It must have been between fifteen and twenty degrees below zero, and the wind would be blowing in squalls and swirling the snow around in the air.

My aunt would go back to sleep, but a few minutes later:

"Get up, Julie! You're not going to miss Mass. You're not going to disgrace us that way. What would Monsieur le Curé say?"

Poor Julie would follow Marie to Mass and very devoutly continue her nap in the glacial and deserted church.

Introibo ad altarem Dei. . . .

When the two sisters returned, it was time for me to get up. After splashing a little water on the tip of my nose, I would slip into my clogs, drink a bowl of milk mixed with a chicory brew, and go outside to have my ears turn red from the cold.

During vacation, when the house was filled with cassocks, I had to serve Mass. I knew it by heart and in Latin, too, and for my labors I used to be given twenty sous.

I was taught by the monks at the parochial school. It was a large gray building next to the blacksmith, or "fabrou," as we called him. His name was Grollier, and he wore a big leather apron. His son Urbain was my age. Urbain was shot after the war at the time of the Liberation. I don't really know why.

With the help of rulers laid heavily across our fin-

gers, Brother Mijoule and Brother Savajols taught us
the multiplication tables and the provinces with their
prefects and subprefects. The balance of the time we
scoured the countryside for something to do. We
scrambled up trees to search for birds' nests; we filled
bottles with minnows; we built huts in the woods; or
we went to fight the pupils from the secular school.
We would wait until they came out of school and
then attack them on the street; sometimes they would
attack us.

We would begin by insulting one another, calling one
another "boursettes"[1] and accusing one another of having only the most insignificant testicles. Our fathers,
naturally, had none at all and had to have help to produce us. From such generalities we passed quickly to
particulars, making up rhymes to insult the adversary
of our choice. Such poetry was always suited to the
stages of the fever of our war with each other. I remember one of the pieces. It couldn't be spoken, but
was sung on three notes like a ritornello, and would always completely infuriate poor Etienne:

> *Estienno boudeïno*
> *La pipo traoucado*
> *Lou bure es foundut*
> *Estienno es foundut.*[2]

Heavy artillery fire always followed this bit of poetry.
Our missiles were for the most part rocks inside snow-
balls, or round stones sent flying from slingshots fash-
ioned of supple twigs.

Eventually we would engage in hand-to-hand combat.
We used fists, feet, wooden shoes. Sometimes we used

1. The word is not really translatable into English. The closest we
can come is "small sacs," presumably referring to testicles, which
doesn't completely convey the French insult. (Translator's note.)
2. This is difficult to translate in English rhyme, but the essence is
that poor Etienne is a sissy little student who is both impotent and
infertile, the language in the original being somewhat less delicate.
(Translator's note.)

sticks cut from hazel trees and sharpened to points. The encounters with the enemy were never long. We employed rapid attacks by small groups of three or four who, when their attack was completed, retired quickly to the position of their major forces, to be replaced by another attack group. Playing the role of the O.N.U.[3]—this was the period of the League of Nations—and with just about as much effectiveness, some of the townswomen, attracted by the uproar of our battle, would shout at us from their windows: "Aren't you ashamed of yourselves, you little wretches?" They tried to exercise some discipline over us by threatening to tell our parents everything they saw.

The side that beat the first retreat was, of course, the side that lost. But the losers never failed to declare stoutly and with conviction that the winners had cheated—for example, by using weapons forbidden by the rules of warfare, such as cow dung.

Girls, who were odd creatures to us and whom we barely put up with, took their part in our combat from a distance. On both sides we boys were in agreement that they should be forbidden to enter into the melee. On their part they agreed that we were all stupid and deserved ten times the punishment that awaited us in our homes. Victors or vanquished, punishment was meted out to all of us for our torn clothes, our muddy condition, our blackened eyes.

All of us, too, had discovered for ourselves the rites of war: take into full account all the wrongs done you and insults directed at you; fight from a safe distance by the use of various missiles; employ rapid and effective commando raids; abandon the territory to the victor.

Some of us went to parochial school as some went to lay or public school: either by tradition or by obligation. Generally speaking, economics required the poor stu-

3. *Organisation des Nations Unies* (United Nations Organization). (Translator's note.)

dents to be largely among the ranks of the skullcap, as it was mostly obligatory for the sons of the constabulary to go to lay school; and traditional for the sons of the political left, who no longer remembered why they were left. The origin was probably the Religious Wars— the Protestant wave that had washed over the land and devastated Mende, and the reflux of Catholics who then formed population islands in the stream. The old beliefs were lost, but not the old feelings of a divided community.

At various times in our childhood wars I had the honor of commanding the parochial cohort. A postman's son, strapping, broad-shouldered, foul-mouthed, commanded the lay troops. He was more than a little annoyed some years later in Algeria to be placed under my command, he a sergeant major, I a junior probationary officer. When I came across him again, he was a colonel, but happily for me, he was unable at that time to take the revenge he longed for. I'd given up the uniform.

When we were fifteen or sixteen years old, these confrontations between those of the parochial school and those of the lay school, between the "reds" and the "whites," were transformed into territorial conflicts, the boys of one village, whatever their individual labels might be, uniting themselves against the outsiders of another village. We waged pitched battles with the young bloods of Malbouzon, of Nasbinals, of Saint-Chély-d'Apcher. As with the Trojan War, the pretext of our wars was always a girl—in our case, usually a girl whom a boy from another village had invited to a dance. That Helen of Lozère of the rosy cheeks, of the awkward manners; that Helen who still smelled like whey and whom we didn't really give a damn about, whoever she happened to be at the time. She was simply part of the territory over which we waged war, part of the claims we appropriated and which we were obligated to defend.

I imagine Konrad Lorenz[4] must have had a childhood as quarrelsome as mine. Not Freud.

But let's get to that discovery I made about war—not war as we played at war, but the real war—when one summer afternoon I opened Pandora's box.

Mamé! Never having known anything but poverty, she was constantly tormented by the fear of greater want. Without really needing to, she went among the neighbors' fields to gather wheat left behind by the reapers, or she went to the communal woods to gather pinecones for the fire. She bought meat at the butcher's no more than three times a year—for the special holidays: the village fair, the fifteenth of August,[5] and Christmas. We lived all year long on the one pig that was slaughtered before winter set in. The occasion of its death was a fête, a bloody and joyous revelry, to which all our neighbors were invited.

On that day Marie Osty showed great generosity, filling all the wineglasses and herself serving the aperitif. Always she was sad the next day at all the money spent, and she would institute a program of limitations and restrictions of which I was always the first victim. She would cut off my pocket money.

For Christmas I was usually entitled to only one orange, which became in my eyes the golden apple from the garden of the Hesperides. I thought it was magic and didn't dare touch it. I was plagued with a lack of any pocket money and lost face before my comrades because I wasn't able, as they were, to buy anything at Mme Bernade's grocery: those boxes of chocolates, a brand of messy licorice, and colored candies which

4. Konrad Z. Lorenz, author of *King Solomon's Ring, Man Meets Dog,* and *On Aggression,* is one of the outstanding naturalists of our day. Having studied in New York and Vienna and received degrees in medicine and philosophy, he became director of the Max Planck Institute for Behavioral Physiology in Bavaria. He has written widely on the territorial imperative and has shed revolutionary new light on the aggressive drive, the "killer instinct," held in common by both man and animal. (Translator's note.)
5. The Feast of the Assumption of the Virgin Mary. (Translator's note.)

came in long glass tubes, all half buried in the store's sawdust.

Suffering over my own poverty, I began to steal.

Mamé didn't understand banks or safes. She hid her money behind the sheets in the linen closet, in "Valda" lozenge boxes, at the back of the buffet; and because she was so absent-minded, she would forget where she hid the money. Each week I filched five francs from her, which allowed me to play the gentleman among my friends.

One day while in search of money I discovered a key in a hiding place, the key to my Uncle Fernand's room. My grandmother only opened that room on special occasions. Then, she would go in and change the sheets and the doilies before the arrival of persons of distinction who had been invited to our house for lunch on the Feast of the Assumption, a time when all our tribe gathered. Profiting by one such occasion, I was able to sneak a glance into the room. I glimpsed a tall bed bathed in somber shadows and covered in a deep red eiderdown, a washstand, a glass-fronted bookcase, and a wall covered with weapons grouped ornamentally: guns, swords, bayonets, pointed German helmets, French helmets. Flanking them were two portraits in oaken frames: a lieutenant of the mountain light infantry in a beret, and an infantry sergeant in a blue peaked cap—my father and my Uncle Emile.

I longed to know more about them. When I found the key to the room I pocketed it, and one afternoon when my grandmother had gone to assist our neighbor with something, I slipped into my Uncle Fernand's room and double-locked the door.

My first rendezvous with war, and already it had taken on the allure of a clandestine meeting, as with a girl. And with the same fear seizing me by the throat.

As opposed to Uncle Lucien, my mother's brother, who'd left his bones in the mud of the Argonne, Uncle Fernand, my father's brother, had died of meningitis in his bed at fifteen years of age. He'd always seemed too

intelligent for his age. Everyone generally agreed that
such was not the case with me and that I risked nothing in that regard.

Because of the military décor of that room, I was certain that it was he who had died at the front instead of
Uncle Lucien.

In deciphering the names of the war victims on the
monuments to the dead from Aumont or from Saint-
Sauveur-de-Peyres, where we came from, I was always
surprised not to discover Uncle Fernand's name on the
long list of Ostys.

Before proceeding further with my account, it would
perhaps be good if I spoke a little of my family. My
place in this history can thus be better understood, as
can my reaction when I entered for the first time into
that sanctuary of war.

In those days the people of our mountains had
many children. It was *all* they had. The land certainly
wasn't worth much. We used to say that the crows
equipped themselves with feedbags before crossing our
land, and the rabbits carried bundles of hay on their
backs. The eldest son of a family retained whatever
land there was, and proudly and miserably lived
there. His brothers shifted for themselves as best they
could. They "went down" to the south of France, or
they "went up" to Paris. In the south they became
"hillbillies"—the poor peasants who worked at sea-
sonal jobs, the itinerant farm workers, such as grape
pickers. Hardened to labor and affliction, they con-
tented themselves with little and saved their meager
earnings sou by sou. In Paris they were charcoal ped-
dlers, café waiters, floor polishers, rubbish men. Before
the Arabs, before the Spanish and the Portuguese and
the rest, they were the "Third World." But they were
possessed by a fierce desire to return to their mountain country with enough savings to buy a patch of
ground and three or four cows. This is what my grandfather did.

In those days our people had few options beyond those I've mentioned. Many joined the army; others became priests or monks; the girls became nuns. My grandfather had eleven brothers and sisters. Except for the two eldest boys, all became priests or nuns. The girls went to Carmel at Valence, where they were kept at those tasks relegated to underlings because they had no dowry. Even so, one of them eventually became Mother Superior. The other girls became Little Sisters of the Poor. One of my uncles became a priest at Saint-Jacques-du-Haut-Pas in Paris; another became Superior-General of the Fathers of the Blessed Sacrament in Rome. Even as servants of God, these tough children of granite had the ambition and the taste for distinction.

Although he was a younger brother, my grandfather remained in menial labor rather than go into the clergy. He had no liking for studies. In Paris he polished floors; then he peddled charcoal on rue Washington, where he earned enough to return to his Lozère.

He acquired four small plots of land scattered at the four corners of the community: the *Champ de la Pèse,* where all the icy winds gathered; the *Mouneïre,* which was overrun with gorse and scrub pines; the *Siagne,* ankle-deep in water; and the *Cambe,* which was my favorite spot. A small brook flowed through it, and there were trout to be found in the hollows beneath the banks, small black ones we could catch simply by rolling up our sleeves and grabbing for them among the reeds. All that no more than three or four kilometers from the house. It was my daily task to take the cows to the fields in the morning and to round them up in the evening, always remembering not to hurry them lest their milk sour.

During the winter my grandfather made furniture in the workshop next to the stable, keeping himself warm with a fire of wood chips. He was modest and abstemious, spoke little, and made few friends, one of them being his cousin Casimir, who resembled him. Then one day my grandfather died, carrying with him all his secrets. I'd really caught only a glimpse of this enigmatic figure, son of that equally mysterious woman who'd been called the "Césarde de Peyrevioles," who had so much nobility and allure and who lived comfortably in a supernatural world peopled with strange noises, apparitions, objects that moved by themselves. Parapsychology owes her a lot. Calling her to mind, a later Osty, a doctor, founded the Metaphysical Institute.

But I'm straying from my subject. Forgive me, for I'm here to speak of war, and I forgot that for a moment.

There was, then, Uncle Fernand's room, with its closed-in smell, its odor of ripe plums, of dried mushrooms, and of wax. And there I was, paralyzed with fear before the pictures of two soldiers.

In a drawer I discovered a pistol, some bullets, and a dagger with a very large blade and, of even more interest, with a groove running down the middle to let the blood run out. The dagger had an American grip. I learned later that this dagger, with its keenly honed blade, was the favorite tool of the mopper-uppers of the trenches.

Under a glass dome there was the Legion of Honor, the Military Cross with palm branches and stars, some other medals of lesser importance, and a red shoulder braid.

I stood on a chair to touch the crossed swords with leather tassels hanging from their hilts, the hooked bayonets, the heavy Mauser whose breech had begun to rust.

There were a pair of binoculars, a map case, a battle plan with latitudes and longitudes by then hardly discernible and from which I read the names of villages, of hamlets, of places whose names no longer held any significance for me: Jouy, Ostel, Broye, the plain of Vauclerc, Chemin des Dames. In a fawn-colored holster there was a regulation pistol, its clip engaged. I imagined my father, sword in one hand, pistol in the other, campaign medals caught by the wind, charging the Jerries, just as I'd seen in a print in a copy of *L'Illustration.* On the very back shelves of the library, I happily found a complete collection of the publication for the years 1914–18.

From a round iron box I lifted out something that looked like a pig's snout, the snout broadened by heavy canvas straps and giving off an awful odor of chemicals. It was a gas mask.

I also discovered five black boxes containing sheets of glass on which the same image was twice reproduced, and an apparatus used to throw the images into relief—a stereoscope. I slipped one of the sheets of glass into the stereoscope and turned toward the window, where a ray of sunshine had found its way between the slats of the window shutters. I focused the apparatus—and then froze in terror at what I saw.

I saw a trench oozing with mud; some soldiers, themselves blocks of mud, loaded down with backpacks and with canteens, with helmets covering their balaclava caps, and with bayonets affixed to their rifles. Against the trench walls were small ladders which allowed the soldiers to mount the parapet to launch their assaults. Two of the soldiers lay flat, arms doubled under them, noses in the mud. Dead. A hand stuck up out of the ground—the fleshless hand of a body apparently just buried by shells.

Despite its nets and screens of branches and reeds, the trench had fallen in for the most part. The soldiers wore puttees, no boots, and their shoes sank deep into the mire. Their rolled blankets were held by crossbelts made of horse harnesses, and their packs, having settled snugly around their waists, looked like life belts.

In the middle of them was my father, bearded like the others and as dirty, his back bent and a pistol in his hand. His sword was relegated, probably, to the supply stores, with other appurtenances fit only for parades.

There was no resemblance to the proud lieutenant of the light infantry wearing the black beret who had transfixed me from the height of his framed picture.

On those plates of sepia-colored glass were inscribed all the horrors of the world.

Next came a battlefield: a razed forest with nothing remaining but a few stumps. It was an upheaval of earth plowed by mines and shells to prepare for some gigantic planting, with the bodies of the soldiers as the fertilizer. They were sprawled everywhere in every position, bundles of mangled, trampled flesh, bodies contorted, or some spread full length with arms crossed, heads always bare, the helmets having rolled away a little.

On another plate was a parapet of the dead, a veritable wall of them, Germans and French mingled together. Medical orderlies wearing the Red Cross badge on their armlets picked them over as at a linen sale— corpses that had been men like you and me, men who had loved girls, who had read Goethe and Heine, Musset and Verlaine, and who, when they looked at the stars, posed the question, what is really up there beyond? Men who lacked altogether the ability to understand what happens here on earth, all that is horrible, unbearable.

"Happy the ripened grain, the mown wheat,"[6] wrote Péguy—though in Uncle Fernand's room I didn't know him yet, discovering him later under the tutelage of the good fathers, the Jesuits of Saint-Francis-de-Sales at Evreux. Have you seen that crop we harvested in the mud and the snow? Among the barbed wire and the shellholes? Are they so gathered for God's granary in heaven?

Another plate. A lookout, crouched low and looking

6. Charles Péguy (1873–1914), French poet, at first a socialist, later a convert to orthodox religion and a French nationalist. His work consists chiefly of long mystical epics in free verse, notably *The Mystery of the Charity of Jeanne d'Arc* (1913) and *Eve*. He was killed in the battle of the Marne in World War I. (Translator's note.)

through a wooden periscope at a vast white plain that stretched downward from the trench and over which shells were bursting. With their white smoke trails, they marked the position of the adversary's lines. Ratholes emerged from the back of the trench; logs shored up the entrance. The earth had been upheaved and was deeply furrowed, crumbled by the explosions. Everything was dirty, gray. A single exception: the weapons, whose breeches shone in the surrounding gloom. All the faces were gaunt with fatigue; the heads looked like those of the living dead. With great care one soldier rolled a cigarette with fingers that were thickly swollen. A cigarette for the condemned.

Still another plate. A narrow communication trench wound its serpentine way through a forest where there remained some skeletons of trees that lifted their mutilated members toward a snowy sky, sandbags forming a burrow that held a man. Living? Dead? And a cadaver halfway out of his hole of clay, arm stiffened, a wedding ring on his finger. And that long procession of phantoms or penitents that filed past him, blankets spread like capes over their backs. A shellhole fitted with shelves on which grenades were stacked. A machine gun that pushed its muzzle out between two sandbags. A mutilated corpse. An overturned camp kettle, the nearby man on cook detail having just died. . . .

How is it that these men were left to lie around as rotting cadavers during that war? Did no one get around to collecting them?

And there—Verdun. Everything had been leveled, rolled flat. In the distance, lost in the haze and smoke, a kind of squat funeral mound: the fort of Vaux. Seven hundred thousand dead, French and Germans, just to take and then to retake some barren and frozen acres of land.

And here—the Eparges. Some grayish saddles of land pocked with mole holes where men hid. Standing in water, they smoked their pipes and, looking bored, waited for their deaths.

It is really too bad it's no longer there—the Eparges!
We could draw up some beautiful balance sheets there,
evaluate our achievements and losses!

I observe that I've used the jargon of today, applied
to the war those reassuring terms of commerce and
technology. You've heard of the undertaker at Place
Saint-Sulpice—Roblot, I believe it is—who dubbed
himself a "thanatologist"? Always the same procedure!
Always resort to trickery. Always play the ostrich! Always make the war vanish or change it into something
else—and with it all the deaths, all the full horror of
it—by a little sleight of hand. One has only to call a
mortician a thanatologist, and a butchery a balance
sheet. That makes it more respectable, makes it
scientific!

Forty years later I looked at the plates of glass
again. And now that I've acquired a certain experience
with war, I must tell you: It isn't only the horror of it
which strikes me, but the futility, the uselessness of
that kind of confrontation; the inconceivable stupidity
of those who directed that war; their total lack of
imagination.

Two armies dug themselves in opposite each other
and massacred each other in short order for a few
acres of land without a single strategic value. They
wore themselves out, they bled themselves white, victory coming briefly to whichever side could supply cattle for the slaughter for the longest period of time.
What the German general Falkenhayn called *Blut
Pumpe*—the blood pump. There was no consideration
whatever of maneuvering their armies. Just the pig-
headed facing off of the armies of two major nations.

I discussed it one day with Bigeard, at that time a
colonel in Saïda, Algeria. He said to me:

"What a mess, that war of '14! Have the foot soldiers
attack in successive waves, throw them against machine-gun nests without those emplacements having

first been cleaned out by night storm troops. Persist in forcing a passage through the enemy's lines at precisely that place where he has the best defenses! Never employ the element of surprise! Mount your attack with men loaded down like donkeys, badly trained men, exhausted men! They had reason to revolt, those soldiers of the Great War. We couldn't wage such a war as that today. Fortunately!"

In *Les Centurions* I quoted the following passage:

> A retired Colonel Mestreville was describing to Raspéguy a shoulder-to-shoulder three-division attack near Douaumont—an attack which resulted in thirty thousand dead and wounded.
>
> Raspéguy jumped to his feet. That kind of story roused him to fury.
>
> "A slaughter! Verdun! You should have your attack troops widely extended. Have thirty meters' space between each man, and each man lightly uniformed . . . men like shadows who slip past too swiftly to make targets. The enemy is demoralized, makes stupid mistakes. At Dien Bien Phu, we found ourselves a little in your position at Verdun, with artillery and trenches. We had let ourselves be so wedged in that we were forced then to maneuver . . . "
>
> Mestreville struck the table so forcefully with his fist that the glasses danced.
>
> "We won!"
>
> "When a million die, it cannot be called a victory."

That was the opinion of Bigeard, it was the opinion of General Ducourneau, and it is mine.

The military critic Liddell Hart expressed much the same opinion when he wrote approximately the following:

> The stupidity and the lack of imagination of the Allied chiefs during the war of 1914–18 can only be compared to the stupidity and the lack of imagination of the German generals.

Let's return to that boy of ten who had just opened
Pandora's box.

Hours passed and I couldn't tear myself away from
those pictures. Fascinated and horrified at the same
time, I trembled with cold, even though it was July.

From time to time I lifted my eyes from the glass
plates to my father and my uncle in their frames as if
to ask for assistance. I would have liked for them to
tell me that it was all a nightmare, that all I'd seen
had never really happened. What I knew of war prior
to that day was what I'd seen in Epinal pictures:[7] of
Joan of Arc at the siege of Orleans; of the sunshine of
Austerlitz; of Marignano in 1515; of the charge of the
Centaures commanded by Murat; of the knight Bayard
who, having commended his soul to God, gave a good
dressing down to the Duke of Bourbon for behaving
badly toward his king; and of Guesclin, that grasping
villain who had pursued the English all the way to our
part of the country to die beneath the walls of
Châteauneuf-de-Randon of a dreadful fever, even
though the climate of the region—as all the tourist
brochures will tell you—is particularly healthy.

None of this had anything in common with what I
had just seen. Which had lied? Which had cheated me?
The glass plates or my illustrated history of France?

But my rendezvous was running out. I heard its
knell tolled in lugubrious notes: the clatter of clogs on
the stone tiles of the kitchen floor. My grandmother
had just returned, and I only had time to dash from
the room, turn the key in the lock, and slip into the
garden by means of an open window.

Was it Portes, or Portal, or Panafieu who had just
died in our town? I can't remember the name exactly. I
only know he was of the same regimental rank as my
father and that he received a military pension for all
the long time it took him to finish the business of dying.

---

7. *Image d'Epinal*: an early form of strip cartoon. (Translator's
note.)

Now I needed to know something more about him. I needed someone to explain to me how one could still die from the war twelve years after the armistice.

I had become friends with a gravedigger. A Hamlet in short pants, I loved to engage him in debate as he dug graves. He always pronounced his sentences as though they were judgments, pausing to spit into his hands before again taking up his spade. He impressed me greatly.

From the cemetery in Aumont, on a clear day we could see in the distance the Margeride mountains, and the freshly turned soil smelled good to me. I loved the place.

One day, after several considered remarks on the weather and on our recent dry spell—one never just came out immediately with the subject one most wished to discuss; it was impolite and tactless—I asked him, "What did he have—Portes (or Portal, or Panafieu)?"

"Poison gas, young man. I was told his gas mask had a hole in it, but it's my personal belief that he threw it aside in order to carry food in its place—you know, in the mask box."

"What's poison gas?"

"Your father didn't tell you? The Jerries fired shells of mustard gas into the trenches. It smells something like bleach. There was a special siren used for a gas alert. I can still remember it: *tara tata taratata.* If you didn't put on your mask, your lungs scorched. Your skin turned green and blistered and burst. Your breathing became difficult, and you spit blood for years afterwards. You always had a fever. You were always thirsty. Like poor Valentin, who drinks up his pension at Prunière's or Mother Chevalier's. You won't repeat any of this, will you? The doctor told me it isn't his lungs that have given out but his liver, because he doesn't eat enough and drinks too much. But it's still the result of gas poisoning."

"And did we—did the French use gas, too?"

"Certainly. Worse than that of the Jerries. We developed a kind of layer of gas, a sort of low-lying cloud that was pushed by the wind into the enemy's trenches. Once you've undergone an attack of poison gas, have had to stay in the trenches for months on end, have been through Verdun or in the Argonne or the Vosges, and have finally been lucky enough to return home, you're never again the same."

And he began to tell me stories which proved that men do in fact remain essentially the same: of men on wine details who returned to the wrong trenches with their stolen wine; of the chickens and pigs stolen from farms, and of how they'd had to be stolen and killed without any noise.

I helped at Portes's burial. Diversions of any kind seldom arrived in Aumont: marriages, births, deaths, and a seedy-looking circus that came our way once a year. Portes was buried according to all the rites appropriate to his status as an old soldier—"victim of the war and one to whom we owe much," declared the mayor, who had prudently gotten himself exempted from active duty. Shirked his duty, my father said.

A delegation of old combat soldiers—"those of the front," as they dubbed themselves—medals hanging, berets in place, marched to the cemetery in front of the coffin. Their regimental colors followed them, carried by a one-handed veteran. His handicap in no way hindered him from holding his flag aloft to the level of the roofs. In place of his hand, he had an iron hook through which he'd passed the flag rope, allowing it full play.

When everything was done, and Portes had been blessed and given to the earth, the one-handed veteran again took up the colors, and "those of the front" retired to empty a few pints together at Mother Chevalier's and to reminisce one more time about their war. They forgot for the moment all the horrors of war, only recalling the "good and sacred moments" they'd shared.

Much later, when I in my turn returned home as an old soldier, I was invited by various groups to take part in what one of my friends called "the great liars' reunion."

He wasn't off the mark. Reunions are held for old war buddies to come together and remember heroic feats of arms and to embellish them, endeavoring not to see that life has changed them all, that they no longer speak the same language, don't even use the same words. For a brief time they cover up the truth.

That which is most unendurable in war, the awful, ordinary daily routine of war, is relegated to those dim regions where men hide all bad memories. But those memories survive, no matter how deeply buried, and sometimes they emerge.

Barbusse wrote in *Le Feu:*[8]

> More than battle charges which resemble full dress reviews, more than conspicuous engagements unfurled like oriflammes, even more than the hand-to-hand fighting you throw yourself yelling into, war is terrible exhaustion, extraordinary fatigue. War is water up to your belly, and mud, and ordure, and unspeakable filth. War is dead moldy faces and rotting tatters falling away from rotting flesh and corpses which no longer resemble corpses, half afloat on the muddy, voracious earth. War is the never-ending monotony of pure misery, broken by intense and bitter dramas. That's what war is, and not a bayonet sparkling like silver in the sun, not the dawn bugle sounding reveille.

I do revere my dead friends, as has been said of me, but not war, which the world crowns with glory. It's courage I revere, and not misery. And I refuse to allow myself that kind of selective memory which makes certain old soldiers incense bearers for war, however unconsciously.

8. *The Fire.* (Translator's note.)

I waited two years before I questioned my father and my uncle about war. Two years—during which I devoured the library's collection of *L'Illustration,* as well as *Les Croix de bois* [9]; *A l'Ouest, rien de nouveau* [10]; *Quatre de l'infanterie* [11], and everything else I could find about the contents of the little glass library dedicated to war.

When autumn came, bringing with it long evenings of sitting around the fire, and I was twelve years old and was allowed to say a few words at the table, I risked asking some of the questions on my mind, pretending that the Great War was one of my school studies.

"What your books tell you will have to be enough," my father said.

"Pah!" my uncle retorted, pulling on his pipe.

Perhaps it's time for me to speak about the two of them.

Albert Osty, my father, did as the rest of his family had done. At eighteen he went up to Paris to earn a few sous, keeping deeply rooted in his mind the idea of returning to his mountains. In Paris he was a café busboy, one of our cousins who labored at similar work having found him work in some bistro. If that cousin had been an itinerant peddler or a newspaper vendor, my father would have followed suit.

In 1911 he was called into the mountain light infantry, where at that time the length of service was three years. He was promoted to sergeant of the Twenty-fourth Battalion, and he must really have merited the rank, for the only thing he had in the way of a diploma was an elementary school certificate from the parochial school, which was recognized neither by the military nor by the government. Officially, he knew only how to "read and write."

---

9. Idiomatic expression for *Killed in Action.* (Translator's note.)
10. *All Quiet on the Western Front.* (Translator's note.)
11. *Four of the Infantry or Four Infantrymen.* (Translator's note.)

He was never discharged, and the war caught him still in uniform. He had a liking for command and was courageous and tough. Since there was a shortage of staff officers, he was sent to an officer training school and graduated at the head of the list of promotions in 1916.

At the battle of Chemin des Dames, as a lieutenant, he was a hero of a feat of arms which all the newspapers of the day seized upon.

He was the only surviving officer of his battalion, and there remained with him only a handful of soldiers—seventeen in all. These were men who'd been fighting for days on end without relief, who'd had enough, who simply could not go on, and who wanted only to surrender. Their orders, though, were to continue to hold the position to the last man. Germans and French were separated by no more than a few meters, and the Germans were fully aware that the troops opposite them were French and knew the sad state of their morale. A German officer came out of a trench carrying a white flag and called to them to lay down their arms. The soldiers were on the point of doing just that when my father sprang to a machine gun and, without further ado, cut down the bearer of the flag of truce. And there we have the "blue devils"—the French light infantry—forced to fight to the end, to go to any lengths, because they had no choice whatever. As prisoners they'd have been as summarily dispatched as the German officer had been.

A counterattack saved them, but during the attack my father received a bullet in his spine.

In the last analysis, his action saved his life. It's my belief that if he'd not been wounded, he'd have reached the rank of colonel or general. He truly loved the army, loved the gold braid, the campaign medals, the honors. It wasn't the war he loved, though he recognized that it had allowed him to hope for another destiny than might otherwise have been his as a common laborer. But only to hope.

Back home again, after months and months in a plaster body cast, he went to Paris with my mother. He had a little cash, his pension, and the Legion of Honor; on the strength of this, he could borrow what he needed. He bought a small pub valued at about three sous at the Pont de Carentan; then he bought a slightly larger one, and finally yet another. When he thought his earnings were sufficient to build a nice home for himself in his own part of the country, he sold everything, packed up bag and baggage, and, with my mother, went back to Lozère. After the house was built, he had nothing to do but read and care for his garden. He read a lot, Bossuet, among others, and everything else he could find about the war. Three years ago, at seventy-nine years of age, he died.

He had just come out of his room, a magazine in his hand, ready to have his coffee. He felt tired and stopped to sit on the steps. The end came to him there.

I put all his medals into his coffin. He valued those above everything else, even above money, which he loved.

He and I could never bear each other for very long. Two or three times a year we'd meet on some neutral ground, never bringing up those subjects we opposed each other on: religion, the Resistance, politics.

There was one time when he became enthusiastic about politics. He found himself among a number of others who, like himself, having had a part in a brilliant war and having fought well, considered themselves capable of leading the country. He was, with Colonel de la Rocque, one of the founders of the order *"Croix de Feu."*[12] On February 6 one year he and several of his companions even succeeded in getting into the Chamber of Deputies, but they were too few in number to get anyone to give a damn for their program.

My mother died in Lozère, too, but much earlier.

12. "Fiery Cross." (Translator's note.)

After the debacle, after I was already in a Spanish prison, she tried to discover what had become of me. She went so far as to demand that the Vatican help her get information (our family was somewhat influential in that quarter). I'm not certain precisely what happened, but her sources were way off beam; they told her I'd been shot. That gave her a shock from which she never recovered. Three years later I learned of her death—a few hours before mounting an assault in the Vosges with a commando group.

My Uncle Emile went first to a secondary school staffed by priests, then to a Roman Catholic seminary, the only way to acquire advanced education if one had no money but had relatives in the Holy Church. My grandfather found the fact that my uncle wasted his time in that manner almost intolerable. When my uncle had received his cassock and was back home, my grandfather demonstrated his disdain by sending Uncle Emile to watch over the geese. Not the cows! In the old man's estimation, my uncle was incapable of the greater responsibility, was too absent-minded, always had his nose in a book. By then my uncle was reading Homer in the original.

At the time I made my acquaintance with war in my Uncle Fernand's room, Uncle Emile was professor of Hebrew and Aramaic at the Catholic University. At the time of the war, though, he was a priest. He was mobilized as a stretcher-bearer, and served in the Balkans. Clearly, my father and my uncle had two very different views of the war.

We spent evenings at our house gathered around the fire in what we called the morning room. We had not electricity yet, and would wait until we could no longer see anything before lighting the huge kerosene lamp I can still picture always smoking and giving off light sparingly. We ate. My grandmother bawled the blessing, an interminable blessing, followed by the Lord's Prayer and the Hail Mary for the intention of all

the dead of our family, of all those anywhere who were
in difficult straits, who were sick, or for whom life was
in any way hard. If a certain person or affliction were
better left unmentioned, discretion dictated that we
say: "For a particular intention." After we'd eaten, we'd
play manille,[13] or we'd reminisce, until it was time to
retire to our ice-cold bedrooms, carrying candle and
foot warmer.

On one such evening I again chanced the question on
my mind: "What was the war like?"

My father didn't like to speak of the war, nor did my
uncle. They sent me from the room, and, by way of
punishment for speaking out, I had to learn one of La
Fontaine's fables and recite it the next day at the table
after the turnip soup.

But finally one evening they began to discuss the
war. It came about oddly enough—apropos some apples
that had been stolen from our garden.

"I nearly missed being shot for having taken an
apple," my father said. "It was during our offensive in
Alsace—on September first, if I'm not mistaken.
Never have I seen such a crop of fruit! The trees were
bent under the weight of plums, of apples, of pears. In
my squad we'd stacked our arms, and while we were
awaiting orders to advance, we'd built a fire and prepared some soup. To improve a little upon that hum-
drum fare for my men—I was sergeant then—I
picked some apples from a nearby orchard. I filled my
beret with them. As I was returning, I stumbled upon
an extremely jumpy captain, who proceeded to deal
with me as a pillager and told me that forthwith I'd
be court-martialed and placed before a firing squad.
Especially since I was a noncommissioned officer and
should have set an example for my men. I tried to explain to him as reasonably as I could that the entire
countryside for miles around had been abandoned by
its inhabitants, that there was no longer anyone to

13. A French card game. (Translator's note.)

eat those apples, and that my men all had hollow stom-
achs. To no avail. He drew his pistol and ordered me to
raise my hands. At the beginning of the war, you see,
discipline was very strict, more so in the light infantry.

"I was saved by the Germans, who attacked us from
the rear. We had only enough time to leap for our
rifles, to throw ourselves flat behind the trees, and to
fire—at random and in the greatest haste. I never
saw that captain again. Maybe he died there. We
suffered severe losses that day, for the enemy
had machine guns and we had none. Three times we
counterattacked over razed terrain, bayonets fixed,
our bugle sounding the charge. I earned my Cross
of War there, with a citation from the Army
Corps."

Another evening my father told us about a bayonet
attack at the Somme. He was bent toward the fire as
he spoke, but I could see that his hands clenched his
knees fiercely from time to time.

"The softening up by our artillery," he told us, "had
continued all night long, until about ten o'clock the
next day. Then only a low rumble like that made by a
train could be heard. A few hours earlier we'd all been
given brandy, along with double rations of food and
boxes of grenades. To us these were bad signs. So, too,
were the new silence and the order that passed from
man to man down the line: 'Fix bayonets! Pass it on.'
We were assured by our superiors that after the artillery hammering the enemy had taken, no one remained alive in their lines. We didn't ask how our in-
formants knew that, but from previous experience we
knew there probably wasn't much truth in the statement. Then came the most difficult moment of all:
when it becomes necessary to leave the shelter of your
trenches. You feel particularly vulnerable at that moment, your flesh crawls, you are overcome with a long-
ing to urinate, and saliva gathers in your mouth but
you can't swallow.

"I turned around to see if my men were behind me.

They were there. 'Advance!' I called. And we pushed forward. We proceeded some hundred or so meters, tearing ourselves free from barbed wire the whole time and stumbling into shellholes. Nothing else moved. Our hopes were raised. Could it be true? Could the enemy really have been crushed by our artillery barrage?

"Suddenly the enemy barrage broke out. All we could do was dive to the ground and wait for a lull. When it came, we ran furiously to cross the enemy's field of fire, but there were fewer of us by then. A good half of my men didn't get up. The survivors and I threw ourselves into the cross fire of the machine guns, but it was impossible to get close enough to the guns to make use of our grenades; and so our assault wave had penetrated to within a few meters of the enemy parapet, to die there.

"All that day I was stuck in a shellhole unable to move, so close to the Jerries I could hear them speaking in their patois. The minute I raised the muzzle of my gun to take aim, bzzz . . . a bullet whizzed past my head. There were three of us left, one of whom was wounded and who constantly demanded water. We couldn't give him any, because he'd been shot in the stomach. He was Marcel X—— from the area of Lille. His parents were rich and had a large farm, and they'd often sent him food parcels which he'd shared with us. He was a decent chap, but taciturn, and no one knew much about him.

"To finish off their barrage, the Germans let loose at us a 'Minenwerfer,' a kind of small trench gun. The French were using their own trench mortars, and with these they dispatched directly at us heavy charges of fire, which made a hellish uproar and shattered the earth uncomfortably close to our shellhole. We crouched down into the earth. They struck to the right of us and to the left of us, and I fully believed that I'd never leave there alive. I desperately wanted a cigarette, but neither my friend nor I had a match. I remember that he said to me, 'We could almost ask those Jerries in front of us to send us a box of

matches instead of their filthy bombs. We're that close
to them!' My friend was a master sergeant, and we'd
gone to officer training school together. He finished
the war as a captain, and they say now he's going to
be recommissioned a general. We write each other
regularly.

"A short time later the wounded man died, whimper-
ing softly like a lost puppy. I collected his blood-soaked
service record from him.

"We had to wait out the whole night before we could
make it back to our lines, where they'd already written
us off as dead. They'd even made up bundles of our be-
longings to send to our families. When we showed up,
our comrades were so beside themselves with joy, they
nearly bowled us over.

"The captain directed me to write to Marcel's parents of his death, because he'd been one of my men and
because he'd died beside me. I asked him if I had to
write, and he answered, 'As I would have done for you,
Osty'—and showed me the letter he'd prepared for my
parents. I copied it: 'Your son died a hero . . . he didn't
suffer . . . he took a direct hit to the head. . . .' In that
shellhole where he died, his body waited eight days for
us—until the following attack wave. When we finally
retook that accursed pit, the rats had half devoured
him. The trenches were always full of rats, fat ones
with red eyes. They gorged on everything: boots, leather
accouterments, even our candles and our rounds of
bread hanging from the roofs of our dugouts. We were
forever chasing them, and we had competitions, the
winner being the one who killed the most rats. Others
among us had similar competitions over lice."

When my father was finished, I asked, "Weren't you
ever afraid?"

"All the time. I was afraid under my baptism of fire
in the orchards of Alsace and just as afraid during the
last attack at Chemin des Dames. You never get used
to that kind of fear, but you eventually learn what
tricks will help you rise above it. I'm going to give you

a bit of advice: if it should one day be necessary for us to engage ourselves again in war, make it your business to become an officer. It's much easier to be courageous with officers' bands on your sleeves, because you're busier than your soldiers are. They have only their fear and their weak, quivering flesh to occupy their minds. You are kept busy with a stack of duties, such as making certain the soldiers' packs are full of grenades, that they have their allotment of cartridges and other supplies, and with poring over your battle maps. It's also much more comfortable at the rear. You're able to leave first. The pay is better, too."

My uncle spoke up:

"The medical officer who ran the field hospital to which I was assigned had found another way to combat fear—if not the horror he dealt with. His entire days were spent using the knife on living flesh, cutting off arms and legs, sewing up wounds, excising other wounds. He was always so tired, he'd fall asleep sitting up, still red with blood, his head in his hands. To be able to hold out, he took to injecting himself with morphine. I surprised him at it one day. He couldn't stand priests, and he looked straight into my eyes: 'This shocks you, doesn't it, Padre? But you see, I don't pray as you do. I have to get through this bloody mess by whatever means available to me.' But I wasn't at all shocked, and I told him so.

"But then I, too, found that prayer was just not enough. Especially when I went out onto the battlefield to collect and bring in the poor brutes who moaned and called for their mothers. And I saw more horrible things than that. At Salonika. An entire army was decimated by dysentery; an entire army was sunk in shit. Those soldiers became so feeble that they could no longer even drag themselves to the bushes to defecate.

"Eventually the medic and I became very friendly, and he ultimately wanted me to leave the priesthood and marry his sister. He owned vineyards in Algeria to which we'd all go.

"The essential tragedy in the story of that doctor is that he loved humankind too much, that he couldn't bear their suffering, and that, more often than not, he couldn't alleviate their suffering, despite all his science. He became a cynic, and coarse. He used to insult me, to call me to account because I represented the Lord on Earth. In his fashion he believed in God, and out of his pain he'd abuse me, saying: 'What the bloody hell does He do, your master? He snoozes on the clouds, is that it? Equally as good as nothing are my own masters, though, the medical service staff, who can't even provide me with the medicines I need!' "

The fire burned out in the fireplace. The wick of the lamp turned red.

"Do you really believe there's going to be another war?" asked my Aunt Julie in her melodious voice.

"No," said my father.

There came a day when they said, "Perhaps."

The Spanish civil war had just broken out.

I immediately made up my mind against France for reasons that had nothing at all to do with politics. It happened several months after I'd assassinated Louis XVI, and that was when I was a pupil studying under the Jesuits of Saint-Francis-de-Sales in Evreux, a smart enough sort of school where everyone there had a title of one kind or another. The titles were like military decorations: they were real enough, but they no longer carried any clout.

I was completely out of place there, but I'd been admitted on the basis of my family's influential connections in Holy Mother the Church. As soon as I arrived I was unhappy. The Jesuit College was a tight little universe where strange plants grew in its overheated hothouse atmosphere—very special friendships, as an example—and since I elected to remain an outsider, I became the victim of informers.

With remarkable skill the good fathers used some of

the boys to spy on other boys, exactly as in the peoples'
democracies or in the Soviet Union. On the one hand
you have the people of the party or the members of the
congregation, who are the "good pupils"; on the other
you have those who are outside the party, who are not
to be trusted, and whom the first are charged with setting back on the right track, the orthodox way.

I stuck obstinately to my path of error, and without
the red cassocks and the black cassocks of my uncles,
I'd have been kicked out. Early in my school career
there I had made an enemy of a titular professor of
the humanities, the Marquis-Father Fernand de
Montrichard, who began the first lecture of his first
course with the declaration: "To the proud title of Mar-
quis I added the proud title of Jesuit." Because I was a
low-born, poor pupil, he always reproached me for my
lack of due humility suitable to my station. But, suitable to my station, I'd been relegated to the back of
the class and ignored, except when it came time to
grill me on the Greek irregular verbs. I pushed imper-
tinence to the limits when I was called upon, and I recited the verbs in an utterly confused manner, mixing
them up every which way with no regard for meaning,
just to defy the marquis-père.

On the day of the anniversary of the death of Louis
XVI—January 21—it was the tradition at Saint
Francis to wear mourning, to sport a black tie and a
dark suit. My first January 21 there I donned a red tie
and a plaid jacket. As we passed in front of the marquis-père, we were duly expected to greet him with a
nod of our heads, at which he would return the salute
with a little wave of his pince-nez. On that day the
pince-nez fell to the floor and smashed when I came
abreast of the Jesuit. He drew himself erect, extended
his arm with finger pointing, and shouted to me, "Out!
Assassin of our king, out!"

And that's how I became the "red" in that class of
ultraconservatives. From that moment on, the marquis-
père could go to hell as far as I was concerned. I

never participated in class again, and when civil war broke out in Spain, the least I could do was to line up on the side of the Republic. Political convictions often do come about through personal friendships and enmities.

I genuinely detest the Jesuits, just as I detest the communist world their order resembles. Didn't Stalin have as his bedside book *The Exercises of Ignatius Loyola?*

After I became a "partisan" of the Republic, a friend and I decided to join the Republican army in Narbonne, where there was a recruitment center for the International Brigade; but my friend took off and left me, and I found myself all alone at the train station. The Paris-Bèziers train came and went, but I didn't take it. I was sixteen but looked thirteen, I didn't have a sou in my pocket, and I wasn't anxious to be taken home between two policemen.

I did become acquainted with Franco's prisons—but that was five years later.

I've not yet forgiven the Jesuits. They can paint themselves pink or red, they can become worker priests, they can have girls, and it wouldn't change my opinion of them.

The day I raised a few glasses with Teilhard de Chardin in a bar on the Champs-Elysées, I didn't know he was a Jesuit. Had I known, I would probably have hesitated to drink with him. But his name told me nothing. He was concerned mostly with the question of China; he was dressed as an ordinary clergyman; and he tossed whiskey off like a trooper. I learned later that he had problems with the representatives of the members of his order. I'm not surprised.

The Republicans lost the war in Spain, and a prison camp was set up for some of them at Saint-Chély-d'Apcher near Aumont, where they were guarded by gendarmes. The prisoners were Catalans who spoke a language close to our own patois, so we were able to understand each other. The girls among them were allowed out during the day, and one day I came across one of them in a barn. We were young; I gave her what I could, and she gave me what she had.

One morning, one magnificent morning in September, two days before my birthday, on the third, the tocsin sounded. It was war.

No one was surprised. Reservists were already being called up in bunches, by entire companies.

"It's spiritless," said my father.

"It's very spiritless," said my uncle. "This war is off to a bad start. Nobody wants it. It's not like it was in '14!"

"You remember, Emile? The wagons and the words across them: 'To Berlin'? The flowers on the rifles?"

"Let's hope this one isn't going to be the butchery the last one was, that the generals will not be as stupid. Gamelin . . ."

"Gamelin! You know we just aren't ready for war yet. You know that."

I decided to enlist despite everything. I wasn't motivated by any noble patriotic spirit. It was just that it seemed the sensible thing for me to do. I had my two degrees; no other career drew me particularly; all around me people were saying that this war would last as long as the one before; so I might as well go in early and pick the unit of my choice, pick my war.

There wasn't any problem of parental permission. In October I arrived at the barracks in Avignon.

PART TWO

WAR
I FOUGHT IN

Avignon. For me it meant a nice little bordello near the ramparts, a family atmosphere, and fine cooking. I still have fond memories of the savory stewed mutton, the beef stews, the chicken fricassees that were served to me. Fond memories of dewy young Burgundian women, fresh and without pretension, without ceremony.

I arrived in the old papal city two days before the rest of my contingent, which had been called to the flag. I appeared younger than my age then, perhaps because my head was still shaven; and I don't know why, but I was mistaken by everyone to be a soldier's son with military school training. A certain Monsieur Julien, a man well past forty who had until then managed to evade all the recruiting centers, had just been caught. Somehow, he nevertheless arranged to undergo his basic training in his hometown. When he met me at the barracks he took me under his wing, because, he said, it made no sense to send a kid my age to the front.

Monsieur Julien was the owner of a tavern and bordello which he operated with his wife. They didn't lack for customers, especially among the commissioned and noncommissioned officers.

Theoretically, we were supposed to remain confined to barracks fifteen days after our incorporation. But the very evening of Monsieur Julien's arrival among us, he took me into town with him to show me his "grand 16," informing his exclusively female personnel that I wasn't a client but an invited guest, and that this entitled me to bed and board. To nothing else! If I wanted "exercise," he said, and if I had the means, I'd have to go to a neighboring bordello, where I'd be sure to become diseased, because that bawdy house, unlike the house at number 16, was badly run, and the women had neither style nor education.

Monsieur Julien was very different from the image of a pander I'd formed from Carco's books or Carné's films. There was certainly nothing about him of the tattooed giant, nor of the unnerving pimp with highly polished shoes. He was a small, neat man, always trim and spick-and-span, even in his private's uniform, which he'd had especially tailored. He was—it has to be said—a terrible marksman, as he clearly demonstrated on the firing range. He wasn't even particularly vigorous.

His passion was cards.

Before I arrived there, I could hold my own sufficiently well at piquet, at écarté, at pinochle, and still better at poker. With just a little luck (I'd been taught by excellent if socially undesirable teachers), I'd been able to trim the young aristocrats of Saint-Francis-de-Sales.

The day that Monsieur Julien first saw me cut the cards with ease, he began to doubt my naïveté; and then, at last, he allowed a woman of the house to take me upstairs. He figured that if I was that able to defend myself at games of cards, I was emancipated enough for games in bed. And because he was partial to me, thinking of me as the son he'd have liked, he didn't charge me. The rest was in the hands of the "gift" he gave me.

Those hands belonged to Clémence, who continued to provide me with her favors up to the day I was assigned to officer training class at Hyères and had to leave that small paradise.

Before I left, Monsieur Julien gave me a terrific blow-out, which made me even more sorry I'd had to conceal from him my formal education, that I was the sort of seed which, he said, achieved rank—became a "lousy bum," in his words. Only reluctantly did he admit that a person of his station and age—one who'd knocked about, as he put it—would soon have to follow the orders of a youngster like myself, have to salute him on the streets. It went down hard, even though he thought me sympathetic and enough of a hooligan for his taste. But he recognized that such things had to be, that even "lousy bums" of officers had to be. We were at war and, however leftist he was, Monsieur Julien was patriotic.

As a parting gift, Clémence gave me a balaclava helmet of heavy wool. She was always cold and was convinced that everyone else was as susceptible to the cold as she. Already she envisioned me mounting guard in the great frozen forests of the East.

I neglected to mention that she was the Negress of the establishment; not really very black, but a delicately tinted *café au lait.* She came from the Antilles in the West Indies.

Madame Julien gave me three packs of cigarettes, and Monsieur Julien gave me some good advice, such as never to tie up with just anyone at all; to make sure I didn't catch awful diseases, or, if I was imprudent enough to catch them, to take care of them immediately. If I didn't, they'd take hold and become incurable.

I was moved by it all. This was the first time in my life I'd had the feeling of belonging to a real family. When the feast was over, we even sang *"La Madelon"*!

So far we'd bothered ourselves very little with the war.

"And you won't have to worry about it now, either," my company's adjutant, who honored me with his confidence, assured me. "Sit down. Let me tell you about Saint-Cyr.[1]

---

1. A military school for the infantry and cavalry. (Translator's note.)

"It wasn't so terrible at all in those infantry classes of 1939," he said. "To the right, right! To the left, left! Quick march! Present arms! Disassemble and re-assemble the 8-mm Lebel rifle, model 1886, modified 1916. Memorize and shout out the sentences from the training manual: 'Discipline is the main strength of the army. . . . What is the importance of your feet? They are the object of all your care. . . . The initial velocity of the Lebel's bullets is 800 meters a second, and its effective range is 800 meters. . . .' And, as though it were a precious thing, they had us view from a safe distance the Bren gun, model 24, modification 29, which, with the seventy-five-pound cannon and the support of England, put us on the side of right and would help us to victory.

"Meanwhile, we were dressed in horizon blue overcoats, the field service color of '14, and hobnailed boots, whose leather under our inevitable puttees was as tough as the hide of a hippopotamus. While we might be lacking a lot in equipment and weapons, we nevertheless all had in our packs a small wooden plate with a hole in the middle, which made it possible for us to polish the brass buttons on our old coats without soiling the cloth. We had to present it at every check of kit and stores."

At Hyères I found everything different from his description. We were dressed in khaki and given working weapons.

The F.M. 24, modified 29, was our long-range gun. We no longer had the 25-pound antitank gun, and could only admire it from a distance.

There were practice approach marches with and without cover, night marches, combat group training sessions, and assaults on positions held by the "enemy"—at one time some of us being the blue party, at other times the red.

At that time the base of the French infantry was a

firing triplet—the firer, the loader, and the ammunition server—all grouped around the Bren gun. We didn't concern ourselves with either armored tanks or aircraft, and for use against enemy planes we had a single weapon, always the same one, the F.M., mounted on a post and equipped with a special sighting telescope.

We had a good time playing war there on the deserted beaches of the Giens Peninsula. We were given blank cartridges, but our canteens held pure unadulterated rosé wine. The wine of the Côtes de Provence was still only a small, unpretentious wine, a little feeble, and it wouldn't stand up to travel or export.

I forgot to mention another weapon in our arsenal: the grenade launcher V.B., which we attached to the Lebel rifle. It had been put into operation in 1916 with the mine thrower 60.

No one, it appeared, had yet learned any lessons from the smashing of the Polish army by the dive-bombing tactics of the German air force, nor from the devastation caused by the autonomous armored tank divisions—the famous Panzer divisions.

"Neither in France nor in Great Britain," wrote Churchill later, "did anyone understand the full consequences of these new events, or that it was possible to make tanks capable of resisting artillery fire and of advancing more than fifty kilometers a day."

Our instructors were young officers, certain staff college graduates, the elite of the army. But they were not much different from the rest of us. They didn't really believe in the new kind of confrontation in the East either. They taught us as they'd been taught, as if we'd all go on indefinitely fighting wars from trenches, as if nothing new had happened in twenty years, as if no new weapons had been discovered.

Poland? Where was that?

There wasn't any real morale, even among us, boys of twenty who had to be enthusiastic, or at least appear to be.[2] Everyone was intoxicated by imbecilic slogans, and because it suited us to believe them, we believed them. "We will win because we are the strongest." "The Maginot line is broken."

It was a "phony war," to use the expression coined by American journalists for a war in which nothing happened.

For me it was all symbolized by a picture that appeared in all the newspapers of the time: a French soldier seated on a chair, his Bren gun, the inevitable F.M. 24, modified 29, posed next to him, soberly mounting guard in front of the Maginot line.

Apparently, however, it was difficult for anyone to impress the members of the general staff, presided over by the apathetic Gamelin and controlled by Daladier, the man of Munich. They went on building castles in the air and dreaming up impractical schemes.

Those schemes were a marvelous collection of unbridled fantasies, fruits of the unreal imaginations of the Allied chiefs, who lived in daydreams until the ice-cold shower of Hitler's offensive recalled them to reality.[3]

We were the ones who were going to have to take that cold shower.

The notions of danger and of death never entered our young heads. We felt secure from all that; we felt protected, but we were like ostriches with their heads in the sand. We were persuaded—our superiors had at last persuaded us—that the Germans were not going to do anything significant, and that this phony war would do little more than lead to a phony peace.

When the preparatory training course was terminated, those who'd failed would become sergeants, and

2. "In a word, France of 1940 was hardly military. One proof of the nonmilitary mind of the day is the fact that the top man of the recent graduating class of Saint-Cyr chose the Quartermaster Corps." Jean Chauvel, *Commentaries* (Fayard).
3. B. H. Liddell Hart, *History of the Second World War* (Fayard/Putnam).

the others, myself included, would go on to military school. Saint-Cyr and Saint-Maixent had been consolidated at Camp Courtine at Creuse.

In *Les Mercenaires* I described the atmosphere of the camp. I find nothing to change in the following account:

> Whiffs of springtime wove their way through the air, and here and there patches of green showed through the sheets of mud. Evenings, the boys drank to forget that there was anything sinister about the abortive war, about a spring which couldn't decide to break out, about the dank and frigid camp. To persuade themselves that they weren't pitiful players in a bankrupt theater, they recited the poetry of Rimbaud or of Apollinaire, discussed surrealistic painting, the plays of Giraudoux, the films of Pabst and of Carné. . . . There was a rumor about that only the outgoing class was awaited for the great offensive to be launched. . . .

Learning that the student officers who tried for Saint-Cyr would have the right to a leave and to sit for the competitive examinations at Bordeaux, I applied as a candidate. While I didn't know the city, a comrade who was born there had promised to introduce me to some sensational girls if I'd go with him. The girls didn't show up for our rendezvous, but I passed the exams and sent a card about it to my adjutant at Avignon.

If I had done a little better than just pass, I'd have returned to Saint-Cyr after the armistice. Nearly all the candidates passed the exams as I had, but I was at the tail end of the list. The oral exam was what did me in. Six or seven hundred passed; I no longer remember the exact figure. After the armistice only about fifty of the top men were kept on.

To return to Courtine.

More covered and uncovered approach marches. We memorized the platoon commanders' manual. We made up our beds and our packs. We waxed and polished. We sang, "France, sweet land of my childhood. . . ."

We were learning how to march in close order, how to mount and dismount the Hotchkiss machine gun with eyes blindfolded, and how to play a good game of bridge, when the new German offensive burst upon us. Just when no one believed in it any longer. It was the tenth of May.

The first reaction was euphoria. Gamelin declared: "They have fallen into my trap." But the defense forts of Liège were surrendering and the tanks of Guderian were crossing the Albert Canal. Our officers raised the cry of treachery, in order not to be charged with carelessness, insisting that thousands of German parachutists had sabotaged our munitions depots and our communications nets.

Parachutists rarely came out of our skies, but they came fully equipped out of the imaginations of the French, who desperately desired to explain our defeat as brought about by treachery, by spies, by the fifth column, not by the incapacity of their chiefs or by their refusal to fight.

There were hasty and contradictory communiqués; pockets of resistance were consolidated; Weygand, who was sixty-three years old, was brought out of moth balls to replace Gamelin. People were soon calling again for the miracle of the Marne and begging for the help of Jeanne d'Arc!

I keep trying to remember just what that period was like. It's difficult. Especially so since I've unconsciously tried to forget it all.

I was unable to believe we could be defeated. I thought I'd viewed the Führer realistically: his lock of hair over his eye, his mustache under his nose, with his crossbelt, his boots, and the way he lifted his hand into the air to every point of the field. I couldn't take him seriously. He was a kind of Charlie Chaplin.

The crowds who acclaimed him, who returned his salute, raising their hands and rhythmically calling,

"Heil Hitler! Heil!"; the immense lines of goose-stepping brown shirts lighted by torches, all seemed to me a gigantic carnival parade. A bad cinema like that just couldn't end with a victorious war.

The war was a serious affair to me. I believed that the generals and chiefs of state who made its important decisions must feel the burden of their responsibilities, must measure the weight of those decisions that were to bring about the deaths of millions of people and to decide the future of the world.

No, it wasn't possible. It was absurd that the future depended on the epileptic of Nuremburg.

I didn't believe in our defeat until the moment I was caught up by its whirlwind.

That began the day when, into our well-regulated camp with its orderly hours of courses and exercises, there swarmed the human debris of the Corap[4] army.

Another brilliant idea of the high command, who wanted student officers of Saint-Cyr to take in hand the untidy hordes of beaten men.

They smelled of fear, of vomit, of red wine. They spoke mechanically and in loud, high voices. At heart they weren't reassured in their new environment, demanding to know if they were to be shot—one in every ten, as in '17—for having fled.

Their officers were worth little more. They were preoccupied with the fear of losing their footlockers!

We interrogated some of these runaways, and we soon saw that they were essentially the same as we were, neither better nor worse; they could have been good soldiers if they hadn't been demoralized by interminable card parties and long days of inaction.

Instead of filling their roles as commanders, their officers played at being their pals, until they were finally giving no orders at all. When we tried to reestablish some discipline among them, it was too late.

4. General Corap. (Translator's note.)

All the men gave us accounts of their battles, especially the last one, and all in very nearly the same terms.

When the Panzers reached them, disorder reigned. The attack was completely unexpected, since their intelligence had told them to look for it at the Maginot line. General Corap, who had once captured Abd-el-Krim, still related everything military to his former experiences in Morocco. He believed that a river as wide as the Meuse was an impassable obstacle. For the Berber horsemen perhaps! Not for a unified German attack force equipped with bridges mounted on rubber dinghies.

Each French division spread itself out along twenty kilometers of the river. They had one cavalry brigade for reserves. Not a tank brigade; not a mechanized brigade—a horse brigade!

The French were crushed under the bombs of the Stukas, thirty planes attacking at one time and dive-bombing. The French planes were nonexistent, and soon even their artillery ceased firing. All communications were cut. No one dared lift his head out of his hole, and the Meuse was crossed.

The tanks of the Wehrmacht swarmed over them, while the French reserve horse brigade simply chucked it and galloped away across the battlefield. Surprise turned to panic. The artillery, which could have done something to reduce the German ground attack, took off first, effectively clogging all the roads with their tractors, their trucks, and their men and equipment. The staff officers followed next. Everyone acted on an order to withdraw that had in fact never been given![5]

Corap's army lost itself among the long lines of civilians and their wagons fleeing the East, all of whom were targets for the hammering Stukas.

---

5. The order was attributed to a certain Captain Foulanges, and he was looked for everywhere—to shoot him. But since he never really existed, the blame for it all was laid at the feet of the famous fifth column.

All the men said, "We were betrayed. We were lost. So we simply did as everyone does—we took off. Then, since we had nothing to fill our bellies with, we got into the habit of helping ourselves to whatever we needed from the locals."

Corap's soldiers soon wanted to do the same thing at Camp Courtine—to pillage our mess halls and our bars.

For my own first feat of arms, I bestowed a citation upon myself:

> . . . for having courageously defended with his section of students the reserves of Monsieur Foyer's wine, for having endured without faltering the rolling fire of insults of certain uncontrollable elements who wanted to seize some of it.

Events were moving fast. They formed us into line battalions; they made us—the fine flower of the French army, her elite—into foot soldiers; and they sent us to defend the bridges of the Loire. Three battalions, one of which was mine, arrived at Fontenay-le-Comte for assignment. Another went to Saint-Maixent. Along with the students of the Saumur and armed only with their training equipment, they were sent to prevent the crossing of the Loire by Panzers, for two days holding a line twenty kilometers long.

Our own adventure was less glorious. We were sent in two sections to a position between Nantes and Angers, and our mission was to prevent the enemy from crossing the river there. When we arrived, the river flowed peacefully before us—"the great sandy river, the great river of glory," as one of our comrades who knew Péguy by heart reminded us.

He even had the bad taste to continue with "Happy the ripened corn, the mowed wheat," at the very time we were feverishly digging our combat emplacements and organizing the positions of the machine guns and mortars.

Night fell. Pink clouds unraveled in the sky and were reflected on the calm waters of the river. We were going to have our baptism of fire in beautiful surroundings. What sweetness there was in the air! And all around us, France was collapsing. The government had fled Paris and taken refuge in Bordeaux.

I was the firer of the machine gun. Seated on the tripod, I practiced lining up the bridge opposite us in the cross hairs of the sight. *They* can come no further than that. *They* will come, but *they* will probably be tanks.

The lieutenant reassured me:

"The munitions you're using have been especially made for antitank combat. The jacketed bullet has a double core, the one, made of a special kind of steel, capable of penetrating armor plating. Pull steadily in short bursts. The weapon has a tendency to ride up."

He gave me a cigarette and addressed me as "dear comrade."

We knew that the famous perforating bullet couldn't make a hole in anything heavier than corrugated iron; that to hold that bridge, the least we required was a cannon; that the war was lost; and that we were going to have to fight for the sake of "honor."

"Honor! Not much to fight for," said a cadet who came from Algeria.

A few soldiers from the engineer corps spoke of mining the bridge, and then disappeared.

And now X—— appears on the scene. X——, the detached, the ironic, whom I admired so much. He was the complete opposite of my naïve conception of his world, everything in nuances, never yes or no, always perhaps. With him around, discussions of the law and of political science prevailed in our gatherings on the embankment. He was elegant, with his matte complexion and the delicious underlying accent he'd brought from Alexandria.

When he'd received his promotion to cadet, he quickly grew to affect all the airs of an inter-Allied staff officer. Didn't he speak three or four languages? And didn't he have great connections?

Not that he revealed them—our future ambassador.

Seated next to me on the embankment, he said to me:

"This resistance is futile and stupid, you know. To kill young men of our age and quality for the sake of honor makes neither rhyme nor reason. France is going to need us very much. We should be reasonable about it; we should speak to the lieutenant about it."

My idol had just melted, had just proved that he was made of wax. I asked him, "What's the matter? Are you scared?"

"Not at all. It just seems to me that an ill-considered action right now could have regrettable consequences for us and for all our comrades. The enemy could consider us guerrillas, you know."

"Well, I'm scared," said Joufflu, a boy with such round cheeks he always looked as if he were playing the flute. "I'm scared of being killed. And I'm not very fixed on what the hereafter is like. All the same, because there are certain things that must be done, we're going to have to fight to our last cartridge."

I, too, was scared. I remembered something my uncle, the canon, had said to me:

"We often confuse fear and anxiety. Both you and I are subject to anxiety, because we have so much imagination. But that anxiety disappears in action, and the very fact of that can precipitate us headlong into something before it's really necessary."

How true that was! And how I wished for something to happen right away.

We were divided into two groups, one behind X——, the other behind Joufflu. The insane and the reasonable. The reasonable outnumbered the others.

Our confusion at first was the result of our long inaction. We were no longer very sure for whom or for what we were fighting. We had also forgotten what it meant to love our country, and had in fact been taught to be ashamed of it. But we had none of those problems when we began to fight. All our enthusiasm was recovered, and the clarions sounded in our heads.

The voices in the night were muffled. Joufflu had come to sit beside me, and the lieutenant rejoined us. Like lost children in a big dark forest, we shared with one another our last loaf of bread, our last piece of sausage.

A lookout spoke suddenly, "There they are!"

We could hear the rumble of motors on the other side of the river.

"They're ours," said the lieutenant. Enemy motorcycles. The advance guard for the tanks. "But what's happening?" he added. "Why isn't the bridge blowing? The engineers have run off without warning! Fire at my command!"

I fired at the shadows. One magazine, another . . . All at once the motorcyclists turned on their headlights. There were cries of rage, insults hurled at us! I understood nothing.

"Cease fire!" ordered the lieutenant.

They weren't Germans! They were Polish! The last troops of them still fighting across the river.

Luckily I hadn't struck anyone. The machine gun, one we had used in our training, was irregular, as the lieutenant had warned, and shot much too high. (In *Les Mercenaires,* I dramatized this incident by having my hero kill three Polish soldiers.)

"It's harrowing," said the lieutenant, "but we aren't the ones at fault. The order was explicit: shoot at anything that shows itself on the other side of the river, or at anything that even approaches it."

The Poles told us they'd been fighting at Saumur when a German tank column came up the Loire toward the estuary they were holding. They'd broken out like a whirlwind and were trying to reach the Breton redoubt. Another beautiful joke!

Our order to withdraw reached us a little later. We rejoined the rest of our battalion, and the bridge was never blown up! From the Loire to the Garonne, the cadet officers retreated, their order and discipline remaining miraculously preserved in the midst of general disorder.

"Little soldier, what have you done with your rifle?" wrote Céline. "I left it on the field of honor." I didn't leave my "fishing pole" on the field of honor; neither did I leave my bayonet. I lost nothing, not even my regulation can of machine grease; nor did I throw into the ditches my ammunition supplies: four magazines with three bullets each.

We lived on cans of sardines and on bully beef; and during our regular halts, after the scrupulously observed fifty minutes of marching, we went into orchards to pick peaches and apricots. But without sacking. We searched out all the owners and offered them money, which they refused to accept.

We maintained a certain dignity in that debacle. This was our monument to the dead. Quick time! March! Eyes right! A salute to those who died "in a war for a just cause." Has anyone ever conducted a bad war?

I didn't know and I didn't give a damn! I was exhausted, but more than that, I was sickened.

One evening I'd had about enough of having to sleep between Durand and Dupont in the barns and stables where we holed up, a little removed from the rest of the army on the run, as though to keep ourselves free from contagion.

We'd been following a canal—my memory has lost the name of it—and I'd noticed a barge moored near three poplars. There was no sign of life on board.

My company was installed in a kind of large depot, but I needed to see the stars, to listen to the sound of the water. I especially needed to be alone. I wanted no more of the other men, nor of the stupid nonsense they kept repeating to one another; for instance, when someone sucked the oil from his can of sardines, he'd say, "Another one the Jerries won't get."

The poor idiot! The Jerries were in the process of gathering up all of France.

I slipped away, and suddenly there I was aboard the barge. I found a bottle of wine and a can of stew, which I heated on a stove, and later I fell asleep on the deck, completely sated, happy, sole master on board, my rifle beside me, my head on my haversack. I persuaded myself that the nightmare would be over when I woke up, that order would have returned to my world, that we would no longer be defeated, and that we'd have the time to learn how to use the famous cannon 25.

When I opened my eyes, I was wet with dew. I grabbed up my equipment and ran to the depot where my comrades slept.

They'd gone in the middle of the night, a farmer told me. It seemed that the "others," the *Vert-de-gris*,[6] had come. He indicated with his hand the direction they'd taken. It was a road that ran straight ahead of us, a deserted road that disappeared into the vineyards.

I took off at a rapid pace, my rifle on my shoulder, the regulation pack on my back, canteen on one side, haversack on the other, helmet set squarely on my head, the flaps of my overcoat properly turned up—all alone. *They* were at my back. I braced myself.

I was overtaken by a German division of tanks and armored cars. Young tank crew members, clean-shaven and with thick blond hair, stood up out of the turrets. They were in shirt-sleeves, some of them shirtless; and they were gilded bronze by the sun, happy in their victory, happy at penetrating so deeply into that France which no longer defended itself, which opened up to them.

6. Verdigris. Having to do with the color of the German uniform, and one of the names given the Germans by the French soldiers. (Translator's note.)

I was the cuckold, the sad and miserable little cuckold. I took to my heels and ran, and in my pitiful condition I provided the tank crews with so much sport that
they didn't even consider taking me prisoner.

One of them threw me a chocolate.

"Here, little wooden soldier, something for your
snack."

I raged inwardly at being the object of their ridicule.
I envied them and detested them at the same time,
these soldiers with their look of genuine warriors, not
of wooden soldiers. For what purpose was I decked out
in an overcoat on the twentieth of June? And with an
old popgun barely capable of firing three shots. With
my bayonet, too, though it was the most useful thing I
had; for with it I could open cans of food.

The war would only be over for me on the day I had
made them pay for the contempt they showed me,
when I'd seen them running away from me.

Hitler was the comic movie at Nuremberg, but he
was also that army of youths commanded by youths
who sped along the roads of France taking two towns
in the same day.

Since they were still fighting in England, I decided to
return to the fight myself.

To begin with, I rejoined my company and my battalion. I learned of France's armistice with Germany
while I was in Brittany at the château of Brède: a
large fortress surrounded by moats in which water
stagnated, and which was topped with machicolated
towers.

My young diplomat X——, who had regained some
of his assurance once he heard the war was over, took
me to visit the library and bedroom of Montesquieu
with all the deference a jurist owed the author of *L'Es-
prit des lois*.

I don't know which of us first got the idea, whether
Joufflu or I, but we decided to spend the night in the
great man's bed rather than in our barracks on our

awful mattresses. We needed to commit some kind of sacrilege. We were fed up with Pétain, who'd made a present of himself to France—which was endlessly drummed into our ears—and especially fed up with all those officers who'd run off early in the war and who were now beginning to strut about again and were appealing to Pétain for aid. We knew that people hadn't stopped lying to us—not the church or the government—and that those old "glories" like Montesquieu and Pétain had taken part in a vast conspiracy that had deprived us of victory for twenty years.

In our studded boots, in fatigues and sword belts, with all our equipment, we slept in Monsieur Montesquieu's bed. Joufflu pretended that I snored; I preferred to believe it was Joufflu. To give us courage, we downed half a liter of rum.

The next day we gave up our military positions. By the terms of the armistice conventions, the Germans had arrived to occupy the zone. Where did we go? Tonneins, in the Garonne basin. I remember a terrace there that overlooked the river, and a tobacco manufacturer. We stole some quids of tobacco and some cigarettes. Cigarettes galore!

Through a friend, I learned that there was a small airfield a few kilometers away where some planes remained. Joufflu agreed that we should take off together and join those still fighting the Germans. It wasn't so much patriotism that motivated us as a taste for adventure. Above all, we were fed up to the teeth with being trapped in France's defeat. We were smothering. I didn't know de Gaulle at that time, hadn't heard his famous appeal of the eighteenth of June. On the other hand, I knew Pétain too well. My father never ceased speaking of him to me. Pétain had eventually been decorated on the very field of battle from which he'd fled.

What we really wanted was to chuck everything. We felt cheated, and we were only twenty years old.

We stole two bicycles, and, after having pedaled

hard and been lost ten times along the way, we finally reached the airfield. And there, nicely lined up, were two full Potez 63 aircraft that didn't seem to be engaged.

We invited the pilot, a sergeant hardly older than we were, to drink with us. A second lieutenant joined us, and I plunged into what we wanted.

I told them it would be possible for us to reach the English coast, that we'd be more than welcome there, and so on and so forth. I grew increasingly muddled as I watched the faces of the two pilots slowly close up. And do you know what they said? That we were completely mad!

"You want to fight on the side of the English who let us go down to defeat at Dunkirk and who refused to support us with their planes on the Somme? Aren't those enough reasons not to?"

"And besides," said the other, "we haven't enough gas. And it's against the conventions of the armistice. The planes have to remain where they are until . . ."

"Until *they* come to find them," I said.

"I know nothing about that. I don't want to know anything about that! I simply obey my superiors. If we'd had a little more discipline, we wouldn't be where we are now."

"If it's just the gas," said Joufflu, "we could find some."

"Haven't you understood anything Marshal Pétain has said?" asked one of the pilots. "That we must defend France with all our energies. Not by playing simpletons. In any case, it can't be done. The runway is barred with gasoline drums. It's impossible to take off. And the police would shoot us if we so much as permitted someone to turn the props. Listen to a word of advice: hold your tongues, boys, before you're rounded up. Go home. The war is finished. We're going to retire in the country."

We got back on our bikes and returned to Tonneins. To our friends who wanted to know where we'd been,

we said we'd had dates with girls, but that they'd
kicked us out.

Now rumor had it that we were going to form a special guard for Marshal Pétain, who was engaged in saving Vichy France. We were trained to parade. Quick
march, march, eyes left, eyes right, straighten up your
lines. They sent us off on a train to Clermont-Ferrand,
and there I was summoned to see the colonel. He informed me that I'd been demobilized, as were all volunteers who'd enlisted in advance of the statutory age, for
the duration of the war, according to one of the clauses
of the armistice.

He advised me to enter one of the youth camps, organizations that had been instituted to enroll young
men like myself, to give them back their zest for effort,
for work, to give them back their love of country. It
would be possible for me to be taken on as an assistant,
which was the equivalent of cadet.

I didn't go. I didn't care much for scouting.

I left with a thousand francs' worth of demobilization
premiums in my pocket, on my back an army overcoat
dyed maroon, and on my feet a pair of regulation boots.

Upon presentation of my place of residence and my
demobilization card, I received a food card and a tobacco
card. I took up my studies again—after a fashion.

The noise of the war had eased. France was curled up
in her cocoon, nice and warm, despite a lack of coal.
Paris had ceased to exist, and the province, wrapped in
silence, had begun again to live in its own rhythm. Each
weekend I made up half of a twosome with a colorful individual who needed a teammate to keep the antedilu-
vian engine of his car running. We drove along the roads
bordered by plane trees and empty of cars, and we
stopped at inns that paid no attention to food or cigarette coupons. Food was so scarce that one had to be a
rich farmer to buy a pound of butter; and we exchanged
a slice of bacon for a package of cigarettes.

We returned home dog-tired from our weekends.

In those days no one wanted to hear any more about the war.

To lighten Pétain's burden, Darlan and some others took charge of our defeat.

After my demobilization, I went to spend some time in Lozère. My father welcomed me with these words, "Well, are you satisfied? You've lost the war. It didn't cause us half so much trouble to win ours."

I wanted to vomit. I collected my clothes and my few books, my mother gave me a little money, and I left.

At Toulouse I managed to keep body and soul together on a scholarship I'd gotten—I don't know how—from the faculty at Strasbourg. Joseph Calmette, my professor of medieval history, had taken me in with him. He arranged for me to get some meager allowances from the B.U.S.—the University Bureau of Statistics—a more or less phony organization which helped financially embarrassed students.

In March 1941 I tried to cross into Spain by way of Hospice-de-France, but I was stopped at the border by the police because I asked them directions; otherwise I'd have made it. That brought me a few days in jail and some good counsel: take another road the next time.

There I was again in Toulouse, and I was up to my neck in the contentions of Charlemagne's heirs and in Roman-Languedocian sculpture, while the German parachutists took Crete, while the Italians took a thrashing in Albania, and while Panzer divisions thrust toward the Caucasus. Armies were tearing each other apart outside Moscow, the Japanese smashed the American fleet at Pearl Harbor, and Rommel seized Benghazi.

To find out which way the wind was blowing, I risked going as far as Vichy, where I had the address of some cousin or other who was something or other equally indeterminate in the marshal's cabinet. He received me briefly, for when I saw him he was an extremely occupied young man. That morning the marshal's wee-wee had not been very clear, and his whole entourage was agitated over it.

> Vichy, the queen city of the Allies and our provisional capital—capital of less than twenty thousand inhabitants. There wasn't even a subprefecture. Source of hot water, of pavilions, of obsolete hotels, of a casino shaped like a herniated bowel, of theater halls of a more pure spineless style. . . . For four years the way of life in that place meant the French way of life to the world. Vichy—the capital. It was not much; let's say it was nothing. Pétain put it well: "Vichy isn't serious."[7]

What struck me in Vichy was the extraordinary number of military men around, especially the naval men, and all of them with the look of victors rather than of the vanquished. Defeat seemed to become them, and they paraded about and decorated each other in turns. In their eyes France's defeat was not their responsibility. What had done us so much harm were "all the lies told us." Those responsible were the politicians, the Jews, the Freemasons, the Popular Front, holidays with pay, and all the young people who thought only of their own comfort and were so lazy they wouldn't fight.

All of this was explained to me at great length when it became clear that I was in Vichy to find a way to reach free France. Crestfallen and without having found the chink through which I might go, I returned to Toulouse. And in Toulouse was Professor Jankélévitch, who'd been kicked off the faculty because he was a Jew and who continued to teach his courses at the Café Conti. He seated himself on a chair near the exit, his hat nearby where we could deposit our meager alms. It was time to leave Toulouse, in order not to be engulfed in the general apathy.

A few months later I left.

7. Jean Chauvel, *Commentaires* (Fayard).

When you don't know anyone, when you have no connections, when you know nothing about how those thin, mysterious escape lines work which permit downed British pilots to return to England, and when you nevertheless are determined to cross over to the other camp, what do you do? You get a Michelin map and you mark the frontiers that would seem to be the easiest to cross. Then you prudently gather all the information available on each of them. The coast of Andorra was too well guarded. Hospice-de-France was where I'd already been burned. There remained Bourg-Madame-Latour-de-Carol. And it presented one difficulty: you had to have an official mission to cross into that zone.

So I arranged an official-looking paper, sealed with the tricolor of France and some stamps, more or less smeared, to do the trick. That time I wasn't alone. I'd found a companion, Alain S——, a Breton, who wanted to make a career in the military, as much by choice as out of respect for family tradition, which dictated that a man be a soldier or a sailor. He wasn't going to let a war go by without being mixed up in it.

Our frontier runner didn't ask us any questions, but his silence cost us plenty. Between the two of us we spent fifteen hundred francs plus fifty pesetas.

Once across, we took a train and then a bus. In the bus were three characters fitted out as though to scale the Himalayas: ski boots, fur-lined jackets, huge backpacks. With all that equipment we hardly needed to ask where they were headed; so when they got off the bus, we fell into step behind them. They would certainly know some of the tricks we needed to know to make it to the other side.

They disappeared into a seedy inn, where their runner awaited them. We followed, and I politely addressed them:

"I believe we're going in the same direction. Do you think we might join you?"

One of them, acting almost as though he were trafficking in drugs and had the police at his heels, looked us up and down suspiciously and said, "Get the hell out of here, beggars. Get out, or I'll shoot!"

With that he drew a pistol on us. It was clear he was very frightened, and a jittery man under those circumstances could be dangerous. With so little hope of reaching an understanding, we cut out.

We casually sauntered along with hands in pockets until night fell. When the lights of Puigcerdá came on a short distance away, we used our map and our four-sous compass to plot our direction due south. By alternately crawling and running, we crossed fields and came to the railroad tracks, where the lines of cars then concealed our movements.

Then we were in the mountains. In our low shoes and ersatz suits, we marched all night through the snow. In order not to arouse suspicion, we had not worn fur-lined jackets or heavy boots; two such poorly equipped individuals could certainly not be planning to go very far. I remember that as we trudged along the roads, cascading streams of icy water from the melting snows were on each side of us. And it was bitterly cold.

We finally had more than enough of dragging ourselves along in the wet and cold, so we tried to board a train at a little station; but the Spanish civilian police arrested us there and led us in handcuffs to the provincial prison in Gerona, after marching us through the whole city.

In prison we were advised: "Since you have no money, no passports, and no visas, you should try to pass yourselves off as English or Canadian. Franco's police expel the French." This was false.

So we spoke English incessantly, Alain and I. And what abominable jibberish it was! Luckily the police were more ignorant than we about the language of Shakespeare.

Gerona's provincial prison overflowed with English and Canadian prisoners—all bogus.

The genuine articles, when they could be found, didn't

remain there long. These were the bomber crews that had been shot down, and the British consul always arrived posthaste to have them removed from our wasp's nest, in order to get them back into combat. Pilots and air crews were in short supply.

We were a crazy damned mixture there on the third floor: young men like me out to try their luck without a sou of their own or without a recommendation; regular officers or noncoms who'd left Vichy to continue the war on the side of Free France; French Jews and German Jews for whom escape was a matter of life and death and who didn't have much confidence in the future of the free zone. Everyone masquerading under an assumed name. Nobody was deceived, especially not our guards.

Mixed among us were Spanish political prisoners, some of whom were condemned to death. Among the latter were a few members of the aristocracy, whose rank earned them a certain deference, but who were nevertheless executed from time to time.

Mass and confession were obligatory every Sunday. At the elevation, a bugle was sounded in place of the handbell, and at the close of Mass we had to shout: *¡Arriba España! ¡Una, grande, libre! ¡Franco, Franco!* (which we changed to: *¡Coño, coño!*).

We were jammed in like animals, ten to a cell, and crowded together in the halls without even a mattress to sleep on. For breakfast we were given a kind of dishwater brew which passed for coffee, at noon a ladle of soup, and in the evening another ladle of soup and one hundred grams of bread. We were constantly famished, despite the few packets of figs we were able to buy at the prison supply store.

I met some amazing men in that prison. One day we witnessed the arrival of a French lieutenant who had escaped from Germany. He had an old raincoat over his uniform, and some legs cut from old slacks and fastened with safety pins over his leggings to hide them. The first thing he asked us was, "How do I get out of here?"

We howled with laughter. We told him that no one
had escaped from the prison at Gerona since the end of
the civil war. Three weeks later he escaped. We never
knew how he was recaptured, but he was caught and
returned to prison. Senseless! But to him it was a kind
of freedom.

Having discovered his vocation in the prison camps
of Germany, he had since that time broken all escape
records. There wasn't a prison that could keep him,
and no sooner would he be retaken than he'd find a
way to escape again—and always in uniform. After
getting out of Germany he was found in Portugal and
again imprisoned. He was constantly preparing to escape, and would have tried even if he had known he
would be freed the next day—merely for the sport of
it.

Later, when he was fighting with his company of Algerian infantry at Monte Cassino, he was shot through
the head.

I've forgotten his name.

In one corner of our prison hall were three boys who
talked of nothing but planes. They knew everything
about the Spitfire, the Junker, the Messerschmitt, the
Bristol. They knew all about the performances of the
planes, their radius of operation, the number of machine guns or heavy guns with which each was armed,
the weight of the load of bombs each could carry.
Among the three boys, the total of their ages was fifty-
five years, and we called them the "aviators." They
knew exactly what they were going to be: pursuit pilots
in the RAF.

Those of us who had declared ourselves to be English
or Canadian received some help from the British consul-
ate: a blanket, a few pesetas, some powdered milk. But
the "aviators," who proudly maintained that they were
French, received nothing and were starving. Loyalty
such as that couldn't really count for much in prison, for
when the stomach is hollow, it's every man for himself.

After we were in prison awhile we learned to organize ourselves better. We learned brotherhood by force, but it wasn't always easy to make some of those among us understand that we were all aboard the same galley ship, that at the end of our trip there was a war awaiting all of us, and that we had to share our resources.

The youngest of the aviators fell seriously ill, and to save himself he had only one recourse: to appeal to the consul of the Vichy government. That gentleman informed him that he'd be repatriated, but with the consequence of internment for the duration. The boy refused.

Even so, one morning he left with his little bundle of clothes.

In 1961 I was returning from a trip to Tahiti and, between the Fiji Islands and Australia, most of the passengers aboard our DC-8 were sleeping. The captain came back to sit beside me, and he told me he'd read some of my books and liked them. He then confessed that he'd done some writing too—poetry. Resigned and once again cursing Saint-Exupéry for having turned loose on the world so many bad scribblers among its flying men, I told him I'd be delighted to hear some of his poetry. I was surprised.

It was excellent—very beautiful. One of the poems was about a boy in prison who wanted to be an aviator. Nights while the other prisoners slept he went to the WC, because through a fanlight there he was able to see a small strip of the sky and one star.

The only place where one could glimpse a star in that damned prison at Gerona was in the latrine. I used to go there myself, and when I saw the night sky, I could even forget the smell.

The captain was one of the three "aviators" of the prison hall. The first had died in a Spanish hospital. The captain and his other friend had succeeded in becoming RAF pilots. The friend was shot down over Germany, and the captain was the sole survivor of the three.

The jet engines droned softly over the Pacific. The

blue night lights feebly illuminated us as we sat together. We were close enough at that moment to understand each other without any words.

When we were over Sidney, the captain returned to
the cockpit. We didn't see each other again, and no
matter how hard I try, I can't remember his name. I'd
like to find him again.

His name had the sound of something Alsatian, I believe.

After the Americans landed in North Africa, the Red
Cross finally showed up. We were then able to obtain
mattresses, the height of comfort for us. They were
rented by the month to those prisoners who were
condemned to death and who rented them to us. We
had cigarettes then, too—very black and very strong.
Smoking them on an empty stomach gave us an immediate high, exactly as though we'd smoked hashish.

I smoked hashish for the first time with the chief of
detectives in Beirut. It was during the 1958 revolution,
when the Christian nationalists and the Nasserian
Moslems were shooting at each other in the city
streets. As they do today, the Syrians, who already
dreamed of annexing Lebanon, were pouring oil on the
fire from the sidelines. But that time the American
marines had landed to strike a balance.

We were tired of being closed in after curfew, and
the police had arranged a few visits to the seamier sections of the city for the journalists—for a remunera-
tion, naturally.

In the hashish I later smoked in a hookah, I
rediscovered the taste of that black Spanish prison tobacco—but without any effect whatsoever. I was now
fat from being too well fed. Sixteen years earlier, my
old flea-ridden pants had hung on me like a sack.

At Gerona we smoked cigarettes like drug addicts
while stretched out flat on our mattresses. And we
dreamed. As our hunger and fatigue increased, our
erotic visions became more and more ethereal. The

girls we dreamed of lost their behinds and their breasts and were transformed into romantic wisps of ecto-plasm. Most of all we were obsessed with food, and we endlessly composed menus for the feasts we'd have when we left prison.

I always had a little fever in prison, but it was al-most pleasant; my friends said it made me look better.

One day the Red Cross arranged with the Spanish for us to be placed under a condition called house ar-rest at a small seaside resort near Gerona—at Caldas de Malavella, the Vichy of Catalan. There was nothing to be seen of the Allied headquarters.

They housed us in groups of a dozen, where we were responsible for one another. If one of the members of our group behaved stupidly or attempted to escape, his comrades would pay the penalty.

The result was that a short time later our group found itself confined to the concentration camp at Miranda de Ebro; for one of our group had found a way to make it with the wife of the leader of the local Fa-langists (which was rather amusing) and was caught (which was unpardonable).

I won't go into a detailed description of the camp at Miranda, as it has been written about in great detail. But it was a strange group assembled there, as you may guess.

First, there were the Spanish political prisoners— the reds; then the Poles, who had come across the fron-tier in full force after the battle of France; then the de-serters from the German Wehrmacht (of whom there were many more than was ever admitted). Then came the French. The French Basques organized themselves separately in a barracks of their own. They had their own water system, their own arrangements for supplies, their own clergy. The Poles did the same. They were the toughest of the prisoners and the most bitter.

The regular officers, or those who pretended to be, demanded special treatment for themselves, which was not intended to include officer candidates. Following the noisy interventions of one Captain Benoist *(sic)*, who later in North Africa revealed himself to be only a second lieutenant, the officers were lodged in what was called the "calabosse," where they received double rations.

The condemned prisoners had lived at Miranda for many years. These were the Spanish prisoners and the German deserters, and they had set up gambling dens where one could play roulette with pesetas and cigarettes. They had also set up *fondas,* or bars, where one could find wine or alcohol. They even had a male bordello—*La Belle Hollandaise*—where blond ephebes were the prostitutes.

Each barracks had a leader, a kind of kapo who was not above abusing his power to gain personal advantages.

Our stinking food was served to us on large trays placed on the floor. The tiny pieces of meat and the chick-peas swam in rancid oil.

The Poles suddenly decided to institute a hunger strike, despite the objections of their officers in the "calabosse." They listed three reasons for their strike: to protest the murder of one of their number who'd been wounded by a guard while trying to escape and had then been finished off; to remind the Allies that the Poles still existed; and to remind the Spanish that they were not stupid, compliant asses willing to be confined for the rest of their days.

The great diversity of interests and of nationalities, along with the almost total lack of solidarity among the prisoners, made such a strike impossible; so the Poles found a solution. Beside every food tray on the floor they placed guards armed with clubs, and anyone who approached to eat was beaten. The hunger strike was one hundred percent successful. Since then I've seen the same method applied successfully in other places.

Nazi reversals and Allied victories caused Spain to

decide to liberate some of her prisoners. I was among the first contingent to leave.

We were given homespun trousers, one shirt, and a pair of espadrilles. Then, after having been counted and recounted a dozen times, we were loaded onto live-stock trucks. A few hours later we crossed the border into Portugal.

The very first thing we saw was an immense inscription written in lime along the embankment of the rail-road tracks: *VIVA FRANCIA!* We all wanted to cry.

We were sent from there to Casablanca aboard a cargo ship.

When we arrived in Casablanca, the recruiters of the two French armies, the Gaullists and the Giraudists, were waiting for us, one and all hawking their mer-chandise: "Come with us," they said, "the soup is good and the war merry."

The Gaullists offered us the battlefields of Libya, the epic of General Leclerc at Chad, Bir Hakeim, and English battle dress; the Giraudists offered us the Tu-nisian campaign, the battles of Bizerta, and the laced gaiters and soft shirts of the American uniform.

One of our comrades, B——, had been very severely tested by prison. When he'd arrived at Gerona, he'd been a strong, husky boy—peaceful, reticent. He'd grown flabby under the prison regime, and his cheeks hung like those of an old cocker. He could hardly keep on his feet.

His uncle came to meet him at our point of debar-kation, and when he saw his nephew, he'd challenged him, hands on hips, "Well, now, tell me. You took long enough to get here, didn't you?"

B——, who'd expected at least to be congratulated on his safe arrival, didn't reply. His uncle was Gen-eral Leclerc.

B—— was killed at the battle of the Second Demi-Brigade ordered by his uncle.

In truth, we'd all had a rough road to travel in

prison—nine months of it! For my part, I would willingly have done without the miserable novitiate prior
to being enrolled under the flag of war.

We'd hardly debarked when we had to submit to long
interrogations about our identities, because it was believed that Nazi spies had infiltrated our ranks. One of
the accused was my good friend Alain, which knocked
me for a loop. It came about in this way:

Because he was provoked by the kind of questions
asked him by another prisoner who wanted to know
what was behind his rejoining the Allied camp, he'd
answered, "In my family we are military men by tradition. I had a choice between Russia and Africa. Being
sensitive to cold, I chose Africa."

The other prisoner, in order to turn something to account for himself and because he had the temperament
of a cop, lost no time when we arrived in denouncing
Alain as a suspect.

Luckily the military security officer was acquainted
with Alain's Breton tribe and the martial inclinations
of the S—— family, some of whom had already rejoined the Cross of Lorraine.

He was amused by the incident, but he also advised
Alain, "Hereafter, be careful what you say. In times of
war, especially in a war such as this, complicated by so
many small personal wars, by rivalries, by clans, by
the secret service, it isn't recommended that you show
too much spirit or give provocation."

I chose to join the colonial infantry, no one coming to
me to hawk: "It's excellent soup."

Those of us who'd been prisoners together scattered
in every direction, swearing to one another we'd meet
again, knowing there was nothing we could do but
leave it to fate to bring that about.

We received our incorporation physical. A radiogram
exam was part of it, and, unlike that of my comrades,

there were complications in mine. I underwent all sorts of radioscopic exams, until finally the hospital commandant summoned me and said, "The army is finished for you, my son. You'll be discharged. You have a hole in your right lung, and you're going to have to be looked after."

I protested. To have come so far. To have spent nine months in Franco's prisons. And now to be thrown aside, to finish up so miserably in a civilian hospital. No! I refused. It was too unfair!

The doctor let himself be moved by me. My condition wasn't too serious, and I wasn't contagious. But there was my low fever, which prevented me from healing as I should. He was willing to compromise: I could remain in the army, but I was unfit for the infantry. I was to be sent to Cherchel to learn to be an officer in the engineer corps.

That was going to be beautiful. I, who didn't even know how to find the square root.

At school they left me in peace to learn what I wished. I understood nothing about the buckling strength of the material used to build a bridge; on the other hand, I was interested in explosives. The different techniques of sabotage intrigued me, especially the tests we made with TNT on an abandoned railroad line.

I was lodged with a very poor and very old lady, the countess of R——, who owned a lovely Moorish house on the edge of a beach. It was surrounded by bougainvillea, which concealed families of lizards. The school paid her a pension for my keep.

At eighty years of age she still had the coquetries of a young woman and took special care of her beautiful white hair. We made festive occasions of our meals around boiled potatoes and a can of sardines.

Her library was full of old books with splendid bindings, though some of them were half eaten by rats. But one day I discovered in still-perfect condition the two volumes of the original edition of *Vies parallèles*[8] by Plutarch, translated by Amyot. On one of the end papers was the great seal of the city of Auxerre, where Amyot was bishop. There were also numerous corrections in the author's hand.

I knew very little about old editions, but was not completely ignorant of the value of these unique treasures. I showed them to the countess, but without hearing my explanations, she said to me, "They interest you? Take them."

She lived miserably, but possessed a treasure that would let her live out the rest of life in tranquility, without having to apply for pensions. I felt I had to speak strongly to her, to counsel her to write to the librarian in Algiers and tell him of the existence of the books.

I don't know the rest of the story, but later I imagined a sequel that would have served as the plot of a novel, one I never wrote—like all the others I dreamed up.

I was the officer candidate Pierre or Paul who had accepted the gift from the countess. I carried *Vies parallèles* with me when I was sent into combat in Italy, at Monte Cassino. I was killed during an attack, and my body lay there on the ground with my backpack still holding the Plutarch.

A German officer recovers the two volumes. He's a university man, versed in the letters, and he knows their worth. Delighted by them, he takes them with him when he is sent to the Russian front. He in his turn is shot by partisans who have no paper and who use the pages of the rare editions to roll their cigarettes . . .

When I left Cherchel I had a double commission as platoon commander in the infantry and in the engineers. From there I went up to patch my health in the

8. Plutarch's *Parallel Lives*. (Translator's note.)

Sahara, and in just a few weeks the dry air of the desert had so completely cured me that I had no trouble passing the aptitude exam for the shock units.

The corps of my first choice, the colonial infantry, took me back, and I found myself in the C.L.I.—Light Intervention Corps—a group of commandos especially trained and prepared for the reconquest of Indochina and for jungle warfare in the Far East.

The Japanese occupied Burma, Malaysia, Indochina, and the Indian Archipelago—all very rich territories. England, France, and Holland each hoped to reinstate their administrations in these countries after the war had been won—in the process, of course, unburdening themselves of the local ballast.

The Americans viewed all this with a different eye, for in their estimation that part of the world was their private game preserve. But *all* these old colonizers were on a collision course not only with the Japanese and their collaborators, who, under the cover of the sphere of Asiatic co-prosperity, worked with the Japanese to keep these territories, but also with the nationalistic liberation movements already under the control of the Communists and supported by Washington's Office of Strategic Services.

America had a monopoly on transports and furnished most of the necessary material for the war in the East, which put her in the position of holding the key to the treasure chest there. This, then, made it necessary for the English, the French, and the Dutch, in order to further their own interests, to organize small units like ours, who compensated by their effectiveness for their countries' lack of material means and who were capable of operating without arousing the suspicions of Roosevelt and his crew.

The originator of this new concept was an exceptional man, Orde Wingate, son of a minister and himself a great Bible reader (he knew Hebrew and could read the Torah as well), who endeavored to reintroduce

into the army two revolutionary ideas which for nearly
a century all the major powers had forgotten, if not actively scorned: imagination and common sense.

After having served in the Sudan, Captain Wingate
was sent in 1936 to Palestine as information officer.
Britain was pro-Arab then, and for religious reasons
and by family tradition, Wingate was pro-Israeli. He
became the Lawrence of the Jews.

When he departed a year and a half later, he left for
all time his stamp upon the Haganah and the remarkable army that came out of it. He had created the celebrated "midnight battalions," had taught the Israelis to
fight in the dark with knives and grenades, to special-
ize in ambushes and hand-to-hand fighting, and how to
find among their adversaries the arms they lacked.
Among his students were Moshe Dayan and others of
the same stamp.

The Israelis would say of this *goïm:* "If he hadn't
died, he would be head of our army." And they gave
his name to one of their institutes.

Repudiated by his chiefs and recalled to England, it
appeared that Orde Wingate had been taken out of the
game; but 1941 found him at the head of the troops of
Ethiopian irregulars who wanted to put Négus on the
throne.

You know his kind: nonconformist, fighting in his
own fashion, with little material means and totally un-
concerned with sacrosanct traditions. But he is effective, and he is best used for diversionary operations,
where there can be called into play all his ability to
improvise, as well as all his "charisma." The kind of
man crazy enough to be a leader of men, to be inspired
by God.

Next he was to be found in Burma, which was nearly
like coming home to him, for he was born on the frontier of Nepal and Tibet in India's state of Ulltar
Pradesh.

Estimating that the war in that part of the world
was being conducted contrary to all common sense and

that it wasn't because the Japanese had "slit eyes" which made them better jungle fighters than the Europeans, he suggested the creation of long distance penetration groups, whose purpose would be to disrupt the enemy's lines of communication and supply. His old obsession: guerrilla warfare and night fighting.

After much shilly-shallying, India's general staff agreed to his plan. They had no other choice, because they lacked the men and materials to wage conventional war, and because they must manage by any means to gain some victories to compensate for the loss of prestige and the thrashing the British had suffered at the hands of the Mikado's men.

Wingate created the famous free "chindit" group, taking the name from the legendary animal—half eagle and half lion—whose statue is found in all the Burmese pagodas. Curiously enough, that animal came to symbolize perfectly the war Wingate waged, which was based on close cooperation between land and air and which brought into play a veritable army dropped by parachute behind the Japanese lines.

Wingate was a professional officer, and he understood the conventional army well—an army where all instruction was directed to kill the young soldier's spirit of initiative, to dry up his imagination, and to replace them with reflexes, where the individual is conditioned to be a tool in the hands of his chiefs. He learns to obey orders mechanically without arguing about them, without even interpreting them. Wingate understood the kind of army that used parades to transform its young men into automatons who all lift their feet at exactly the same time, the kind of army that believes its quality is seen in the way it marches.

Wingate was opposed to all of this. He believed that instead of castrating the individual soldier, instead of training out of him all that made up his personality, one could cultivate the whole man—all his good and bad qualities, all the weaknesses he brought with him from civilian life—and still obtain a better return, a

better performance. In exchange for leaving the man
a whole man, the army could ask of him even more
than could be asked of the ordinary professional
soldier.

He ran counter to all the teachings and manuals of
the war of 1914–18. He refuted the notion that men
were expendable "human material." Not because he
was a humanist, but because he abhorred waste. He
was going to do the impossible with his men, going to
launch a new kind of war. And because he had relatively few men at his disposal for the kind of operation
he envisaged, it was necessary to be economical with
them and to teach them how not to throw their lives
away stupidly.

He said to himself, "I'm going to recruit my soldiers
from among the worst soldiers, or those the army con-
siders to be the worst, because they are the ones who
feel uneasy in the old army of Queen Victoria, the
army of the Bengal Lancers, of the Charge of the Light
Brigade (which still exists today, even in 1942). I want
with me those men who believe we've earned our defeat because we've let ourselves be had by the Japs,
those who've no desire to recommence fighting under
their old leaders and to take the same licking. I'll teach
them to think. I want them to manage their war themselves, to improvise, to decide their course of action according to the circumstances. I'm going to propose a
dangerous and exciting game to them. They will all be
Kims in the jungle. They'll wage a hard fight, where
everything is permitted. They'll learn to conduct themselves like assassins, with trickery, with ambushes,
using all the weapons of their adversaries. Exactly as
the political wars are being waged to serve the minorities who have been oppressed everywhere in Asia and
who now have accounts to settle with their governments. My men won't be robots any longer, but they
will fight because they want to, because they've elected
to fight that kind of war."

Another great idea of Wingate's was that any soldier

trained to suit Wingate was capable of fighting in the jungle equally as well as, if not better than, those who'd lived there many years. *La Jungle est neutre* is the title of an excellent work by another Englishman, Spencer Chapman, who'd himself practiced jungle warfare in Malaysia and in Burma after having escaped the disaster of Singapore.

At Djidjelli, our instructors of the Light Intervention Corps—the C.L.I.—worked to put commandos into action who would operate according to the principles elaborated by Wingate and Chapman. And we would have two objectives: to chase the Japanese and their allies from Indochina; and to replace in office the old administration of Colonel Decou, compromising in this with the enemy. This was the least expected of us.

We would be supported in our efforts by a certain local resistance group (very self-important) and by the local minorities (who were far less favorable to us than we could have imagined). With these minorities we should be able to make up small armies in the country's interior, using some to spy on others, and vice versa, with ourselves the recruiters of these armies. One exception was made: we'd forget the Vietminh—the Communist resistance group—of which we'd heard only the worst.

Assembled in the camps scattered around Djidjelli were a number of colonial administrators, such as Messmer and others, who would later play an important role in the "reconquest" of Indochina. There were also those who would play a part in its destruction, specialists in destruction even as I was, and other colorful individuals such as Captain Dewavrin, Colonel Passy's brother. All were volunteers, naturally.

In application, what we'd been taught was to set afoot "sticks" of intervention, small groups of four or five men, who would parachute behind enemy lines with a single precise mission: blow up a road, a bridge, a dam, burn an enemy base.

This kind of operation presented unknowns: we didn't know how we'd be welcomed on the ground or by whom. The worst possibility was that we could be brought down before having been able to open our chutes.

For want of accurate information, many of my comrades were blindly dropped over Tonkin, over Cambodia, in the mountains, on China's frontier, and died as a result. Some of them took a long time to die.

The "sticks" could not expect to be recovered when their assault was completed. They must remain where they were and try to organize camouflaged bases in the forest from which to launch raids on the enemy. They had to count on living for weeks or months in the jungle with nothing but local resources, because they'd be completely cut off from supplies, and drops of rations could be expected only in very exceptional cases. There would be no planes, or very few, and priority was given to arms and munitions.

In a situation such as that, you'd need to know how to render water potable; how to find and dig edible roots; how to hunt and fish without being spotted. You'd need to learn how to recognize herbs, lianas, and berries, which, for lack of something better, would allow you to survive; how to filter water through your hat, which, however, wouldn't help you to avoid dysentery; how to care for your wounds and injuries. We went through various stages and trials which concluded, as in the scouts, with a final exam and the awarding of badges. Did you know that scouting is, first of all, a school where you are taught war?

In training, you are armed with a compass, a map, and a can of lightly salted water. You have to cover two hundred kilometers in forty-eight hours, alone and shifting for yourself. You decide for yourself your periods of march and rest. Or you might be stuck alone on a raft at sea and be required to manage not only to survive, but to keep in shape, with only a canvas tent to serve as your roof, as your sail, and as your receptacle in which to catch rainwater. It had better rain! To be honest, we couldn't resist cheating. We carried bundles of TNT with us on the raft and made underwater explosion tests to gain us good catches of fish.

A doctor had persuaded Wingate that humans needed far less sleep than they thought. Only the first hour of sleep was important, it being the time when sleep is deep and refreshing. The rest of sleep time is lost time.

Wingate had then instituted a system of training which interrupted the rhythm of our sleep and had limited its duration. We were trained to fall asleep anywhere, anytime, in any way, and in any position. Never more than one hour at a time and never more than four hours a day.

We were taught to fire "instinctively," to shoot without either aiming or bringing the gun to the shoulder, and without knowing ahead of time what weapon we would be using.

You'd be placed somewhere alone in the middle of the night, and suddenly you'd be tossed a weapon— French, English, American, Japanese, a rifle, submachine gun, F.M. 24. In a few seconds you had to be able to find the safety catch and to know if the weapon was loaded. With the speed of lightning, targets would light up around you—in front of you, behind you, near or far—and you were required to hit them.

At first the exercise was a catastrophe. We didn't react swiftly enough, and we became enraged. But at the end of several weeks and after hundreds of batches of cartridges, the miracle happened, and we *could* hit a fly. We acquired the reflexes necessary for firing "instinctively."

You must also learn how to throw a knife, and it isn't done the way you see it in the movies—with the blade held at its extreme point between two fingers and thrown from the height of your head.

On the contrary, the blade must be held flat across the palm of the hand, the point turned toward yourself.

If the weapon is properly balanced, when it is thrown it will turn of itself before piercing the opponent. A word of advice: Always aim for the belly or the back. Watch out for the belt or other articles that can have a buckle.

Nothing is easier than strangling a sentinel without noise. You place yourself beside the path he walks, and you wait until he passes you. You leap. You seize him by the edges of his helmet and pull it toward you. The strap strangles the jugular vein and prevents him from yelling. Then, the knife you place at his kidney penetrates quite naturally.

We were allowed to eat our meals only after we'd spent ten minutes toughening up the edges of our hands on the table of heavy wood.

Another game: A friend plants his Colt in your back, bullet engaged. You must disarm him with a rapid turn of your body, accompanied by a quick chop to his gun wrist. You dare not miss hitting your mark, because your friend will really shoot. You will do as much when it's your turn. At the beginning we had a few accidents. They were included in the normal percentage of expected training casualties. I no longer know whether it was three or seven percent.

We grew used to playing with danger.

Once I was sent right through the canvas roof of the bell tent where I slept, along with the board that supported my mattress, propelled at top speed by the TNT a friend had ignited under it.

You learn to move without making a sound, coming down first upon the heel and then the rest of the foot. Until you're used to it, that can be terribly fatiguing, because you stretch muscles you're not accustomed to using. And to let yourself be recognized by your cohorts, you learn to imitate the cries of certain animals or birds. In *La Jungle est neutre*, Chapman tells how he used the sound of the clacking of the tongue with which one urges on a horse.

On a quiet night, such a sound can be heard for a

very long distance. It attracts hardly any attention; it could be produced by any bird or insect; it could be fruit falling from a tree, a branch breaking.

Chapman also used the ululation of an English owl, perceptible even in a dense forest, which could never be confused with any other cry of the jungle.

In case your flashlight batteries die, you learn how to produce a light sufficient to read a map by or to light your way. You place glowworms or luminous millepedes in the flashlight's reflector. The Viets often used such a method, and it's long been known to old bush runners.

You learn how to make probes and pincers out of bamboo with which to extract bullets; how to apply tobacco, which coagulates blood, to leeches to make them release their bite, as the Chinese have always done.

You are taught to fear and distrust the savage ox of Malacca and the gaur of Indochina, the most dangerous of all animals, because they will attack on sight; even when wounded, they will not give up.

You are warned never to forget that distance in the jungle is very difficult to evaluate correctly. If you should stray from the path, it takes several hours to progress a single kilometer, for you must hack your way through with a machete. If you're white, you're too easily seen and must camouflage yourself or dye your skin. The worst thing you can do is to be overconfident. All you have to do to be completely undone is to forget only once a single precaution you've been taught, under the pretext that there's no one around, that the jungle is empty. The jungle is never empty. The jungle is full of eyes.

During training we were forbidden to smoke, to drink alcohol, and to amuse ourselves with girls—all brain waves of that old Puritan, Wingate.

But the war we were trained to fight was nevertheless far better than Verdun, the trenches, and the bayonet attacks, even though we had to do without red wine and girls.

These units cost a great deal to train, but, as in roulette, when the right number comes up, it pays you
twenty times over. Three or four of these soldiers with
enough luck and nerve can do the work of a brigade of
infantry: three thousand soldiers who have to be trans-
ported and provisioned, with all their equipment, their
rations, their heavy arms, and their vehicles. And if
the mission of a "stick" is aborted, another unit can be
sent in until the mission is completed.

Generally, the "stick" is composed of a lieutenant or
captain in charge of the group; a second lieutenant or
officer candidate; a specialist in destruction; a radio
and radioman; and two specialists in the knife and
high-powered rifle, all at least noncoms.

More often than not the radio units were equipped
with heavy and cumbersome generating sets with pedals.
It was always recommended that prisoners be taken as
quickly as possible to help transport and pedal them. A
commando unit whose radio was out was considered lost.

After several months of that kind of life, some of our
men began to look for reasons for the kind of war they
were fighting, reasons other than using the techniques
they'd been taught and the sport involved. They wanted
other criterion, too, than just the successful bringing off
of a coup. They needed better justification than what
they'd been given. Despite all their training, they remained in a sense fragile—especially after they were
removed from the security of group discipline, of the
traditional military environment, of being surrounded
by men of their own race and kind.

Our man had been asked to understand the motives
of the adversary he confronted, to impregnate himself
with his enemy's theories, in order to fight him better
on his own ground. And now here he was, far away
from home, obliged to adopt another way of life, different manners of dress. The war was total, and it was all
mixed up with politics. It confused him. Why was he
really fighting? Generally it was to reestablish an

old-fashioned colonial power no one wanted, not even his own partisans whom he'd barely recruited before he'd had to lie to them, who'd been promised independence no one intended to grant. Lies. Always lies. Lies, above all, to those men who lived and died beside him because they believed him. It was becoming insupportable to him.

There were some who succumbed completely, who began to believe the enemy's catechism. Others had fought so long they went out of their heads. They began to dream of becoming kings, and they sometimes involved themselves in strange and sordid adventures that always ended tragically. And still others sought death, because it seemed the only solution for them. Victory was as hard for them as defeat.

The old Colonel Blimps, who clung to their beliefs in the F.M. 24, modified 29, lost their wars, but they did it within regulations. These others, the children of Wingate—the red berets, the black berets, the green berets—wanted to win their wars without bothering their heads about regulations, which didn't keep them from losing their wars and themselves, into the bargain.

The tragedy of the Centurions.

It was 1971, after the Tet offensive. I followed the Lam-Son operation, that tentative effort to cut the Ho Chi Minh trail with nothing more than the support of American planes and helicopters.

The helicopter that carried me became lost in the fog, and the pilot had to land. He set me down on a path, a sort of trail he'd glimpsed in the middle of a jungle so thick it was impossible to tell on which side I'd landed—the Viets or the others. I wondered then if I'd be able at fifty years of age to extricate myself with what I'd learned at commando school. I was finished, washed out. I'd grown fat; I was easily winded; all the plants around me resembled one another.

On the other hand, I am still able to blow up a bridge in such a way that it would take a very long time to rebuild it; I can sabotage a railway track or a dam; I can blow open a safe without messing up the whole bank—all with nothing more than a correctly placed hollow charge. Does one ever know what the future holds?

I was a specialist in destruction and only had the chance to put my expertise to the test, alas! on rare occasions and in the least spectacular places: setting and clearing mines under enemy fire.

Brrr . . .

When the first stage of my commando training was completed, a few days before I was to embark for the Far East where I would finish my training, I left the C.L.I. A memorandum came down stating that all French escapees were free to join their units before sailing.

Going to the Far East would be fine and was one thing, but to be legitimized and to return to France a victor was something else again. To be able to say to my father: "You see? This time, I, too, have won my war!"

So I rejoined the battalion of shock troops and studied explosives and the clearing and defusing of mines. Later I was again assigned to the commando group from Africa, which was then based at Agropolis in Italy.

I missed the debarkation to the coast of Provence by a hair, though I wasn't at fault. All our reinforcements missed the convoy, and I was even late in reaching Naples.

Some ships wouldn't take me aboard for fear I'd blow them up with my TNT, my plastics, my blasting caps, my delayed detonators, my mines, my flamethrowers, my cans of napalm. Not surprising. More than a few subtle traps were set by the handymen of the secret services.

The whole port of Naples had been completely destroyed.

We went ashore in amphibious carriers which crossed the harbor like a fleet of ducks on a debris-covered lake.

A friend of mine had come to meet me, a *pied-noir,*[9] the best guy in the world, but given to annoying exaggeration. I asked him, "What's Naples like?"

"Not much," he answered. "A squalid and disgusting place, in fact. The only place you can find anything decent to eat or drink is at the English or American mess. If you go into the "off-limits" areas, keep your gun hidden, or you'll lose it. And with it your belt. And your trousers. And your boots. As for the girls, though, it's a miracle! You can have all of them you want. All of them, do you understand? Providing you can pay the price."

"Aren't you stretching it just a bit?"

"Pick out any girl you want. Offer her three thousand liras, and she'll go with you. I'll bet your salary against mine."

I accepted the wager. Even in a country at war and plunged in misery, even in a city with as unwholesome a reputation as Naples, it still had to be possible to find honest women.

The next morning my friend and I waited for the finish of the first Mass and the exit of the worshipers into the square in front of one of the innumerable churches with an overblown style of architecture. I saw a young widow in her black veil come out of the church. She was tragic looking, pale, with red eyes. I decided on her and told myself, "You're going to earn a couple of good slaps for this, but it would be worth much more to prove that even in Naples all the girls aren't whores."

I approached the young widow and spoke to her brutally, "Will you sleep with me? Three thousand liras."

9. An Algerian-born Frenchwoman or man (Translator's note.)

She looked at me, bit her lip, and, in singsong French, said, "When? But give me some cigarettes, too, and some milk for my children."

I fled, red with shame and furious at myself and all the other men. I had just discovered the other side of the picture, the one on the underside of every war.

"You were right to leave her," my friend said. "She wasn't so great. For a thousand liras you can find better and younger girls. Pay up!"

In Naples I saw what can become of a city grown rotten by a war and by occupation. I can still remember the lovely nun who came to beg alms outside the bistros, accompanied by two schoolgirl boarders of her order. They were perhaps twelve or thirteen years old. Holding the sister by the hand, they made eyes at the soldiers; for a little money they'd lift their skirts and show their panties.

In *La Peau,* Malaparte writes that there was in Naples at that time a hovel where a madame would show you "a real virgin." The soldiers were allowed to examine her to verify her virginity. I believe that story, and others of the same sort. I've seen the parade of young boys—less contaminated than the girls, it was said—who'd just come from servicing the Moroccans, who preferred boys. They used to fish inside the pants of the children to handle them before accepting or refusing their services.

I remember the smells of urine, of rancid frying oil, of bad perfume in the alleys of Naples. I remember the cats and the children who ran to avoid the slops and ordure descending from the windows above. What was there for us to be so proud of, we defenders of the Occident against the Nazi barbarians, we who had come with our black mercenaries, our Berbers, and all the jailbirds let out for the occasion from American prisons and disguised as Rangers?

We returned to Agropolis, our rear base, to wait for the convoy that would land us on the shores of France, where some of our comrades had already gained a foothold. They'd been the first to reach Cap Nègre on the coast of Provence, and while we were becoming familiar with all the bistros and bordellos of Agropolis with the Rangers from Sing Sing, they'd taken Condom and the battery at Mauvannes.

We rejoined the commandos at Marseilles, which had just been liberated. I use the term loosely. I've never seen such disorder. Everyone sauntered about with brassards and weapons. There were the genuine Resistance fighters and the phony ones, those who'd adopted the Resistance on the eve of liberation, who two days before had been collaborators with the enemy.

There were even "Chinese commandos," who took their turns of duty on their convoy trucks, sleeping on the running boards in grotesque positions, guns in readiness. All second rate, a bad crowd trying to replay the Spanish War.

But in Spain they'd fought. Here, this bunch ran rackets and black-market operations.

Our men were the only ones who went about without arms in this city of insanity.

We went to the movies once, and two walking arsenals came to sit next to us. They wore the insignia of captain or commander. One of them, a boy of about eighteen, let his Sten gun fall—a filthy piece of botched work, that weapon—which then shot a burst of rounds into the ceiling of the theater. Someone yelled, "The militia is attacking!"

The Wild West wasn't just on the screen, it was in the theater, too. What a free-for-all!

The young gangster lost no time in recovering his arrogance, rigged out in all his military trappings and the brassards of the F.T.P. or the F.F.I.[10]

10. "Superbly slovenly, 500 F.F.I., which became 20,000 after the victory, fought at the side of the Allied forces." Raymond Cartier, *La Seconde Guerre mondiale.*

The F.T.P. were the *Francs-Tireurs Partisans* (free marksmen and partisans), and the F.F.I. were the *Forces Françaises de l'Intérieur* (French Forces of the Interior). (Translator's note.)

The commandos, the shock groups, and the parachutists were no longer the babies of the choir. They'd grown up, and when they were presented with the bill for a black-market meal they'd eaten, they simply left without paying. They conveniently forgot the "gift" promised the girls they'd picked up, and were then angered when they were told the Germans had made better clients.

With so many elements jammed together, something was bound to give. And the soldiers were bored. Once it happened that one of them was shot in the back as he left the nightclub where he and his friends had eaten and drunk at the unwilling expense of the house. His comrades returned in force, backed up by a half-track with a heavy machine gun. They blocked off all the adjoining streets and let themselves into the nightclub—all of them recognizable by their bearing, even in their ragtags of uniforms. They closed themselves in and turned the place into a sieve.

Assuming the role of recruiting officers, some of our men made it their business to beef up the effectiveness and the numbers of the group. They tried any means: getting the target drunk as a boiled owl; telling him stories of impossible heroic feats; even blackmail. Not very difficult, given the quality of the merchandise! It was in this way that a few important pimps landed in the commandos. As soon as they could they escaped, but were retaken and made to walk through their bailiwick—the narrow hot streets behind the theater—with signs hanging from their backs that read: "I'm a coward." Bad publicity for those toughs who lived by their fearful reputations.

It was thanks to some of these "recruiters" that a certain Cohen, as he called himself, a native of Algeria or of Medes, became a hero.

He'd been assigned to the transport unit. Three commandos, who knew all the good bistros, had easy access to *pastis*, [11] were good talkers, and appeared to be

11. An aniseed apéritif. (Translator's note.)

knowledgeable about all the plots and plans hatched in the high command, invited him to have a drink and engaged him in conversation.

The three began by asking Cohen to which unit he'd been assigned. The transport? They complimented him on his courage—or was it his obliviousness? The transport unit comprised those lines of trucks that carried munitions and fuel, and the enemy concentrated its artillery and its aircraft to smash them. They had seen such convoys blown up and burned in Tunisia and in Italy. Going back up the Rhône River was going to be much worse. In high places they were already saying that only three trucks would arrive intact out of the whole convoy. With luck!

Who had given the three this information? The general staff, you see. On the other hand, because the commandos had gone to the islands of the Mediterranean: Pianosa, Elba, Corsica—then to the coast of Provence, and had suffered serious injuries, because it was decided they'd done enough, and because there were no more debarkations planned, they'd been placed in "general reserve." They were going to be used to form personal guards for the great leaders: de Lattre, Juin, de Gaulle.

Our recruit, who didn't really feel that he had the soul of a warrior (which was why he'd let himself be assigned to the transport unit in the first place), began to feel uneasy; especially more so as the three associates played their game to perfection, taking their time, staging their plans well.

Finally Cohen could take no more, and asked how he could get himself out of the mess he was in.

"We're going to give you a little tip," the three told him. "Join the commandos."

Cohen formally requested his transfer, and so found himself with us, where he quickly learned that he'd been tricked.

He was assigned to an assault group, learning to handle flamethrowers and other devices. In that environment he became a remarkable soldier, was wounded, cited for bravery, and given the medal of the army. Covered with glory and with medals, he triumphantly returned to his home.

I heard that later he became one of the "toughs" of the O.A.S.[12]

Which seems to prove that the ambience of a fighting unit like ours, with the record of all its past feats of arms—or those it has borrowed—with the myths it has created (made up partly of lies and exaggerations), can bring out hidden courage in men. Well-hardened men, men made self-confident by the oft-repeated assurance that they are lions, will not bray like asses and run away in the middle of combat. They will behave like lions.

I remember those "quiet little dance halls" of Marseilles, where the "Admiral" trained us. Hardly had the dance begun when the call would sound for a free-for-all, with chairs and bottles the weapons of attack and defense, in the style of *Don't Shoot the Piano Player.* We preferred to fight the Yanks, but in a pinch we'd take on the compatriots of any other flag.

The "Admiral," Louis Laguilharre, was an engineer in the marines and had seen active service in Burma, an extraordinary adventure straight out of Kipling.

He was responsible in that part of the world for the Schlumberger Geophysical Society, and he'd brought all his prospecting material through the densest and most inhospitable jungle in the world, even having to make his way through the territory of the headhunters. It is said that after what was acknowledged as a unique accomplishment, his material was out of date! More than that, it was all thrown into the sea!

Laguilharre was the hero of a celebrated communiqué of General Wavel's general staff: "The last units of the rear guard of the British army have finally reached

12. *Organisation de l'Armée Secrète* (Secret Service). (Translator's note.)

our lines. They are composed of a French madman
(Laguilharre), a red Irishman, and a spotted dog. . . ."

I owe my pseudonym to Laguilharre. After the war
we tried together to write a series of articles about his
prodigious exploit. Since we were both still in the military, we couldn't sign our own names without asking
for authorization from a dozen colonels or generals.
Osty and Laguilharre, combined, became—I don't
know how anymore—Larteguy. (It was the Admiral
who was bent upon our endeavor; I had not done the
things he had.)

No one wanted our narrative. It was too exotic for
some, too long for some, too badly written for others.
At that time the newspapers were only four pages long,
and most of them were run by amateurs, some of
whom barely knew how to read.

Some of my comrades of those days are especially remembered. There was Delvigne, who came to us from
the cavalry, and who polished his boots until they shone
like mirrors. He even wore gloves, which irritated the
rest of us. He had absolutely the most puffed-up ego of
our group.

And Boulanger, who came from Algeria, and who
later lost a buttock in the Vosges. And Massé, who had
a noble Russian bass voice, and who spoke Arabic like
a priest of the mosques and wrote it like a member of a
Moslem ulama.

And the old fellows: Colonel Bouvet of the nutcracker
jaw, who walked with a cane, and who tried with feats
of arms and with the dead and wounded that he
chalked up to equal the record of his archrival in the
shock troops, the diminutive Commander Gambiez;
Commander Rigault, who had a deep husky voice, and
who swore vulgarly; Faré, who'd lost an arm at Elbe;
and Ruyssen, the organizer, who did his utmost to
maintain some semblance of order among us.

And Captain Ducourneau, the best soldier of the
bunch, one of the great French parachutists. With
Bigeard—I've mentioned him—he was my model for

Raspéguy, the Indochina colonel in *Les Centurions.* A true Basque! Later, when he was a general in the army, he was struck on the head by a helicopter blade and slept through the night he was to become chief of staff.

And François de Leusse, who came to us from the First Demi-Brigade of the Legion, and who loved women, fun, and war. And Métivier of the Legion's First Cavalry Regiment. And Merindol, who had a Russian accent, the voice of Chaliapin, and the thirst of a moujik.

And Suti—Suzanne Tillier—who saw service in Verdun as a nurse. As an aviatrix, she was Maryse Bastié's copilot during his raid on Russia and Siberia. As part of an ambulance unit, she was one of the first to enter Bizerta. She was the first to land, disguised as a man, on French soil. There she took a young German prisoner, who cried with rage when he learned he'd surrendered to a woman.

And all the cadets and second lieutenants of our group who loved to laugh, to fight, to take towns and girls, to surprise their friends and to surprise themselves, and to whom there remained, as with Massé, but a few days of life. All those hussars in blue for whom death lay in wait in the great forests of the Vosges, in the snows of Alsace, and later in Indochina.

It seems to me sometimes that Massé must have taken my place in the landing that I missed. How I would love to have written the letter he sent to a friend, a letter written in that easy and elegant tone that was so much the style of our men.

30 August 1944

This year I'm vacationing on the *Côte d'Azur,* on a delicious little beach with not a pebble in sight.

The crossing for me and my section was effected by means of a motor torpedo boat which traveled at great speed, and

in the company of American marines we found the trip
extremely pleasant. The mission of our first commando
group was to go ashore in rubber boats, to proceed stealth-
ily, and to take the battery holding the beach. Everything
went off exactly as planned.

Our training had been intensive, so much so that we were
able to scale the nearly vertical cliffs of Cap Nègre (110
meters high) with seventy men and all our equipment.

. . . I received radio orders to take the fort at Condom,
which dominated the entire plain of Toulon. But the Germans were well camouflaged in the fort and could, at
their pleasure, rake us with machine gun fire whenever
we moved. The drawbridge was raised, and we had no
means to penetrate into the fort; so without any hesita-
tion whatever, Captain Ducourneau undertook to climb
the ramparts by clinging to protruding stones.

. . . Suddenly afraid, the Germans took refuge under the
arcades. That left the walk above free, and we quickly
encircled the center of the fort. . . . I set all my grenades in
the holes of the chimney, and the noise of the explosions
was deafening. . . . The Germans rapidly changed positions
and began shooting at us from the rear. We gave chase
and finally, after we'd pursued them for a half hour, they
hid themselves in the cellars, first firing a green flare,
calling for artillery fire. We'd have been done for if we'd
remained outside, so we, too, rushed for the inner halls
and more obscure galleries. The captain was wounded.
Through a miracle I got off without a scratch. . . . I closed
the eyes of the dead myself. . . . Since yesterday we have
been at the seaside. . . .

Don't let me lead you to suppose that the landing was an
easy thing for the commandos. Very many are missing at
roll call.

The commandos from Africa were more a free corps
than a genuine specialized group such as the C.L.I.
(Light Intervention Corps). It was born the Free African Corps and won wide renown under Monsabert in
the Tunisian campaign.

There were men in the corps from every shore, from every army, from every walk of life, of every age, some of them with prostitutes trailing after them.

Among the most astonishing of the men were Lieutenant Bietti and Sergeant Major Rocca. Rocca had twenty-seven citations with seventeen palms. The Germans so admired him that when they thought they'd killed him at the landing in France, they paid tribute to him. A commander of the Legion of Honor, he never wanted to become an officer. Bietti didn't wear his marks of rank. He won the Victoria Cross for having single-handedly defended an abandoned trench against a battalion of the Afrika Korps. Once he mounted an assault braying *"L'Internationale"* with his squad of Spanish Republicans. He also later joined the O.A.S.

When de Gaulle arrived in the south of France, they confined Bietti to the monastery of the monks on the Iles de Lérins. Then the prefect came to make his apologies for such treatment. Driven back to Saint-Maxime, Bietti swore to kill the "grande Zorah." His service records showed him capable of doing just that.

What became of my friends? Dead, dead, dead. Like Laguilharre, de Leusse, Ducourneau; like Massé and so many others whose names I've forgotten; all the old clowns, all the old heroes of what we used to call the "circus."

And what was really extraordinary about the whole fantastic affair was the friendship we felt for one another. Sometimes to the point of forgetting the other face of war.

I received my first real baptism of fire during the indecisive battle of the Vosges.

It was the task of our group, of the shock battalion, of the commandos, and of the First Regiment of Parachutists to infiltrate deeply behind the enemy lines and to wait there for the army commanded by General

Monsabert. Our particular mission was to make the Wehrmacht believe by the noise we made and by repeated surprise attacks that they were outflanked and surrounded. The attack by our regular divisions would then break a front already weakened by our efforts, and the end result would be a rout of the Germans.

The first part of our program went as planned. Our guides had marked the forest routes we were to take, and after dark we crossed the enemy lines without great damage to ourselves.

It began to rain—a torrential rain, hard and cold. I couldn't see beyond the end of my nose. By way of Cornimont and Saulxures, we reached our designated objectives: the heights of Tonteux and of Grosse Pierre. At daybreak the Germans began fighting.

Mortars bursting with the sound of smashing crockery. Lines of humpbacked soldiers under their rain ponchos. Soldiers who staggered and stumbled and swore. A sky so low the clouds cloaked the tops of the tall firs.

The half boots of the Americans became slick with mud, and their rubber soles could gain no hold on the slippery earth. We took falls in the mud where our weapons and packs were lost, our ankles and wrists sprained. For a while there was an overwhelming silence, the rain never ceasing to fall and to add to the thick silence. Suddenly we were engaged in a brutal skirmish—rapid, unexpected. Weapons cracked, grenades fused in midair and burst deafeningly. A mine exploded. A long cry of pain. A rush to the safety of the trees. And the fighting went on.

I thought I was hit, and I saw Massé crumple to the ground. My feet grew heavy. I knew nothing more until someone came to drag me away.

When we returned a few minutes later, Massé was dead. A bullet had severed his femoral artery. *Adieu,* Massé!

With my section I pressed behind a stone wall, letting

myself think for a moment that we'd reached protection. I felt relieved. And I was hungry. I took the opportunity to open a can of rations.

But they began firing at us again. Next to me, a soldier jerked convulsively like a rabbit whose spine has
been snapped. The Germans held a hill that overlooked our position, and they repeatedly raked us with
fire.

It was useless to jump to the other side of the wall; it
was equally vulnerable. I didn't know what to do or
what order to give. I was responsible for the lives of my
men. I'd taken all the courses for such responsibility at
school. But my head was empty. I was paralyzed. I
could remember nothing. And I stayed glued and trembling against the moss-covered stones, which offered no
protection.

I the agnostic, the atheist, recalled from my distant
childhood some musty whiff of God. I prayed. I asked
God to enlighten me, to help me out of the desperate
fix I was in—me and my soldiers.

We eventually got out all right. Taken from behind,
the "Chleuh"[13] had pulled back.

I'd been afraid, had known real fear, the kind that
can turn you into a wet rag, unable to do anything.
That can happen to everyone. That *has* happened to everyone. I forgive myself for my fear, but not for my
failure—not for having prayed in my panic for help
from a God I no longer believed in!

Monsabert's army never did link up with us. They'd
been put to use at all sorts of combat, and they were
worn to a thread—bled white. The Moroccan sharp-
shooters counted scarcely thirty men, the Tabors[14] a
dozen men; and Monsabert's tanks were useless. They
were barred by mines and blockades and became mired

13. "Chleuh" had replaced the word "Boche" (1914–1918). During
the Occupation, we also said *"Vert-de-gris"* and *"Frisés"* to designate
the Germans.
14. A corps of Moroccan troops. (Translator's note.)

in the sodden terrain. All the rivers were flooded, including the Moselette.

When the parachutists finally took Thillot, there were so few reserves that it wasn't possible to press the advantage and pursue the Germans to Alsace, where they were preparing to evacuate.

General de Lattre was to call the battle "bad luck."

On our part, we were confronted by really excellent troops: the "Edelweiss" Light Infantry—the 269th Elite Mountain Division—which had just arrived from Norway. They were rested, highly trained, accustomed to the cold and the snow, and provided with arms and equipment especially designed for forest and mountain combat. They had long-range rifles and light mortars. They had remarkable radio transmitters. And they had warm clothing, hobnailed boots, and tents of double thickness. Everything we so cruelly lacked.

After the first moment of surprise at seeing us—as soon as it became evident that we were a mere handful of men—the "Edelweiss" pressed their attack. Still, we held our position for a week without any artillery or air support, shivering in our thin, sodden clothing and lacking almost everything we needed—food as well as munitions.

The rain, mixed with melting snow, never stopped, and the great forest of the Vosges became more dank and sinister.

Using sophisticated radiogoniometers, the "Edelweiss" located every one of our positions. (The way people keep on talking in a war is insane! They never cease to chatter away in front of the microphone, using, too, all the pretty names of flowers for indicatives. At one time or another I was Jonquil, Petunia, and Primrose.) Before we could even complete a radio message, the Chleuhs would have intercepted it, located us, and turned volleys of mortars on us. They burst through the branches of the trees and fell on us in a rain of iron so heavy it was futile to try to hide behind the trees.

It took us two days to realize our error and to stop our useless dispatching of patrol after patrol to try to seize the enemy sentries we'd believed were watching our movements through binoculars. We imposed absolute radio silence. But then, how were we to know where we were in all the confusion? We were all mixed up together in the forest—both French and German—to the point where we were even bumping into each other, staggering around like drunkards who'd lost their way.

We *were* drunk! Drunk with fatigue and hunger. One night I slept in a ditch of water for an hour—or it may have been two—close up against a friend to keep warm. I believed he'd kept me warm. Only later did I discover he was a corpse.

A German came out of his foxhole one night and moved a few meters apart to urinate. It landed all over one of our commandos, who was crouching in his own hole and sleeping like a log. Brutally awakened, our man exclaimed to himself, "What d'ya know, it's raining warm water."

I heard that story later. True? False? Exaggerated? In a war there is really only what one sees: which amounts to very little when most battles appear to the combatants as contests among black men fought in a tunnel. Or what one does: the action itself, the combat, generally very rapid, a few minutes for all the days and nights of march and fatigue. And, lastly, what one relates afterwards: in those stories a man has seen everything, done everything. Except that he's forgotten the backpack that cuts into his shoulders, the helmet that weighs so heavily on his head, the loaf of bread transformed into a sponge, the weapons that drag at him. And the long nights when the least noise starts a man to shaking with fear. And dawn—that terrible hour of dawn, the cursed hour—when everything is discord, when the exhausted sentries give in to sleep, and when the enemy attacks.

We named him "Saint John the Baptist." He was a Christian mystic with the tormented and greenish visage of a Spanish Christ, and he'd brought in three prisoners. What do you do with prisoners in a situation such as ours? Our only chance to get ourselves safely out was to continue bluffing; to make the enemy believe we weren't eight hundred miserable wretches, of whom two hundred had already fallen, but that we were at least a division.

If a prisoner should succeed in escaping, he'd inform his unit of the truth of our situation, and they'd lose no time in cleaning us out.

We couldn't even consider sending the three Germans to the rear, as provided for in the regulations. We were encircled. (We'd already tested their lines.) We gave Saint John the Baptist the order to liquidate his three prisoners. He refused, throwing at us pellmell his faith, the Geneva Convention, the rights of man, and the rights of the combatant. Over and over we told him that it was them or us, but with the obstinacy of a saint, he would listen to none of our arguments. He would absolutely have died where he stood to defend the lives of his prisoners. And in line with his Christian tradition, he was perfectly right. But in our particular case, I leave you to judge all the principles at stake. The intellectual in the warmth of his library or on the terrace at Flora can decide between us as he likes; but we were to be forgiven, I believe, for wanting to hang onto our dirty skins. And there was no time to lose.

Those Germans were as innocent or as guilty as we were. We didn't know them at all. And they were good-looking men, probably Austrian Tyroleans.

Our commandant, B——, came up with what he thought was a solution to the impasse. He ordered Saint John the Baptist to take his section and scout out a hill that might be held by the enemy.

Now, Saint John the Baptist wasn't only as obstinate as a saint, he was also as suspicious as one. He left on patrol as ordered, but he took his three prisoners, loosely secured at the end of a rope, with him. At the very first opportunity, of course, they escaped and returned to their unit. No one need ask the results: a counterattack in force by the enemy.

Saint John the Baptist received a blast in the stomach that nearly tore him in half. I fastened what was left of him onto the back of one of our nearby mules, though without any grand illusions. He was nearly done for and would probably shortly join that ancestor whom the church had just sainted in Paradise. He'd earned a halo for himself, as he had earned all the trouble he'd have received had he returned intact from his patrol.

I've no idea how the mule made it, but he found the way back to the French lines. Saint John the Baptist was stitched and restitched a considerable number of times, and, after several months in the hospital, he was put back on his feet.

After the war I saw him again, looking almost like his old self. I was stone-broke at the time and asked him to lend me a thousand francs. He had to refuse me in the name of I don't know what new principle to which he paid homage. I reminded him that he owed me his life (he really owed it to the mule); for several days this reminder allowed me to sponge off him, though very sparingly, because he was practicing asceticism and a few other esoteric disciplines in which meat and wine were forbidden.

It was a good thing for all of us that we had our mules. They were in the care of bearded Moroccans as stubborn and as indefatigable as their beasts, and they were of immeasurable service to us. Seeking out impossible paths, climbing the sides of mountains, escaping the ambushes of the Tyrolean infantry, they came through with our rations and our munitions.

One of these convoys of munitions came under an enemy fire of mortars and was blown up. A Moroccan picked himself up out of the rubble. He had not let go of his animal's lead strap, but at the end of it he had only the head, the rest having been pulverized. I can still see his huge round eyes.

One morning I was sent out on liaison. I became lost in the forest, as alone in the fog and rain as little Tom Thumb, and went round and round in circles. Suddenly I found myself nose-to-nose with an "Edelweiss" who was lost as well, who was also going in circles. We were only about ten meters apart. He had a machine gun; I had my Colt. We remained immobile, each behind his own tree and watching each other for several minutes—interminable minutes. I disengaged my Colt and he aimed his gun. But no one was there to see us or to make us fight. We felt no hatred for each other. We were just lost and exhausted. Two poor slobs who didn't know each other and who had no particular reason to fight it out.

We each made a little gesture with a hand and left, each to his own side.

That kind of adventure happens more often than most people know. But it's better to keep quiet about it. There's always some overzealous clot who'll tell you: "It was your duty to fight, to take the guy prisoner. He might have been carrying important information."

Except that he had the machine gun and I had the Colt. He had the weapons advantage, and we no longer live in an age of chivalry. Our single combat of arms in that filthy forest would have had no rhyme or reason. And there would have been no one to applaud the winner.

The situation grew worse and worse for our African Corps commandos. We were worn out. Our feet rotted in our boots. The condition is called trench foot and takes a long time to heal. We were unable to evacuate our wounded, and our dead piled up in front of the hospital tent—or what served as one.

We were being hunted down like wild game, followed in our tracks by mortars.

Shivering under his tree, a blanket over his head,

chewing on canned beans, our colonel looked like an old lady. Without stopping, he recited his long list of those whom the bullets, the mortars, the rain, the fatigue, and the rest had put out of action. All at once he turned to his adjutant and said, "At least they can't say we fought badly. Seventy percent lost. Even de Lattre, who has no love for us, will have to congratulate us."

Seventy percent lost is more than honorable. It's glorious, isn't it?

For me there remained one more dirty moment to get through. It was my job to mine all the positions we abandoned.

With the help of my men, I buried antipersonnel mines on the heights of Tonteux and on Grosse Pierre, and I booby-trapped the pillboxes.

Those mines were filthy things, undetectable, going off under either pressure or traction, and linked to one another by nylon threads as fine as a spider web.

I arranged them in alternate rows, placing a tank trap between each row. To be certain of my work, I carried a plan of their emplacement with me. The mines were buried and then covered with moss, or sometimes they were hidden under stones. I had to work quickly, with no time to be finicky. One after the other, the commandos were withdrawing, and the soldiers, backs bent, feet dragging, passed before me in silence.

Then it was time for my section to disappear into the fog and the rain. All I had to do now was to remove the security pins from the mines, and it was better for me to be alone when I did that; better, too, for me to be blown up alone. Once fused, those hellish things were extremely sensitive. They could explode over nothing at all.

Night fell. Captain Ducourneau, who'd remained to the last to be certain his men were all out, laid his hand on my shoulder and said; "Give me your plans of the mines. They'd better not fall into the hands of those gentlemen who'll be here before long. You could have an accident. Your identification papers, please. And your tags. Wouldn't like them to know with whom they've had business here. A simple precaution. Routine! Good luck. A jeep will wait for you at the bridge at Saulxures until midnight."

And his bouncing gait took him away. I removed my overcoat, my helmet, all my equipment, everything that could catch on a thread, pull down a branch. I armed myself with only pliers and a flashlight whose light was camouflaged with a piece of cloth. There could be no more question of my giving way to fear, of trembling, of being clumsy. My life depended on the control I exercised over my muscles and my nerves. I could very well have left there without pulling a single pin. No one would have questioned me. Why was I laying a field of mines, in any case? Who was going to come? No fools, those "Edelweiss"; they'd know full well we would plan an unhappy surprise for them.

The whole forest was theirs. They could pass through to the left or to the right. This was but a tiny patch of mined forest in the middle of all the Vosges. Deer would explode these mines, or wild boar, when they finally returned to their green home; or woodcutters, when peace returned. When the damned war was all over, the mines would be waiting.

But it was still my job to prepare them. Crawling along on my elbows and trying not to catch my nose on a flimsy thread, I began to pull the pins. Some came out easily; on others I had to use the pliers.

I was so caught up in my task that I forgot my fear.

To conquer fear, one has to perform those small tasks that demand attention and that require some dexterity: roll a cigarette; fiddle around with a motor; shuffle cards. To be avoided are charging in or hasty movements of any kind. Fear is like a fawn: ready to leap at anything that moves and to take off running.

Despite the cold, I dripped with perspiration; my mouth was dry, and I longed to urinate. Yes, I was

afraid. Only I had placed that fear in a cage somewhere deep inside me. She clawed at the bars and
snarled, but not loudly enough to unnerve me. Soon
enough, when my job was done, I'd let her out.

It took me a long time to finish. Occasionally I
stopped, my muscles in knots, my hands frozen. I'd
carefully turn onto my back and rest a little, testing
that cage where my fear was locked in. It held. I
recommenced.

I don't know how I reached Saulxures. The jeep was
there, hidden behind a barn; but the enemy was sending in a harassing fire, and shells fell all around me. I
ran! After a while I stopped and smelled the air, redo-
lent with moss and pines. I'd succeeded! I hadn't folded!
And I hadn't begged any God to assist me this time. I'd
behaved correctly.

I slept so soundly at a farm near Cornimont that I
didn't even hear the night-long bombardment. A heavy
sleep, without dreams, during which the neighboring
building was completely destroyed.

At the crack of dawn I just had time to spring into
my jeep. The Germans had arrived with their tanks.

After the first few battles, I began to understand a
little something about war.

I'd been struck particularly by the confusion, the
chaos, the almost total lack of communication prevalent at every level. The result was that we lieutenants
or captains had to resort to constant improvisations.

At the top of the hierarchical heap a magnificent
plan had been incubated, but it hatched out a different
breed of bird than was foreseen. They'd figured everything out, down to just how many shells would be required to crush a certain position to be won. To kill X
number of soldiers and to bury them at a depth of Y,
you'd need Z number of shells of such and such a cali-
ber. Since the equation was resolved by an intellectual,
it must of course come out even; there must be no re-
mainder of any kind after the projected bludgeoning

of the enemy. The assault on the target can then easily be made. It will amount to hardly more than a military parade, weapons slung.

Certainly! The problem is that the bombs and shells usually land off to the side of the target. Artillery and air support never come when they should. And the enemy is waiting for you with machine guns and mortars intact. So you do what you can to extricate yourself. Then you keep the ubiquitous telephone wires humming to acquire what you need, encouraging this person, abusing that one . . . . After that comes the real battle, not the paper one; the rapid combat, brutal and deadly.

The rest of the time we just had to contend with— pit ourselves against—this immense, antiquated, creaking machine no one knew how to operate.

Who was the victor? Who the vanquished? On the spot it would have taken an unusually bright individual to know the difference. It's very similar to those horse races where a photograph is needed to determine the winner; and at most reprisals, it has been my experience while standing in the camp of the victors to wonder if I wasn't in the opposite camp, and vice versa.

And when it's all over—with all the battles replayed on maps and on blackboards—the time comes for the staff officers to shine. All the sloppy work, all the accumulated errors are erased; and laid before us is the fiction of the various subtle maneuvers where there'd been nothing to do but to improvise, where only happy or unhappy chance determined the outcome. They depart covered with glory, inspired, throwing out their chests, making a fine leg, the masters, the great chiefs, who had in reality been way off the mark, who had understood nothing.

For the simple private or the lowly head of a section, war is, above all, wearisome. There may be a few exalted moments—when you are able to advance or during heavy fire—but then you find yourself in a pillbox, or in a ruined farmhouse the 77s or the 105s have turned into Gruyère cheese. You warm yourself a little over the fire you make with gasoline in your can, which is now your stove. And you play cards.

You have a foursome? Son of a bitch! But it's the luck of the devil you really have. S—— had a royal flush the night before a mine blew him up. Keep a watch out for your men of the *Bataillon d'Afrique*. Belote and more belote. There—a flare lights up the sky. Three kings. The pot is mine. The patrol hasn't returned. Still, if they'd been caught, you'd have heard. Ten o'clock at night. You're on the radio with P.C.[15] Petunia calling Authority. I do hear you—four out of five times. Nothing to report.

Grand slam, 421. Who bought this disgusting wine? It's so sour it burns holes. It's too hot. It's too cold. It's taking a damned long time for daylight to come! What are those shadows? I fire at them. An illusion. Oh, how I'd love to be in a real bed. I can imagine no greater pleasure than that of being able to fall asleep in a bed. And beside me a silky-skinned girl who isn't a tart. Someone with a light lavender perfume, not the heavy odor of patchouli. I dream.

> "Red wine, a feather bed, a dame;
> the Africans are coming home again."

Escape to Paris, where I'd been given three days' leave. All anyone could talk to me about were the many difficulties they faced in getting supplies of any kind and of all they'd suffered under the Occupation. There was no more coffee, nothing but chicory. And you couldn't get dairy products at all. I was the foreigner dressed as an American from another planet. My jeep was full of rations; so I distributed them, playing Lord Bountiful with things that didn't belong to me.

15. "Post de Commandement" (fighting post headquarters). (Translator's note.)

I had a terrible desire to do silly things while I was there. I've always been beset by a need to provoke, to challenge, and that need still plays tricks on me— makes me take positions sometimes that are absolutely opposed to everything I believe. In politics, for instance. I'll do anything to stymie those politicians with their parish-priest faces, their stupidity, their conceit, their nest-feathering symposiums; all those who label the coming together of four friends to drink, a "conference," and the bowling games of the same four, a "collective"; all those who, with the jargon and the philosophy of a banker, preach what I'd like to shout in plain language: that society is a complete mess and needs to change.

In October 1944 the only fantasy I allowed myself to make real was to travel up and back on the Champs-Elysées at a slow speed in my jeep. *But* to go up on the right-hand sidewalk, to pass under the Arc de Triomphe, and to return on the left. That great avenue was empty but for me, and I must have been taken as a drunken Yank who'd made either a wager or a vow. The three or four policemen I met on the way said not a word to me.

Today, when I find myself jammed in the sea of cars on the Champs-Elysées somewhere between the traffic circle and George-V, I remember that long-ago morning when I exorcised Paris in my own way. My bad temper leaves me, and I split my sides laughing.

I picked up a young Hungarian girl. She was ravishing, she had huge eyes, and she seemed to understand me. I recited Apollinaire's poetry to her and kissed her, standing in the snow at Place Furstenberg. I was in love with her, in love with all girls, with Place Furstenberg and with its streetlamp and the snow falling all around it, in love with all of Paris. I was a little insolent soldier—in the eighteenth century I'd have been called a cornet, a lovely word—who'd come back from the war and who, before he returned to it, thumbed his nose at the world.

I swore to myself that if it ever became possible, I'd live in Place Furstenberg. I kept that promise. But I had to wait thirty years, and I was no longer the same, no longer the cornet. What we desire often becomes something else once we obtain it.

My ravishing Hungarian was only a common decoy. She dragged me to a low gambling house where her entire family, with infinite distinction and with carefully marked cards, was engaged in plucking all the pigeons she flushed out and brought in. They preferred Allied officers, and dollars to francs. The stakes mounted dangerously, and, under the pretext of going to my hotel for more funds, I disappeared.

After the Vosges, we were sent to recuperate at Salins-les Bains in the Jura Mountains, our line of departure at that time.

The rumor having somehow gone abroad that I'd died, my landlady, an extremely good woman in other regards, had laid heavy hands on my personal effects— just in the event I should not have a family—and she didn't quite greet me with open arms.

A few memories are still with me of those days, but they've all faded to sepia, like old photographs.

A large house; an open fire; a few beautiful women who granted us their favors, even taking us ahead of the officers; the obsequious officers who wondered how long they were going to be kept waiting.

François de Leusse showing up and thundering:

"All right, then, what'll we do? Jump them?"

And then making up for it with his hand-kissing to the right and to the left.

The captain Merindol, thoroughly drunk in the deserted streets of the small village, singing *"La Ronde de Nuit"*[16] in his bass voice. And the rest of us who followed him with our torches and our bottles.

The bender I went on in Arbois. I'd been sent to buy

16. "The Watch Patrol" or "The Watch." (Translator's note.)

wine for our mess, and I found a cellar, which had this inscription over the door: "The more you drink, the straighter you stand." I wanted to put that to the test, and I proceeded to drink both rosé and straw wine with scrupulousness and application.

On my way back *I* remained straight, but my jeep loaded with bottles tangoed, waltzed, and gave itself over to swerving and skidding on the slippery roads like an ice skater.

And we liberated a city. Not just any city; one of the great borderland cities of France with a proud name, a city where men had been killing each other for centuries: Belfort. It hadn't started out to be an objective of ours, but we had the nerve to take the place; and our unplanned success helped us to forget a little the thrashing we'd taken in the Vosges.

All the French divisions were hurling themselves toward the East: the First D.F.L., with its marines in pom-pom berets who manned tank destroyers, and with its Moroccan Tabors and its mules; then came the B.M.C., accompanied by their girls in gold jewelry and colorful dresses; then the Ninth D.I.C., commanded by Salan, the tank groups from Italy and Africa.

There was an incredible military traffic jam on all the roads that converged on the eastern fortifications and on the Belfort Gap. The shouting and fighting and trampling! Especially around Delle.

De Lattre had a fit of shouting and hysterics, his echoes reaching all the way to us. Seems he dismissed a worthless colonel and danced with rage, made a huge scene; and then, when he'd already gone too far, he kissed the man he'd just finished treating like a dog. All because of reaching Colmar and taking it before Leclerc did.

I found a lean-to where I might sleep in some warmth, wedged between a chaplain and a Tabor who smelled like rotten meat.

Driving rain, snow, and sheets of ice. We were ranged along a grade with seven tanks lined up in

single file, regulation distance between them all. They
were thirty-two-ton Shermans, and they were all
destroyed. Across from us was the villain: an ugly Jagh
Panther on caterpillar tracks, destroyed in its turn a
little later on.

We commandos had been badly trounced, with no
time to re-form our group; but we were given another
assignment within the range of our particular talents:
to take the fort of Salbert, one of a line of fortifications
needed to defend our positions.

We prepared for the assault as for an attack upon a
medieval fortress.

We were given long wooden ladders, climbing ropes,
hurdles, and all the other gear we'd need, both eccentric and picturesque. We carried pitch, pans of oil, mus-
kets, round shot heated red-hot, hollow charges, two
flamethrowers, and especially Gamon grenades.

For those, you soften some plastic and roll it between
your hands until you've formed a ball. You slip this
ball into a cloth pocket affair, at the top of which is a
sort of stopper, much like that in a hot-water bottle. It
holds an inert detonator: a tiny loaded ribbon that un-
rolls when the grenade is thrown. The best place to
throw one is down a ventilator shaft. The blast is such
that everyone in the pillbox is flattened like pancakes.

Flamethrowers: In my opinion they're highly overrated. Let loose two or three bright squirts of napalm—
the flamethrower is fed by that dirty-pink jelly—and
you're a marked man, yourself having become a target.

We lacked nothing that goes into the gear of assault
troops. We were ready. And our throats were dry. The
fort at Salbert had the reputation of being impenetrable, and the Germans had had plenty of leisure time to
fortify it. But this time luck was going to be on our
side.

We moved off at three-thirty in the morning, passing
through the deserted towns of Essert and Le Coudray,
towns we believed to be evacuated by the Germans so
they could concentrate their forces at the fort. Then we

were at Salbert. We reached the sheerest of the walls, picking it so as to effect the greatest surprise. It was successful—for us!

The fort had been evacuated a little beforehand, and the Germans had positioned themselves elsewhere outside the fort. Why? We could only imagine that one of their strategies had been to await an expected attack on their flanks and not inside the fort. By dawn the fortress overlooking the entire countryside was ours. One of our sections and then another descended toward Cravanches. They found nothing. They pushed on further to Valdoie and reached the Alsthom factory. It was at Belfort. They were setting themselves up in the factory when they came across a group of German soldiers on commissariat duty carrying rations with them: quarters of meat and loaves of bread. They were unarmed, and they were all old enough to be our fathers. They were now our prisoners and, if the truth were known, relieved to be. Acting entirely without orders, all the commandos made their way to Belfort. And when, from here and there, the Germans returned to close their pincers, they closed them on a void.

We had a few brief encounters along the way. We came very close to two regiments, but fortunately we didn't know that. Even so, twenty-seven of our men were killed. Then we were in the ancient prefecture, which had become the Kommandant's office under the Germans and was guarded by two corpses in the hall. Across from us rose a hostile fortress—the Château, with its somber halls, its iron gates—where the Germans still holed up. We looked everywhere for anyone from the F.F.I.[17] who could give us the information we needed, but we could lay our hands on only two of them. And what a pair! The one looked as though he'd stepped out of a picture book of what the smartly dressed officer should wear: a blue helmet, well-cut

17. *Forces Françaises de l'Intérieur* (French Forces of the Interior). (Translator's note.)

officer's undress, silk brassard, elegant fawn-colored gaiters. The other: dirty, slovenly, loudmouthed, and emphatically demanding that we give him a machine gun so he could settle accounts with the Germans. We found a few girls, too, happily more of the style of Jeanne Hachette than of Joan of Arc. They welcomed us warmly and gave us information.

The two "Fifis"[18] were angry and jealous and claimed that the girls had much to be forgiven for, that they'd slept as often as they could with the *Vert-de-gris,* the Doryphores, the Nazis, and that it was only for that reason they made such a show of zeal. They urged us to mistrust the girls, insisting that they could be spies.

It was a very strange night. The town was completely encircled, but Belfort, except for the Château, was ours. We confined ourselves as tightly as we could to preserve as much as possible what remained of those houses destroyed by Allied bombardments, the torn-up streets, those few hundred terrorized inhabitants who continued to live in their cellars, coming out to hang their tricolor flags at the whims and the pleasures, at the comings and the goings, of one side and the other. And, of course, those girls who'd welcomed us, but about whom we had no illusions.

A dialogue between the "Admiral," a true gentleman (his golf clubs and his split-bamboo trout fishing rods accompanied him everywhere in his footlocker), and one of the young ladies he'd sought out went like this:

"So you're from Belfort, mademoiselle?"

"Do you mean *Baisefort,* [19] sir?"

One of my men came back from the prefecture absolutely stoned, and when he walked he made a weird noise. He'd filled his pants with wine bottles.

Two of the girls from "*Baisefort*" decided they wanted

18. Nickname for those of the F.F.I. (Translator's note.)
19. This is a play on words in French that doesn't work in English. Belfort can also be *forte belle*—very beautiful; and *baisefort* is a play on a coarse expression, seldom used, meaning a good fuck. (Translator's note.)

to be our regular companions, despite the bullets and shells that struck the walls of our shelter and showered us with plaster. The Fifis were looking everywhere for them, and they preferred the plaster to having their heads shaved.

There was no way we could escape the trap we found ourselves in, and our colonel, who'd been delighted at having taken the town out from under the nose of a fellow colonel, began to feel uneasy. He sent an officer —one of my friends—to the tank group that had just broken through the German defenses and reached our lines, asking them for support at Belfort.

My friend went through the lines without any trouble and found the aforementioned colonel—the one ours had beaten out—at the Command Post. They were the Hussars, or the dragoons, or something of the sort, who'd formerly been a horse brigade. Now, fallen from high places, they crawled along on caterpillar tracks. Still, they'd kept something of the old manners and bearing of the cavalry: the crop under the arm, spanking-fresh gloves, here and there a monocle.

The colonel sat before a huge fire, a glass of port at hand, and informed his staff of the situation regarding Belfort:

"It's intolerable! De Lattre promised Belfort to me. It was stolen from me. The commandos took it. By what right?"

One of the commanders tried to reassure him:

" 'Took' is really too strong a word. Actually the situation is that a few drunken commandos are dragging the streets. By dawn they'll have the place cleaned out and we can go in."

My friend announced himself:

"Second Lieutenant X—— of the commandos. If you don't intervene immediately, sir, we'll be wiped out; and when you enter, your tanks will roll past our corpses. You'll also be greeted by enemy bazookas at every intersection and from behind every house."

The tanks came to Belfort. Only two or three were

incinerated, shelled by German grenadiers holed up in
some ruins we'd been unable to clean out.

In the meantime the fancy Fifi played his own kind
of game with me—as a way, I suppose, of getting even
for the girls. The idiot came to me and said, "The *Vert-
de-gris* have left. They've abandoned the Château."

I asked him, "You're absolutely sure?"

"We saw them take off."

My men and I invaded that filthy fortress from
which we'd been so continuously under fire that we'd
been unable to gather up our dead. That had been
demoralizing. Weapons slung, we looked around to see
what we might find to take as souvenirs: a P-38, a
knife, a helmet, any one of the things we all collected.

The Germans were only just packing their bags. Furious at being disturbed, they greeted us rather badly,
and everyone fired at everyone else. The uproar in that
fortress full of echoes and resonance was appalling. It
was impossible to orient ourselves. The lights went out.
Bullets rebounded from every direction. All we could
do was take cover, keep shooting, and wait for the
party to end.

At last, though, the Germans surrendered, and we
took possession of the ground—or the concrete. So there
I was with my unit the first to enter the Château of
Belfort, the one who had, in the words of those who explained our "strategy" after the fact, ". . . with flanking
maneuvers after the manner of Serre-de-Rivière,
dealt the master stroke which broke the back of the entire right flank of the enemy counteroffensive. . . ."
(General de Vernejouls in *Autopsy of a Dead Victory*).

Our colonel was exultant. He awarded me my second
citation.

The fancy Fifi should have been the one to receive it.
All that evening my men and I looked for him to kick
his ass.

I came very close to being in a great deal of trouble.

I received an order to inspect the prefecture, which

had been the Kommandatur under the Germans, to see if the Kameraden had left behind any mines or traps. I tested the walls, the ceilings, the floors. I went over everything with my "frying pan"—my mine detector. Nothing.

The day after our departure, when the cavalry colonel had finally succeeded in getting us to leave the occupied areas to him and his men, the prefecture blew up. Nothing remained but a pile of plaster and rubble.

Those filthy Germans had lowered a delayed-action bomb down a chimney. Luckily it went off in the middle of the night, and when no one had yet moved into the building. A lone guard was struck on the head by a stone; but since he was a soldier of the cavalry, not a sloppy commando, and fully garbed in helmet and other protective equipment, his injury amounted to no more than a lump. And he received a citation.

From there to saying *we* had deliberately left the bomb in the prefecture was but a step. That step was taken. The party responsible for the criminal negligence, or for that act of sabotage, had to be found. That party could only have been me. I wondered then as I do now if military security hadn't gotten itself mixed up in the affair, hadn't exaggerated the whole incident, to settle accounts between two units, two colonels, two concepts of war and the way it is fought.

Then the whole thing blew over.

There was another bad affair which we got ourselves out of only by resorting to that kind of disobedience which, fortunately, is widespread in so many armies and which can be defined as acting as though a particular order had never been received.

After having taken Belfort, our colonel was confident of himself and wanted to push forward. One of our four commando units, a hundred lightly clothed and armed men, was sent in pursuit of the Germans. In the woods near Arsot they were caught between two SS regiments backed up by tanks. Our men were overwhelmed, and the SS were taking no prisoners. All the wounded were shot through the head.

In reprisal, our colonel ordered that all our prisoners be lined up against a wall and shot. These were our good old "grandfathers," whom we'd found in the factory carrying meat and bread, these who'd been so relieved at their war being over. And they'd had nothing whatever to do with the massacre.

We never executed that order. We crammed our prisoners into a truck and delivered them to a prison camp. Our colonel never brought up the subject again.

If the commandos hadn't been the eccentric medley we were, each involved in fighting the war while maintaining the maximum in individual initiative, the maximum critical sense; if we'd been machines drilled to obey; if we'd been fanatical partisans of a political faith, that order would have been executed.

Was it because we were freer than all the others that we were later dealt with as mercenaries?

We made a vain attempt while we were still at Belfort to recruit volunteers to fill the gaps in our ranks. We learned why it was in vain one morning when we found posters on the walls of the city we'd just liberated. They were notices inviting young men to rejoin the regular army by enrolling in the local F.F.I. (French Forces of the Interior), which had at last come out of the shadows. They offered the same pay and the same benefits as the commandos, but with the added glamour of the unit in question being charged to restore order in the region . . . notably, to shave the heads of the girls.

We were assigned to Giromagny, a charming canton near Belfort, where we made our winter headquarters. We were tired and anemic, badly in need of rest and recuperation. We were also promised reinforcements which never arrived.

War, as I think I've already told you, is like Proteus: she can take on many faces. By turns, she can put on the mask of defeat and the mask of victory: the Vosges and Belfort. She can finish off our comrades in the woods at Arsot and then try to drag us down into the endless cycle of reprisals. We give her our devotion, and she gives us at twenty years of age the exhilaration of freeing a city.

Roger Caillois once wrote:

> To a high degree, war possesses the essential characteristics of sacred things. She forbids an objective consideration of what she really is. She paralyzes the spirit of investigation. She is formidable and impressive. People both curse her and exalt her.

I will add that she can also disguise herself as a clown and make her appearance in some highly entertaining stage numbers. Here is war playing the buffoon.

In our judgment we commandos were short of jeeps and trucks, our allotment of vehicles always falling far short of our needs. But when our unit was dissolved, we realized that we had three times the number of vehicles assigned to us!

We had acquired the surplus by rather questionable procedures.

Whenever a commando went on leave, he knew—it was written nowhere in the regulations—that he could return three days late without being declared a deserter on the condition that he brought a jeep with him when he returned. Four days meant a four-wheel drive; five days a General Motors truck.

One time two of our soldiers were coming back after a five-day delay without a valid excuse or a medical certificate. They'd gone all the way up the Rhône Valley without finding anything to steal, and they were desperate. They knew they'd be in for it, believed that at the very least they'd be court-martialed—though to my knowledge no commando was ever court-martialed, no matter what stupidity he was guilty of. Finally the

dreamed-of opportunity presented itself to them—one
made to order. Two GIs were drinking a bottle of wine
at a table in front of a bistro, with, or so it seemed,
their machine guns at their shoulders. Across the road
from them was their vehicle: a large gray truck, completely empty.

"A mobile workshop," said one of our desperate men.
"If we could take something like that, we'd have no
more worries. We'd be congratulated."

They slipped around behind the truck and then into
the cab, where they crossed the ignition wires and set
the truck in motion. As easy as falling off a log. They
gave the truck a burst of speed, at which the two GIs
began firing round after round at them with weapons
that were indeed at the ready. They began howling,
too, at the top of their lungs. Our commandos were
convinced that they'd tangled with a couple of particularly ugly customers and increased their speed. They
got away, and as a precaution took only back roads and
narrow streets.

Two hours later they delivered their mobile workshop to the motor pool where the Admiral, by virtue of
his having been a naval engineer, had only recently
taken command, though all he knew in the family of
motors was the oil turbine.

Completely happy with his new acquisition, our sailor
absolved the two late arrivals and didn't give a thought
to opening the truck.

An order came down from Allied general headquarters to close off all roads immediately. German parachutists operating in our region, they said, had seized a
truck with the maps and plans of the American Army
Corps. Their whole offensive was on paper in that
truck. So we set up barriers at the entrance and the
exit of Giromagny, even doing the same for nearby
Rosemont. This last initiative was the brainchild of the
aspiring lover of one of the maids at the inn. He profited by the occasion by setting himself up in the inn,
where he could advance his suit.

We thought the whole thing was simply a joke on the part of the bored general staff. In combat units there is always the tendency to look upon the general staff as a bunch of pathological liars, of paranoics, and of other such nuts, just as for them combat units were made up of mental deficients, illiterates, and goldbrickers. The result was that their orders were written out to include the tiniest detail, no matter how preposterous, with the obligation on our part to give an exact accounting of the execution of every detail at every instant.

A large, flamboyantly new and shiny American car pulled up to one of our barriers. On the registration plate were three stars and on the windshield a caduceus. The sentry signaled the car to stop, but the driver either misunderstood or simply wanted to ignore the signal. He ran through the barrier. The sentry sent bursts of fire into the tires, and the car skidded and rammed a wall.

A general of the French medical corps jumped from the car and yelled at everyone in sight. Our colonel charged up to the scene and came strongly to the defense of his men, who had for once scrupulously respected a sentry's instructions.

The argument reached fever pitch, with our colonel the most heated of all. Someone had stolen the truck with the maps! It contained no less than the plans of the whole new offensive! Did the general want more? It was a coup of unequaled audacity! Skorzeny himself had to be involved in the affair! Why wasn't it possible that he'd disguised himself as a French general? The sentry who'd shot away the four tires of the car was to be commended. He was going to receive a citation. He was going to be promoted to corporal. Why not to sergeant?

When our colonel finished, the beautiful American car was towed away to the motor pool for repairs. They changed all the tires and repaired the radiator grill grid by grid. Off to the side stood the large gray truck.

The next day an adjutant needed another piece of machinery or a tool for the repair job and went to the truck to see if he could find one. He broke the lock at the back. It was, of course, the truck with the maps and plans.

That night we took it out and lost it a few kilometers outside Giromagny. Then we conveniently and happily found it again early the next morning. Our group was congratulated by the general staff.

We were increased by a battalion of the F.F.I. and by another of the F.T.P., and our colonel could convince himself that he now commanded a full brigade. Except that essentially each battalion maintained its own independence and accepted only those orders which suited it. Most of the officers of the two new battalions were only recently promoted themselves, and they knew nothing about war and hardly anything about guerrilla tactics. Their men had no confidence in them.

That ill-assorted army of men was thrust forward onto a snow-covered hill at Cernay and up against solid German entrenchments held by tanks and SS troops in winter-white wear. It was a massacre of our men. The F.F.I. and the F.T.P. battalions broke up, and what remained of our old commando group was pinned down.

I wasn't among them, for a few days earlier I was returning to base in a jeep along an icy road and was involved in an accident which fractured my shoulder. I was sent to the hospital at Dijon. I hadn't even been driving the jeep.

After my convalescent leave, I rejoined the commandos in Alsace. Colmar had been taken, but there wasn't much left of my old unit. The entire First Army was in a similar state. It could do no more.

Strange rumors then began to circulate in the mess halls and barracks, rumors that Alsace could have been liberated two months earlier than it had been; that thousands of lives and enormous amounts of supplies and materials could have been saved; that the ruination of cities and towns and the crushing of so many civilians under bombs and shells could have been avoided. All this if only General de Lattre de Tassigny hadn't envied the glory of his rival, General Leclerc, so much that he'd brought a halt to a successful offensive.

The commandos had no love for de Lattre. We hated his excesses, his cult of the personality, his narcissism. But it was nevertheless difficult to believe that in a fit of temper and jealousy a commander in chief had been able to sacrifice so large a part of his army.

Since then all the evidence points in just that direction, whether the testimony comes from General de Vernejouls commanding the Fifth Demi-Brigade[20] *(Autopsie d'une victoire morte),*[21] from the Generals de Langlade, Bethouart, Monsabert, Gribius, Valluy, or Leclerc, or from the American Generals Devers and Eisenhower.

It was like this:

At the end of November in 1944, the Wehrmacht was in full rout. At Mulhouse, the German divisional general staff waited only for the arrival of French officers to surrender. (This information was received in a communiqué sent by the Chief of Resistance of the Upper Rhine area of the Second French Bureau.)

At Colmar the archivist had let it be known that the crippled Germans there were ready to do the same.

General Oberst Weise, the German commander, wrote in his log:

26 November: Cloudy weather, occasional clearing. Reserves: none.

27 November: Reserves: none.

28 November: We must be prepared for an enemy breakthrough in the area of Sélestat from the 2nd French Armored Division and the 36th American Division.

Everywhere the enemy is falling upon our beleaguered garrisons, taking them from behind.

20. The Fifth Armored Division. (Translator's note.)
21. *Autopsy of a Dead Victory.* (Translator's note.)

The armored divisions of the First French Army had nothing in their way to prevent their advance, and they had all the means to press forward. But Leclerc, who'd taken Strasbourg, had now left there and was approaching from the other side of the Vosges—from the direction of Sélestat. He was twenty-two kilometers from Colmar, and the Americans were only fifteen kilometers away. They were set to take the city as soon as they knew they were protected by an epaulement of the armored division of the First Army. It was then that de Lattre annulled the attack of the First and the Fifth armored divisions, who were to give Leclerc the support he needed to liberate Alsace. De Lattre decided to take "a shorter route," to cross the Vosges with his own troops, and to enter Colmar as the sole victor. His order to annul was so surprising that General de Lenarès, his chief of staff, had to personally deliver it one by one to each commander of that huge unit to ensure its execution. De Lattre didn't hide the reasons for his change of orders: "Leclerc liberated Paris and Strasbourg. It's the First French Army that is going to liberate Colmar! It's going to go straight down the Vosges to Colmar." This, despite the orders of his superior, the American General Devers, whom he totally ignored.

The Germans were now going to have the time they needed to recover themselves, whereas they'd expected at any moment to be dealt the fatal thrust. They were already evacuating Alsace and recrossing the Rhine with their artillery when they were accorded this undreamed-of respite.

On June 11, 1946, at the request of the United States Historical Service, the German general, Heinrich Bürchg, who'd held the front opposite the First Army, wrote in his operations report:

> Our infantry could no longer maintain itself under those worst possible combat conditions in the mountains and in the forests. . . . Our effective strength all along the line had fallen to twenty-five, thirty men. If our regiments

were still armed at all, it was thanks to the severe reduction in their numbers. . . . We had very few field batteries, few radio personnel, few transmission apparatus. . . . It was questionable if our weak front could resist a new assault by the adversary. Questionable whether we could withstand a massive breakthrough if the main thrust of the enemy's forces was directed at Cernay-Thann. . . . In my opinion, a united enemy attack striking at our Mulhouse-Cernay line in the direction of Colmar on the 29th and 30th of November, 1944, would have been crowned with success, because the attack would have come up against my 159th Division, which was in a deplorably weak condition. But two days later our whole front was able to strengthen itself. . . .

And then, because even the enemy had been aware of the widely publicized dissension between the generals, he added:

In the matter of the counterorder of General de Lattre de Tassigny, an explanation could well be his jealousy of another general, or the rivalry for reasons of prestige between the two. If that's the case, however, it was a mistake that could never be compensated for. . . . One must never stop pursuing a beaten enemy in retreat, lest you would see him recover his effectiveness, refortify himself, while you lose what may be your last favorable opportunity.

I repeat what I wrote in my report on the situation of 30 November and 1 December 1944: I expected a united attack on Cernay. Happily for us it didn't come. The counterorder of de Lattre will probably remain a mystery on the order of our having been stopped at the Marne in 1914. . . .

The Germans took immediate advantage of the respite de Lattre accorded them simply because he wanted Colmar for himself. Himmler personally saw to it that reinforcements were sent: five thousand men, four regiments of the SS. And the Luftwaffe reappeared in the skies.

It was fifteen degrees below zero in the Vosges and

there were two meters of snow on the ground when de Lattre undertook his attack, certain that now Leclerc would be unable to do anything more than maintain a defensive position between Sélestat and Plobesheim.

De Lattre sent his armored units out onto the snow-bound roads in small groups. The First Cuirassiers, which started with an effective strength of 300 fighters, lost 206 officers, noncoms, and soldiers; 25 tanks out of 65 were destroyed. Another group lost more than half its tanks: 51 out of 89.

Soldiers died in the snow by the thousands.

In order that Leclerc not take Colmar!

General de Vernejouls, commander of the Fifth Armored Division, wrote:

> And so it was that Alsacienne victory died in December of 1944, to reappear only in the blood and suffering of a new birth in February 1945.

The offensive of the Vosges was checked!

> The harshness of the elements; the snow; the cold; the fierce resistance of an enemy who is a past master at large-scale defense maneuvers in mountainous and heavily wooded terrain; openings slammed shut by enemy artillery; the slaughter; the destruction; the mines; all combined to halt one by one the last feeble efforts at an offensive. . . .

But Leclerc had not entered Colmar!
In Alsace:

> . . . the sick, the infirm, women in labor, without medicine, without care, without doctors; children and old people without milk, without bread, without fire, without beds; public buildings ransacked by soldiers; the dead hastily buried, without prayers and without clergy. . . . the strain, the exhaustion, the hunger, the filth, the over-work, the terror, the constant menace of Himmler's SS on

the one hand, and the raining shells on the other. . . .
[The Chronicles of Wittenheim.]

But Leclerc hadn't entered Colmar!
Eisenhower himself said:

> The liberation of Alsace could have been realized,
> should have been realized in three days. It wasn't because:
> 1. General de Lattre didn't want to unleash his armored
> divisions so they could go to the aid of Leclerc.
> 2. He wanted no other corps but the one he desig-
> nated to free the bridge of Ansbach and to profit from its
> exploitation.
> 3. He didn't want to because, whether one likes it or
> not, he never had known how to adapt himself to the
> proper use of an armored division, as evidenced by the
> way he cut the one he had to pieces. A lamentable mis-
> take, borrowed from the not-so-long-ago one of 1940 for
> the benefit of infantry brigade groups.

Eisenhower also asked that de Lattre be relieved of
his command. De Gaulle and Juin opposed him "for
psychological reasons" that Eisenhower was obliged to
understand and accept.

General de Lattre de Tassigny entered his Colmar a
victor, and with all the pomp he so well knew how to
display.

Why am I telling you all this? So that you'll understand how, under the influence of de Lattre—and it
was considerable—the French army finally lost its
unity, a unity already compromised by the fights between the Giraudists and the Gaullists. Its troops
would be gathered together again in Indochina when
at Tonkin the same de Lattre—"King John"—created
his field marshals, flattered them, excited them to
envy, pitted one against the other. To their mutual destruction they all used those methods of the Master in
Alsace when he thwarted Leclerc. That same spirit was
also perpetuated in Algeria until the well-known

thirteenth of May, and culminated in the putsch of the
generals and in the formation of the O.A.S., which at
best could only act as a check to the ruthless rivalries
among units.

If de Lattre had known what it would cost for him to
take the hills of the Vosges in the dead of winter, he
would probably not have permitted himself the decision
he made.

But for three days, blinded by jealousy, he let his
chance for real greatness pass by.

The dispute between de Lattre and Leclerc was not
the only one of its kind. At a higher level, Montgomery
and Patton hated each other, were jealous of each
other, opposed each other's battle plans. And in September the Allies missed their opportunity to end their
war with Germany when Montgomery persuaded Eisenhower to cut Patton's supply of gas because, in
Montgomery's eyes, Patton was going too fast and gathering in too many laurels for himself to suit Monty.

Patton exploded: "My men can always eat their belts
if they have to, but my tanks cannot move without
gas!" And he stopped his advance at the Moselle because Eisenhower "placed harmony before strategy and
sacrificed the best chance to obtain an early victory in
his desire to appease the insatiable appetite of Monty.[22]

Liddell Hart added:

> The best chance to arrive at a rapid end to the war
> was probably compromised when in the last week of Au-
> gust, Patton's fuel supplies for his tanks were cut, just
> as he was 115 kilometers from the Rhine and its bridges.
> . . . The Allied armies paid a heavy price for having
> missed the opportunity. Of the total of 750,000 men lost
> in the liberation of Europe, 500,000 died after the check
> upon Patton in September. And because of the prolonga-
> tion of hostilities, humanity paid a still heavier price in
> the many millions of men and women who died after

22. Liddell Hart.

that, either caught in the war or in German concentration camps. On the other hand, if one wants to stand back and look at things wholly objectively, in September the tide of the Russian armies hadn't yet reached central Europe. . . .

That these generals belonging to the same army were able to uselessly massacre thousands of young soldiers merely to reap for themselves, as the Quaker Bigeard said; "a scrap of glory" is intolerable.

Whence the necessity for always having a supervisor, a chief, placed over these officers; a civilian chief who holds them with an iron hand, who will praise and decorate them, but who will also dismiss them at the least mistake they make and will do it with éclat. Whence the celebrated reflection of Clemenceau, who in 1918 was just such a man as I speak of. Churchill agreed with Clemenceau that war was far too serious an affair to leave in the hands of the military, but he could still not rid himself of Montgomery.

As for Stalin and his generals and marshals, he stood them up against a wall if a mistake was made, even when it was he who'd made the mistake. But he operated from a very unusual point of view, one very close, besides, to that of his old ally and accomplice Hitler, who hung his officers on meat hooks when they wanted to desert him in defeat.

To return to de Lattre.

One day there was a big review, a parade of troops at Strasbourg. I was there, but I don't remember what the occasion was.

The troops were in their places at four o'clock in the morning, those men who had shortly before been engaged in hard combat in order that Leclerc not take Colmar. They were scrubbed and polished; the home army was accompanied by its brass bands; and the North Africans had their noubas, the Algerian military bands with their raïtas and tambourines. The motorized

units had painted the sides of all their tires white. Nowhere was there so much as a gaiter button missing.
The guests and various authorities began to arrive
about eight o'clock, and the parade was scheduled to
begin at nine o'clock.

Nine o'clock, nine-thirty, ten o'clock. And still no
general-in-chief. We shook in our places from fatigue,
but there could be no question of breaking ranks. Our
places were marked with chalk.

At last the great prima donna arrived. Smiling,
charming, taking care that the photographers only shot
him from his best side. Already he was "King John,"
surrounded by his courtesans. He acknowledged no one
who was not in high favor, who'd ceased to please; he
was followed everywhere by the favorite of the day, of
the week.

He beamed. He ruled. Suddenly there was an air of
unease. Where was the cardinal? His Eminence, Monsi-
gnor Tisserant, who'd been specifically invited because
de Lattre felt that a cardinal would be a good touch in
such a review and would add a nice spot of color. De
Lattre needed him for the *combinazione*—the arrangement—he'd planned.

Tisserant carried considerable weight as well, was
even shown into the presence of Charles de Gaulle. De
Lattre was worried.

The aides searched everywhere for the cardinal, but
he was not to be found.

A good half hour passed, and then he appeared at
last. And what an awesome sight he was! What bearing
and what a grand manner! An energetic and rugged
face, a little reddened by the cold; a magnificent, full,
white beard; the large gold cross on his chest; garnet-
colored stockings and sash; patent-leather pumps with
silver buckles. And over all that, hanging regally from
his shoulders and sweeping the earth far behind as he
walked, was the *capa magna,* an immense red cape like
that of the caesars.

None there could hold a candle to him. He held the

stage, filled the arena. Every eye was upon him. The Generalissimo was altogether effaced, relegated to second place, and he didn't like it a bit. It was apparent that the cardinal loved it, was laughing into his beard, though he controlled it well. He pulled out all the stops, played all his tricks, even to graciously stretching out his hands and offering "King John" his ring to kiss. And de Lattre could do nothing about it, couldn't let his feelings show. He called himself a good Christian, but more than that he badly needed the support of the Resistance; and the cardinal was highly thought of in the Resistance.

Fortunately I was in the front row and in a position to see and enjoy the stage number of those great whores.

(I found de Lattre contemptible, but later on when I became a journalist, I grew to appreciate that damned monster. With him around, no one ever lacked for copy. Isn't that right, Bodard?)

I was in seventh heaven when I heard that the Generalissimo had been ticked off by Leclerc, who'd been placed under his command shortly before. The army! An assemblage of gossips! As everyone knows.

De Lattre had summoned Leclerc to his office to put on one of his shows for him to let him see that after all he was only an underling.

Leclerc was on time, as his habitual good manners dictated. De Lattre let him wait in the outer office half an hour before giving the order for Leclerc to be shown in. The orderly returned, highly embarrassed, and said, "General Leclerc waited five minutes. He checked his watch and then left."

Another fit of temper. But what could de Lattre do against the enigmatic and aloof victor of Koufra, of Strasbourg, or Paris, the liege man and companion of the president of the Provisional Republic? He couldn't even place him under arrest.

Later that same day, de Lattre was able to retrieve a desperate situation in Indochina, despite his monstrous defects, his megalomania. Because he had a sense of grandeur; because he was a scene-setter of genius; because he knew how to make use of the press; because he was an impossible demagogue, impossible to ignore; and because when ambition, his mania for glory, and his envy of others didn't blind him completely, he knew his trade.

I think you can see why I had no desire to remain in the army. I couldn't accept de Lattre and his breed. I couldn't accept his style for myself, more especially after I'd been assigned to the officer school at Rouffach. Another idea of "King John's" was to throw into the same mold the young officers of the regular army and those of the Resistance.

And what was it he offered us there? A rehashed version of the old-style officer school of the National Revolution. It wasn't for me. I'd been denied my adolescence, and what I needed most was to make up for lost time. I wasn't going to spend an eternity in that hearty-muscular-Christian universe.

How beautiful Alsace was in that springtime of liberty! Wine flowed in the streets; girls waved their handkerchiefs at us and were easy to kiss. They cried as easily when we left them.

Then, we were across the Rhine and into the Black Forest. We had a few last skirmishes there with fleeing elements of the Waffen SS; also with the "Charlemagne" division of Frenchmen and Belgians.

When one of these latter SS was taken armed, he was shot as a traitor. Those were our orders. But we burned his papers so his family would be spared.

One of these we caught was still a boy. He was to be executed like the others. But the cadet in charge of our operation was struck by the boy's resemblance to one of our comrades, a second lieutenant who had recently distinguished himself by being the first to cross the Rhine under enemy fire.

The cadet called the second lieutenant on the radio

and explained the situation to him. The officer came
running.

It developed that the boy was his younger brother, of
whom he'd had no news in over three years—ever since
the officer had left France to fight with the Allied forces.

The young idiot, in order not to be left out of things,
to fight as his older brother was doing, and finding no
slot for himself in the Resistance, had enrolled in the
SS at seventeen years of age. He'd been to Russia and
had seen the end of the campaign there.

We gave him a uniform and dumped him in the mess
hall to work.

There was a section of Alsatians and their officers and
noncoms repatriated by the Russians, who came to us in
the uniform of the Wehrmacht. They changed uniforms,
sewed on new stripes and patches, and lined up on our
side. At first they lapsed into German in their training
maneuvers and bellowed their orders in their patois.

What can I tell you about the occupation of Germany? We were still half boys, and they made us responsible for the country people in our area, for the village mayors, and I don't know what else. We drove
around in huge old cars, Mercedes we'd stolen and
which our jealous superiors stole from us in turn. The
pretty maids hired to take care of our barracks joined
us in our beds, more for the chocolate we gave them
than for the pleasure of it—though there was that, too.
We never did believe that the good country folk who so
resembled our own were monsters—war criminals.

The commandos were dissolved. They were in any
case only a volunteer corps. Though they were useful
in time of war, they were an embarrassment, and in
the way in time of peace. As thick as thieves, they
acted as though they owned their zone of operations;
and they were completely lacking in respect for those
fine, fancy-plumed officers one saw joining the rat race
and rushing for the spoils. They respected even less the
older officers whose uniforms had just come out of hiding and still smelled of naphthalene.

Those commandos who wanted to remain in the army were sent to Pau, where they did some practice jumping before leaving for Indochina and the heated-up war there. They parachuted over Namdinh. Few of them returned alive.

I didn't want to go to Rouffach, as I've said. I didn't want any more of the army. I knew I could never be a good officer in the active service. France was free, and I had a fierce desire to live.

I was demobilized.

PART THREE

WAR
I WROTE ABOUT

Contrary to what you might think, I never wanted to be an actor in the Korean War. I really only wanted to be a witness, a privileged spectator, on the stage and in the auditorium at one and the same time.

The journalist who had been unable to make his place in the sun took on the disguise of a soldier, and that brought him luck—though I still classify Korea among the wars I wrote about and not among those I fought in.

But we haven't come that far yet.

I was demobilized on August 15, 1945. In addition to a month's pay, I drew out my savings: 300,000 francs, an enormous sum at that time. Especially for me.

It was quickly spent. I loved bars and the night life, and I loved the singular encounters one made there. I desperately needed to feel myself at home in my own country, and at night, as you know, after a certain number of glasses of wine, you discover a world that the magic of alcohol peoples with boys and girls, men and women who seem to understand you, to love you, who are your brothers, your sisters, and all your lost friends.

In offices, in agencies, at newspapers, in all the rest of the free-for-alls, I met too many men who wore me out with inexhaustible barrages about their heroic feats of resistance during the war, their brilliant acts of daring—all to explain how they'd acquired the numerous stripes on their sleeves. If there really had been so many acts of heroism, so many exemplary feats of arms; if all those prisoners really had escaped from the Germans; if all those workers and students really had refused to work for the S.T.O.[1] during the Occupation, the Germans would have been whipped long, long before they were. There'd have been no need whatever of *our* assistance!

My record was a poor one by comparison. I'd taken three years to go from cadet to second lieutenant. Near the end of the war it had taken three months for others to become commanders or colonels.

Do you remember the story? De Gaulle was reviewing the Fifis (F.F.I.). They had stripes up to their ears, one of the colonels even having six stripes. Lost among them was a pitiful creature with only two stripes.

"What's the matter, my friend?" asked Charles de Gaulle. "Don't you know how to sew?"

With several friends from the commandos, who'd also thrown aside their uniforms and who were, like myself, dissatisfied with life in France, we'd formed a kind of community unto ourselves, just waiting to leave for Chile and to remake our lives. One of my friends had an uncle who owned a stretch of pampas near Terre-de-Feu and who didn't know what to do with it. He'd written to ask for our services.

We lived together in a large villa at Bois-Colombes, and we threw numerous parties there. The parties attracted girls to us, as the girls were also attracted by our band of young men who dreamed and spoke together of their adventures. That last also disturbed

---

1. Compulsory labor service. (Translator's note.)

them. They couldn't bear to know we loved adventure above them, that we'd escaped them.

In the first version of *Les Mercenaires,* "Blood on the Hills," I described how, when our pockets were empty, we had to take roundabout routes to the train station to avoid those stores where we'd run up debts—until the day came when we were completely broke and, not having heard anything more about Chile, found it necessary to go our separate ways.

Some returned to the army; others followed the girls and looked for work.

For many reasons it was hard for us to part. We'd all carried a few things over from the war: a special sense of friendship, of clan; a certain madness; a taste for adventure and wide open spaces. And we were all out of place in our own land. We'd dreamed of a welcoming France, of a generous France, of a rejuvenated France. The reality was that the Germans had raped her, had done her a great deal of damage, and the Resistance—the genuine Resistance, those who'd really fought—hadn't managed at all to cure her of her disease: occupation by foreigners, secretly tolerated.

We found a mean and divided country where everyone lied and cheated, paid off old scores, and lined his pockets. And we returnees were welcomed rather badly into that scene. We'd come too late, besides, and all the jobs and positions were taken. It had never occurred to us that either the war or the Resistance was to be thought of as a sound bargain, a situation one could manipulate and turn to account.

Proud of my uniform and of my medals, I went to see my father, who at first wasn't above showing me his own pride in me. One day all that was spoiled. In one of our conversations, I'd said to him, "There's something to be said for us. We won our war after all."

"Listen to him talk!" he answered sourly. "What would you have done without the English and the Americans? You'd have been like the Fifis: stealing chickens, robbing the farmers blind, hiding out in the woods to avoid danger. Just like them!"

He was entitled to some of his rancor. The F.T.P., who'd managed to avoid all combat and who believed they'd had a political mission far more important than fighting, had grabbed my father and stood him, along with my younger brother, against a wall to shoot him because he was a member of the Legion of Combatants. He was spared only through the intervention of the local chief of the Resistance, who was a friend of his.

Even so, the Spaniard who commanded the horde of the F.T.P. had stolen the officer's uniform of the Light Infantry that my father had so treasured; had stolen, too, his front-wheel-drive Citroën, which meant even more to him. To add insult to injury, the Spaniard's troops had helped themselves to my father's stock of wine.

It drove him wild to think of his great old bottles of wine being tossed off by those thugs with no palates at all. Those barbarians! Those latter-day Fifis couldn't recognize good wine, deserved nothing better than poor wine, sour wine. And we didn't dare try to cheer him up. My brother and I had a bit of lying to do on the subject. We'd made some serious inroads into his stock ourselves, that lovely wine he so piously kept for special occasions that somehow just never seemed to arrive. We'd buried some of the wine in a cave in the cemetery, where it was safe for us to go to satisfy our thirsts.

To put the entire situation at home briefly, each of us was taking up old quarrels, making new ones. In Aumont it was no better.

The town was divided into two clans: the Pétainists and the Resistance. The Pétainists—the good guys—spread the rumor around, for whatever reason, that I'd gone over to de Gaulle's camp because I was guilty of something or other criminal or unpatriotic, and that the police had been chasing me. On their part, the members of the Resistance hesitated to acknowledge me as one of their own. At Marvejols, one of them asked me, "Is it true that you belong to de Gaulle's Praetorian Guard and that he counted on using you against the Resistance?"

So you see? That's where we stood. Divided. Dog-eat-dog. "The Sorrow and the Pity" going on and on.

I had to get out of there. Once again.

Now here and now there, I went around looking for work. Then one day I came across an old friend I'd known in Toulouse who worked for an agricultural newspaper, H. Déramond. He suggested that I go to work on his paper, and I accepted.

It was called *La Libération paysanne*,[2] and was an organ of the General Confederation of Agriculture, which had recently been created by Philippe Lamour. And it was not very exciting. As for myself, I'd never given a thought to working as a journalist. I really should have met an old friend who made cosmetics, should have gone to work in the cosmetics business, at Puces, where I might have become a salesman. It would have suited my temperament far more at that time. I was footloose and fancy-free, with a pronounced taste for girls, for daydreaming, and for idleness. I certainly had no natural tendency or ability for agricultural journalism.

My Toulousian friend took all that into account and introduced me to Max Corre, who, with Yves Krier and Marcel Haedrich, edited *Samedi-Soir* and *Paris-Matin*. Max asked me if I'd like to be a journalist, a true journalist. By then I wanted only that, but honestly confessed to him that I was worthless, knew nothing whatever about it. My sincerity either touched or amused him, and he said he'd like me to try my hand at writing fillers. But he went on to advise me that since I was healthy and had ambition—health I had; ambition he attributed to me—I should be on the lookout for a big story, a sensational story that would get

2. *The Peasant Liberation*. (Translator's note.)

my foot in the door. This is called a "scoop" in the profession. So I set out on the quest of a scoop.

I learned—I no longer know how—that the Catalonian underground had organized to overthrow Franco. I suggested to Max Corre that I investigate the story up close, and he gave me a train ticket and several thousand francs so I could go to Perpignan.

I had a "contact" there, a very refined young man with the long, fine hands of an intellectual, who was deeply involved in the Catalonian separatist movement. I played the big journalist for him, and he played the big revolutionary for me. In truth we were both very small potatoes, but our act gave us pleasure.

He sent me off on an exciting enough affair. One of the men of his organization named Solair, a remarkable individual, was going to cross the border to manage a large operation in Barcelona. After having subjected me to a lengthy interrogation, Solair agreed to let me accompany him. What decided him was that he enjoyed playing the parts of all the characters in the stories of Malraux,[3] and I was able to recite for him entire pages from *L'Espoir*[4] and from *La Condition humaine*.[5] That formed an immediate bond between us. We left, and I soon found myself with him in Latour-de-Carol, in the very place where, in 1942, I'd set out for my first great adventure. This time, though, I felt more assurance than before; there was an entire organization behind me, and Franco was as good as done for. It would take only a few more weeks to finish the job. Everyone in France was already talking about the expected overthrow.

When I questioned my friend about the heavy bag he

3. André Malraux, French novelist, known for his Marxist beliefs and his novels dealing with Communists in Europe and in Asia during the twenties and thirties. (Translator's note.)
4. Written in 1937 and translated as *Man's Hope* in the United States and *Days of Hope* in England. (Translator's note.)
5. Written in 1933 and translated as *Man's Fate* in the United States and *Storm in Shanghai* in England. (Translator's note.)

carried everywhere, he said—it should go without saying—that it contained dynamite. With it he was going
to blow up the statue of Christopher Columbus, which
stood at the port in Barcelona and faced out to sea. It
was a symbol, he said, of the Castilian oppression.

The idea pleased me well enough. I'd never liked the
overrated Christopher Columbus. It wasn't he who had
discovered America, but the Basques and the Vikings;
and they'd done it much earlier.

When I asked why he limped, his answer was laconic
and grandiloquent: *"La guerra civil."*

Without hindrance—*with* the complicity of the
French police and, though I didn't know it at the time,
that of the Spanish *Guardia Civil* —we made our way
across the railroad tracks at the International Train
station at Puigcerdá. I was shaking with fear over that
damned suitcase of dynamite, which seemed much too
heavy for explosives. To make matters worse for my
peace of mind, the car that was to be waiting for us at
Barcelona wasn't there.

Suddenly a patrol sprang into the road and confronted
us.

"We've been betrayed," said my *compañero.* "I've already been condemned to death. If they take me, I'll be
shot. But you could lead them away; you could help me
by drawing them after you. No, leave the suitcase here.
¡Salud!"

"¡Salud!"

Malraux to the end. Or this time a Hemingway
matinée.

All night long I had the police and their dogs at my
heels. I'd been taught that if you wanted to escape
track dogs, you shouldn't just plunge stupidly across a
stream; you should move up along it, close to the bank,
for several hundred meters. Then you could cross and
proceed on the other side. The dogs wouldn't be able to
find you then. I did as I'd been told and evaded the
dogs. I'd also been well trained in endurance and held
out until morning, when another patrol grabbed me.

I stood there with my hands in the air and a machine gun poking me in the ribs. I played the dimwit and claimed to be a tourist just taking a little ramble in the mountains and that I'd gotten lost. I continued with the joke and pretended not to be able to speak a word of Spanish. No Spanish! After a nine months' stay in Franco's filthy prisons! I even had an admirable collection of oaths I used to reel off under my breath: *Coño, hijo de la grande puta . . .*

They put me in handcuffs and took me to their post. There followed a long discussion between the commander of the patrol that had first followed me and the captain whose men had captured me.

"Why take him all the way to Barcelona?" said the adjutant. "Shoot him now. We could say we caught him crossing the border and that he refused an order to halt."

"You might be right," said the captain, "but what if he's really with a bunch of tourists? At the *Segunda bis*[6] in Barcelona, they'd be able to loosen his tongue and teach some Castilian to the little bastard."

For two hours the discussion ranged back and forth, with nothing decided one way or the other. Finally, as usually happens, the captain had the last say, since his rank was higher.

"We'll take him to Barcelona," he decided.

I breathed a deep sigh of relief. A chain of command did, after all, have its value. For the very first time I blessed it. In a little train that wound its slow way between the mountains I traveled between two guards with their machine guns in readiness. They told everyone on the train coach about me; that I was a particularly dangerous terrorist, as well as being a foreigner. A Communist! And they embellished the story further. A nun eyed me with terror in her eyes and rapidly said her rosary. An old woman dressed in shabby black offered me a piece of cold omelet—a *tortilla*. With my hands

6. The Spanish Secret Service. (Translator's note.)

tied behind my back I couldn't accept it, so she fed it to me as though I were an invalid. My guards let her do it. And one of them offered me a black cigarette that reminded me of the third floor of the prison at Gerona.

When we were at the mountain post, I'd heard my fate discussed among the police, and my stomach had knotted up. It was nearly unbearable, worse even than mounting an assault. I could only stand there and listen and wait. I thought of those prisoners of "Saint John the Baptist," who'd had to listen as we'd urged their deaths. What if, after all, "Saint John the Baptist" were right?

Then, on the train, I was furious more than anything else. To be returning to a Spanish prison at the end of 1945! To spend Christmas there! What a stupid fate!

They took me to an old convent—San Elias—which had been transformed into a prison. An easy enough prison, compared to the provincial prison at Gerona; and the men confined there were largely the French SS and the old militia, who were all waiting for visas to South America—primarily to Argentina.

I was welcomed into the group with open demonstrations of kindness and friendliness:

"What were you with? The 'Charlemagne' division? The Waffen SS? The Wallonian Legion? The L.V.F.? The *Sturmbrigade Frankreich?* How were you captured? It doesn't really matter, and don't worry. This is nothing more than a marshaling yard, a place of passage. We're parcels being processed for someone to pick up, and the veterans of the Azul Division haven't forgotten us. They'll help."

They took me out for my first walk on the *"patio"* of the prison, for the ritual *"paseo"*—a name I remembered, as I remembered *L'Economato,* packets of figs, those little sardines grilled over a newspaper flame. And when in answer to their questions I revealed, "Matter of fact, I was in de Gaulle's camp, with the commandos," I created quite a sensation.

They didn't want to believe me, but one of the guards

was happy enough to confirm that I was a real *"rojo"*—
a red.

Surprised, the other prisoners began to laugh. One of
them, an old leader in the P.P.F., even took it upon
himself to get word out to the French consul on my be-
half. (The consul received the message, but did nothing.) The P.P.F. leader collected old Catalonian furniture. He loved it and devoted a lot of time to it. Those
men defeated by the Liberation, those whom I'd have
shot during the war, as they would have me, shared
their rations with me and then sent a letter to France
for me.

We spoke together of our wars: theirs in Russia, mine
in France and Germany. Our arbitrators were some Republican prisoners of the civil war and the commander
of the guards who'd lost an arm in the *Requetés.* War
gathered us all around her like an evening campfire.

One of them told me about the battles he participated in along the Dnieper.[7] Another described the
agony of the Wehrmacht on the Baltic Sea and of their
encirclement at Tcherkassy. A third described the last
hand-to-hand fights in Berlin, which by then was
defended only by foreign volunteers. One of the prisoners was a Spanish veteran of the old anarchist
brigades; he'd come to the prison from the battle of
Ebro[8] and the reconquest of Brunete, where he'd lost
his arm—and where twelve thousand men of the
brigades had lost their lives.

A strange gathering of men! Not one among us had
been in the top brass. All of us had been footsloggers.
We all somehow sensed that politics had no place in
our discussions; and while politics might be the reason
for our being where we were, it was irrelevant to our
present association, something to be kept in the background.

If I had been a good journalist, I'd have taken notes

7. A river in West Soviet Union. (Translator's note.)
8. A river in Spain. (Translator's note.)

on all I heard there—would have recorded their
names; weighed their stories learnedly; censured the
histories of these defeated men; written a sacred account for posterity.

But I wasn't able to remain aloof enough for that
kind of reportage. I had been too battered by my own
experiences in the war, by all we'd done in war's name
without having comprehended a thing. On the other
hand, I knew I'd already chosen the group in my field
with which I'd stand: that of the witnesses, not the
judges. Judges are necessary, certainly, but I could
never be one. And true witnesses, alas! are in shorter
and shorter supply in our profession; whereas any dimwit at all who has seen nothing and suffered nothing
will set himself up as a supreme judge of what has
transpired.

But this isn't the time for me to lose my temper.

Paris-Matin, having been notified of the turn of
events for me—and the amateur collector of Catalonian furniture having somehow coaxed them into it—
decided to supply the *Segunda bis* with proof that I was
neither a lost tourist nor a terrorist; even less an officer in the intelligence service (like an ass, I'd retained
my officer identification papers). I was finally released
from prison.

Next I was in Barcelona, unable to leave and followed by this one and by that one; embroiled in the
intrigues of the secret police about which and about
whom I knew nothing at all; artlessly working as an
extra in a Clouzet film, *Les Espions.*[9]

Then, after detaining me a month in prison and a
month under house arrest, they deported me.

When I returned to the newspaper, I conscientiously
wrote a report of my adventures. I wrote it with no
excuses, no exaggerations, but exactly as it had all happened. Max Corre read my report, wrinkled his nose,

9. *The Spies.* (Translator's note.)

called it crap, and called me a "Tintin" in the Spanish underground. I hadn't found the underground! I'd only invented them! He gave my report to the paper's re-write man, Jacques Robert, with instructions to do something with "that."

For "that" I'd nearly been shot!

At least I believed I'd nearly been shot, that I'd been in grave danger of losing my life; until the day my con-tact of the long, fine hands, my "correspondent" of Per-pignan, found me in Paris.

He told me that my dynamiter with the suitcase was an officer in the Spanish Secret Service, the famous *Segunda bis,* and that he'd infiltrated the ranks of the separatist movement. He'd never had the least inten-tion of blowing up the statue of Christopher Columbus. The suitcase held no explosives; rather, it held parts of cars; for, as well as being a double agent, dear Solair was active in the black market.

In order to shake me off and not be exposed, he'd sent me on my trip into the mountains. The police who were sent in pursuit of me had been in collusion with him, and not for a single moment had my life been in danger. Everyone had known exactly who I was from the beginning of my adventure.

On his way through Paris, the head of *Segunda bis,* who'd been in charge of my "case" (I may give his name: Lopez Moreno), left his card at my hotel—at that time I lived at Place du Panthéon—with these words: "Forgive us for having given you such a run-around. Solair (the phony dynamiter) adds his apolo-gies to mine. The report you wrote is worthless. We expected you to write such a report."

On the other hand, the Catalonian separatist of Per-pignan thought my report excellent and said, "People are finally talking about us. That's what is essential. The little mistakes are nothing by comparison." He married a very pretty girl and eventually became a naturalized Frenchman.

In any case, the final report as it appeared was not mine, but Jacques Robert's.

As for Max, he fired me.

"You know how to play at cowboys," he told me, "how to land yourself in jail, how to cause, or very nearly, a diplomatic incident, how to fight in a war, but you have no future in journalism. And believe me, I know whereof I speak!"

Later, when he'd changed his opinion of me, he claimed to have discovered me.

In addition to these activities in a profession that appeared so ill-suited to me, I became involved in politics. But always in the "infantry," always with the footsloggers; because I estimated that it was the footsloggers who won the wars, and that it was essentially the same in politics. Everything depends on the advance guard— the spearhead.

In what lay the major strength of the Communist party? Certainly not its philosophy, not Moscow (its Rome), not Papa Stalin. Its advance guard! I joined the S.F.I.O.,[10] whose liberal and hazy ideas suited me then. The ideas—nothing else.

I'd really have been more comfortable in the Communist party; but because of their inquisitorial style, which to me smacked disagreeably of the Jesuits, their want of any sense of humor, their didacticism, their meek submission to all the orders out of Moscow, I found their "cocos"[11] at the head of the French party unbearable. As Guy Mollet said of them: "They lean neither to the right nor to the left; they lean to the east."

The branches of the Socialist party were rather flabby, especially in the fifth arrondissement. There were a few

10. *Section Française de l'Internationale Ouvrière* (French branch of the Workers International). (Translator's note.)
11. Nuts. (Translator's note.)

militant young people there, but they were oppressed and could do little more than keep their mouths shut and listen to the eloquent rhetoric of practiced orators, of the humanists who knew much more about Plato than they did about Karl Marx.

When I asked that we get out of the lecture halls and down onto the streets, that alongside every vendor of *L'Humanité* there be a vendor of *Le Populaire,* the learned orators looked at me as though I were a dangerous animal. Still, they made excuses for me: my youth, my overriding enthusiasm.

I persisted in my obstinacy and, with a friend who'd graduated from the same school as I—the school of war—I went down onto the streets; I went to the Boulevard Saint-Michel, where we sold *Le Populaire.* To the great amusement of the "cocos," who lined ten or twelve vendors of their papers opposite us. And to the bewilderment of the public.

Moving on to other diversions. The A.E.P., a news agency run by Yves Morandat, took me on and sent me to Iran. The agency was already on its last legs, but I was unaware of that. I also represented some makers of perfume, of scrap iron, and of other such trifles. Not armaments. That came later.

At the end of just a few months the A.E.P. broke up, and I was left high and dry. But I was content in Teheran and had no desire to return to France yet, even though the ambassador of the moment, who dealt in oriental carpets (helped by his diplomatic pouch), let it be known that he thought me an individual of questionable character. Hard to say why. I never sold any carpets, never competed with the ambassador. Luckily Jekiell of the A.F.P.[12] and my friends the Godards helped me to survive. But that's another story.

The true head of the country of Iran was the chief of

12. *Agence France Presse.* (Translator's note.)

staff, General Razmara, a powerful dictator and an old graduate of Saint-Cyr. He heard of me, became interested in me and asked if I'd find him some other "good boys" of my kind to be trained to form a special unit. One that would act as his personal guard and on which he could count under any circumstance.

I requested time to think it over. I'd have to make contacts, find out what had become of my old friends. But I never had the time to reflect or to make contacts. Razmara was in the midst of preparing to overthrow the Shah and to take his place. The Shah beat him to the punch and had him assassinated.

I returned to France bearing a can of caviar, which my brother ate for his breakfast, and one carpet, which I lost no time in selling.

I wrote a series of articles on Iran, relating those events I'd witnessed and which I thought interesting and extraordinary enough for publication: the revolt of Mollah Moustapha Barzani's Kurds; the return of the Shah and the Iranian army to Azerbaijan, which had been occupied by the Soviets (up to the very last minute everyone wondered if they'd leave; the Russians' fear of the American atom bomb convinced them to give up their hold on the city); the revolt of the southern tribes, the Kashgaïs, which the British Secret Service manipulated; the misadventures of the Iranian Communist party—the Toudeh—which Stalin had just let loose and whose leaders were going to become intimately acquainted with the rope; the marvelous world of the bazaars, of the secret sects, and of the Zurkanés, those prisons where there were recruited all those paid assassins and other such unsavory characters of the south district.

Le Parisien libéré accepted my articles, published them, and paid me very poorly. But they did promise me the *prix Vérité*. That prize was going to be won by a fraud for purely imaginary adventures.

I did free-lance writing here and there (most notably

I found the third man in Vienna for *France-Soir*); and I
was working for *C'est la vie,* Jean Nohain's newspaper
and the offspring of a broadcast sponsored by *Le Chat*
soap, "Queen for a Day," when suddenly war broke out
in Korea.

I was waiting to meet a girl on *avenue de la Tour-
Maubourg.* The girl being late, I bought a newspaper,
Le Figaro, and learned that voluntary officers were
being called up. In order to sign up, one was to go to 51
bis, avenue *de la* Tour-Maubourg. It was only a matter
of a few steps for me to enlist. Did the girl arrive for
our date? Frankly I don't know. I was impelled neither
by the desire to throw myself against Soviet imperialism nor by the desire to go to the aid of American imperialism. I had no stake whatever in the matter. I
knew only that the aggressors were Communists. After
an ambiguous statement by the American secretary of
state which led the North Koreans to believe that the
United States would not intervene, they invaded South
Korea.[13]

The pay was good, half to be paid in dollars. Korea
was on the other side of the world, and I loved to travel.
I hoped, too, to find in the Korean battalions that same
generous and free spirit I'd known before with the commandos. All these things played a part in my decision;
but more than all else I wanted to succeed in writing
sensational news reports, to become a true journalist, à
la Kessel, to show Max Corre and others like him how
wrong they were about me.

At that time Max headed *Paris-Presse.* I told him
where I was going and suggested that I send reports
back to him. He accepted. What was *he* risking, after
all? I would regularly send him my articles from Korea
under an assumed name; I'd be the secret correspondent for *Paris-Presse,* hiding in the bosom of a French

13. On January 12, 1950, Dean Acheson declared that the defensive
perimeter of the United States was from the Aleutians to Japan
and from Riou-Kiou to the Philippines, which clearly excluded
Korea.

battalion; and I'd prepare a whole series of articles that could be published on my return. If my articles were good, they'd take me on as a regular reporter. If I were wounded or killed, that was my own problem.

On the strength of my past record, I was accepted into the military and went to the camp at Auvours as a lieutenant with two stripes.

I'm not going to repeat what I've already written in the form of a novel, *Le Sang sur les collines,* which later became *Les Mercenaires,* nor in the series of articles published by *Paris-Presse.*

The Korean battalion I was assigned to was not at all what I'd hoped for, but a monster: one with a large head and a tiny body. It was commanded by a four-star general, General Montclar, who was assisted by a whole general staff of observers that counted among its members graduates of the war college with irreproachable records, as well as a number of adventurers pure and simple, some of whom would end up in jail. They were all jealous of one another, all got out of as much as they could, all sought to create a personal following. The regular officers despised the reservists who, in their opinion, had only joined to steal the glory belonging to the regular officers.

The picturesque—and there was that, even in the Korean battalions—was to be found almost entirely among reservists. Among them were veteran parachutists, some of whom were old friends of the Liberation, who were ill-suited to civilian life; more than a few cuckolds, who believed that the best way to get back at their wives was to be killed fifteen thousand kilometers away, leaving them war-widow pensions; some rather good Legionnaires; some veteran SS members; a police officer who'd been involved in the assassination of Lemaigre-Dubreuil at Morocco; a doctor whose reputation had been compromised in a lamentable abortion affair. There were men hunted by the police and by the Internal Revenue Service. Or those who had creditors of a wholly different character on their heels.

Our group of reinforcements sailed on the *Mar-seillaise,* arrived in Japan a month later where we celebrated the fourteenth of July, and was decimated two months later on the place the Americans called "Heartbreak Ridge."

As we were crossing Japan by train, a night steward shook me awake in the middle of the night. He'd mistaken me for an American officer.

"Here it is, sir. We're passing Hiroshima."

I asked him, "And so?"

He answered, "Americans like to be awakened as we pass Hiroshima."

In reality, it was the Japanese who'd given the instructions that the Americans be shown Hiroshima. Five years after the bomb, they clung to their memories of it and reminded whomever they could.

The Korean War was of the "classical" type. Everything behind the front lines to a depth of fifteen kilometers had been cleared of all civilians. The military could thus at least be assured of no guerrilla activity in that zone.

The two enemy forces maintained their front lines as they'd been held in 1914–18, digging themselves more and more deeply into their trenches and leaving themselves at the mercy of artillery and air bombardments. At Bilan, 800,000 North Koreans were killed or wounded and 400,000 South Koreans. No one spoke of Chinese casualties. No one thought of counting them. Just as no one thought of counting the civilians who died of cold, of hunger, or who disappeared under the bombardments.

At least two million civilians died.

To no good end and for two years of palaver at Panmunjom.

The monster Stalin had to die before peace could finally come.

The North Koreans and their Chinese allies paid an especially heavy price for having let themselves be talked into fighting their "classical" war, for having let themselves be influenced by the Soviets, who placed their faith in heavy fighter battalions and in the kind of tank groups that had won the day on the Steppes.

Everyone wanted to go on and on waging the kind of war they'd won before: the French that of 1914–18; the Russians the great armored battles of the Steppes.

When I arrived in Korea the Chinese had just launched a huge attack in force, and hundreds of thousands of men swarmed down over the hills. The Americans and their allies—all those who'd sent brigades, such as the British and the Turks; or battalions, such as Belgium, France, and the Philippines—retired twenty or thirty kilometers to the rear in "Operation van," as it was called. It was a catastrophe for the Chinese. With bombs and with napalm, the American air force wiped out that ant hill of men.

Later I went along our lines and through those valleys of the dead, and what I witnessed was atrocious. The Chinese had not had time to dig any foxholes, hardly had time to scratch at the earth. They were taken completely by surprise, and their charred bodies lay strewn upon the ground by the thousands and thousands. They lay in blackened tatters of clothing, bodies hideously twisted and commencing to decompose, to stink of rotting flesh.

I imagine that later in those valleys the harvests were beautiful and plentiful. There had been enough good fertilizer!

Another face of war: Seoul and the ravages made on it by the American dollar. The green sickness which prevailed in Indochina and which caused the fall of South Vietnam.

In that city of Seoul, three-quarters destroyed, everything was up for sale. The GIs came in from the front and threw themselves with their dollars upon anything alcoholic or female, placing a premium on the market in schoolgirls—students either real or made to look real with their braids, their blue dresses, their flat shoes.[14]

I'm no Puritan, far from it, but it does seem to me that nothing at all is served for one country to defend another militarily while at the same time destroying its very substance with currency.

The American soldiers had too much money, too much of everything. Life for them was too soft. Besides, they didn't at all like the wars they were obliged to fight. (And it took Pearl Harbor to make Roosevelt declare a state of hostility.) Their government considered America the world's policeman, but they remained essentially isolationist. Their world was the United States. They knew or cared little about the rest of the world. For them, communism represented only a vague threat somewhere else.

The United States at first sent only its professional army to Korea, but that wasn't enough. They had to mobilize contingent forces, draftees.

The selective service system that was carried out on college campuses and in universities was at one and the same time logical, functional, and unusually cruel. America would send to the war only its ignoramuses, the bright students to be kept precious and safe at home. Those students old enough to bear arms had to undergo a certain number of tests. As a questionnaire unrolled from a machine, in the space for each answer the students were to insert either a circle or a cross. Those whose answers were not good enough were sent to war.

One such student whose name was Montfort—probably of French origin—and who was the brightest student at his university—a "young lion"—refused to take the tests because the idea of them was abhorrent to him. He was automatically sent to Korea.

14. The Koreans and the Japanese would learn to resist the dollar—the green sickness. After having once been contaminated, they became immune. The South Vietnamese would succumb completely.

One morning upon orders, Lieutenant Montfort was leading his company in an attack on the slopes of what would come to be called "Heartbreak Ridge." A stupid, pointless attack, a banzai attack like those of the Japanese in the islands of the Pacific. He was killed. The next day all the reserve officers of the division—all those who'd failed their tests—went into mourning for their friend, despite the fury of their general, who saw their action as the beginning of subversion.

To return to the tests given at the schools: they were worthless. Einstein, who died four years later, secretly took one of the tests. On the basis of the results, if he'd been a student, he'd have been sent to the bloody hills of Korea. A failure!

In truth, those tests thought up by average men were only valid for average men. Too high an intelligence, too lively an imagination, too creative a spirit could not be pegged by those tests, by that form of selection. Even there, war knew what she was doing. She could never be content with half-wits. She had to have the best, the youngest, the handsomest, and often the most intelligent to feed upon. Only these satisfy her appetite.

Tests and surveys! What stupidities! Booby traps!

In Korea we fought a war of the rich in a land full of misery.

In the zone behind our lines—in that area cleared of all civilians—there were piles and piles of cases of rations and of munitions along all the roads. They were heaped in veritable walls two stories high. As you passed by, you helped yourself to whatever you needed or wanted. Eventually we became very hard to please among such an excess of supplies, opening a case of rations to find a can of fruit salad, then throwing the rest of the case away. An incredible mess! Meanwhile, at Seoul and at Fusan, the people were starving to death; and in the streets, sanitation crews gathered up the bodies of children and of old people.

How I sweated and struggled my way over those peaks of Korea! Forever climbing and crawling my way up, achieving one crest and then seeing from there all the other crests and mountains we'd have to take sooner or later; mountains that lifted themselves serenely into infinity all the way to Siberia.

The Americans weren't prepared for that hard mountain warfare. They'd have preferred to run about in jeeps. But they learned. They fought well, in fact, out of pure patriotism, out of loyalty. (It would take Indochina for that spirit to die.) And they left fifty-four thousand men on the mountains of Korea. All to return everything to the *status quo ante*.

That autumn was a magnificent one, and the country mornings were soft and lovely. Sheltered behind our sandbags, we watched the ballet of the planes in the sky as they attacked each position with bombs and rockets.

Talk of peace had begun. The front had been stabilized, and activity had been reduced to that of patrols— or so it was said.

We held all the mountaintops forming a sort of great arc that we called the basin, with the exception of a section to the north of us, a kind of spur dominating the area. It was this spur that would soon be known as "Heartbreak Ridge"— *"la Crète du coeur brisé."*

It disturbed the general commanding that sector, a perfectionist, that his men didn't hold that spur. It bothered him to see that tiny red spot on his battle plan neatly colored in blue.

So one day he decided on an attack on the hill—a futile attack on that red spot, on that spur, on Heartbreak Ridge, that was of no strategic value whatever.

Later, when peace had come to Korea, I climbed Heartbreak Ridge with two friends—two battalion captains who'd been wounded shortly before I had. The ambassador of France accompanied us.

At that time, Heartbreak Ridge was in the demilitarized zone, and we needed all kinds of authorizations from both North and South Koreans to get there.

I quote from an article I wrote at that time:

It was only a hill like all the other scrub-covered hills.
We came across some ruined blockhouses, some cartridge
cases, a rusted helmet.

And beyond that hill were other hills, thousands of hills
disappearing into blue infinity. Higher and higher they
climbed, all the way to Manchuria. It had served nothing,
nothing at all, to take Heartbreak Ridge. . . .

In that month of October 1951, two entire American
divisions were thrown into the assault on Heartbreak
Ridge and were massacred. Fifteen hundred American
corpses remained on its slopes. The Chinese and the
North Koreans were solidly entrenched, and they put
their artillery to its best use. It was impossible to cut it
off. Individual artillery pieces were brought out from
under cover—from a cave or overhang—one at a time.
Each fired two or three rounds and then withdrew,
while another took its turn. They were never grouped
in a battery—were always isolated. Their losses were
thus slight.

The North Vietnamese, molded and trained by the
Chinese, employed the same tactics at Dien Bien Phu.
Our 105s, which were set up in the cove and neatly lined
up together, were useless against the strategy of the
enemy; so useless that the colonel commanding the
French artillery committed suicide by putting a bullet
through his head. It's just too bad a few of the chiefs of
staff didn't follow his example!

The colonel in question had even been sent reports
from Korea on the new Chinese tactics. But no one on
the general staff was interested in reading what had
taken place somewhere else.

I saw the parts of the American units that had survived coming back down all the little twisting trails from
Heartbreak Ridge. The GIs carried long bamboo poles on
their shoulders and bore the bodies of their friends like
hunting trophies. Many, many soldiers had gone mad.

Stupefied by their experiences, some would suddenly begin to howl, or to leap about in a frenzy, until it became necessary to stun them in order to quiet them.

Then it was our turn to attack.

The First Company mounted an attack and took a licking. Then the Second. Finally, just before dawn, I and my men of the Third advanced into a charnel house. By some rare chance we made our way through a barrage of grenades and found ourselves on Heartbreak Ridge. I had no more than a dozen men left. The others were either dead, wounded, or had fled. A company of Americans that had come to our aid was pinned down.

At nine o'clock on that same morning, I left Heartbreak Ridge in a helicopter. I'd been hit in both legs by a grenade. My war was over.

I was operated on in a field hospital across the valley, and I was lucky. My life was saved.

Then followed Osaka, Tokyo, and Saint Luke's Hospital.

I participated in a curious kind of experiment in that hospital.

A team of doctors had been devoting themselves to research into the healing of wounds. They certainly had a remarkable choice of men for their experiments: young men wounded in battle, and from a wide variety of nations, such as Turkey, the Philippines, Portugal, Belgium, France, Greece, and the United States— Americans of every origin.

The doctors discovered that they couldn't break their research down along racial lines, or even just along lines of origin; they could, though, in large part, along national lines. Wounds didn't heal in the same way for all nationalities. All Americans, for example, unless they were Puerto Rican or were otherwise recently nationalized, healed more slowly than any others. Why? Because their dietary habits had been so altered in Korea? Not at all. They still had all they needed, all they were used to: their Coca-Colas, their fruit juices, their frozen turkey.

It was all in the mind. And this is what happened in an American soldier's mind: The United States of America was like a mother to him. For her he had done his duty, and he'd been wounded doing it. He depended on her entirely. He'd abandoned himself to her, if you prefer. Now, his wound was no concern of his, not his responsibility; it was hers—America's—and it was up to her to take care of it.

On the other hand, those who belonged to older nations, such as the Greeks, the Portuguese, the French, healed much more rapidly. And it was because—the doctors whom I interviewed confirmed this—they didn't have the same behavior patterns in relation to their countries, the same freedom from constraint, the same confidence. For the Latins, for all the men of the Mediterranean, the state is not a mother; she is the enemy. In no instance can he place any real confidence in her. He'd been lied to and fooled by her too many times.

As a consequence, his wounds become something that concerns him and him alone. You can't in any case count on anyone except your clan, your family. The farther away from you the state remains, the better off you are; too many times she has revealed herself to be a thief, a swindler, someone who preys on the helpless, a sadist who hides behind incomprehensible rules and regulations in order not to have to keep her promises to you. If she should happen not to take your life from you, she'll at least steal the shirt off your back.

Out of these centuries-old and deeply rooted sentiments of the Latins have sprung organizations like the Mafia, created as a sort of insurance against the enemy—the state.

I left Saint Luke's Hospital on crutches, and I was sent to the old imperial city of Kyoto to convalesce. I

was the first French officer to land at the Myako, a
luxurious hotel reserved for officers, and a kind of celebration was arranged for me.

Thirty or so Americans leaned on an immense bar,
and I had to have a drink with each one of them. Not
something really to complain about, I'd say. A Lafay-
ette, a dry Martini, a Tom Collins, a Patton, some of
what we called *les petites femmes de Paris,* a gin fizz, a
whiskey sour, and so on . . . and on.

In addition to the wounded who were there on convalescent leave, there were among us a number of aviators who fought the Soviet planes in the skies over
what was known as MiG Alley. The two sides came together and clashed as in medieval lists, and the dance
began. A colonel told me that the American Sabre Jets
were faster than the MiGs, but less maneuverable. The
planes met and passed one another at two thousand kilometers per hour, and the pilots knew they were engaged in a fight when their machine guns, which were
automatically triggered, began to fire. All the engagements were filmed by cameras attached to the machine guns and rocket launchers, the cameras starting
to roll as the guns fired. Both the Russians and the
Americans studied these films to improve the operation of their planes and equipment, to perfect them, to
find better armaments to throw against the enemy, as
well as new and better aerial combat tactics. MiG
Alley was a test-bed for both sides. At each encounter
some of the planes were brought down, though the
Russians never risked flying over territory controlled
by Americans or South Koreans, making it impossible
to prove that they had ever directly intervened in the
Korean War.

The colonel told me that this kind of combat demanded excellent physical condition. "For that reason,
every two weeks we're given eight days of rest and recuperation in Japan. We're like boxing champions.
We're well cared for, superbly fed, so that we'll be fit to
climb back into the ring. A very serious problem con-

fronts the U.S. air force, and it's up to us to solve it: Should they equip our pursuit planes with rockets or with thirty-millimeter guns? So against 'Ivan' we try out the rockets at one time and the guns at another. Likewise, they experiment with their weapons against us. We are all not so much combat pilots of this war as research pilots for the wars of the future. Since war is inevitable, we might as well take from her all the information we can get, the best lessons she can provide us. The greatest progress made by science, its most important advances, are made because of war. Without war, humanity would be at a standstill for centuries at a time. No, I'm not an insensitive military machine, not just a crazy technician; I'm just relating facts. I'm not one of those crass ignorant Yankees everyone in old Europe makes such fun of—even though he's there to deliver your countries from bondage, and even though he remains there to protect them. I'm a southerner. I love books. I'm a nephew of William Faulkner."

At the Myako bar, as well as at the hospital, I was able to gather much better information for my articles than I'd been able to do while I was with my battalion.

I was on hand and ready to talk to a splendid choice of officers from all branches of the military—reservists as well as regular officers—who, with that freedom and openness of Americans, tried to explain to me how they felt about things, how they saw themselves and their roles. They were, for instance, gratified to have become the world's foremost power. At the same time, they'd have preferred not to have to pay the price required of them for that position of power, not to have to be involved in the world's far-off wars, which was repugnant to their essential isolationism: a deep-rooted instinct which led them to think of the United States of America as an island that all the currents of the rest of the world couldn't quite reach.

I dispatched my first series of articles on the war in Korea and on new weaponry and techniques. I was then asked for articles about Japan.

At that time Kyoto was a very beautiful city, like some old dead cities are beautiful. It's no longer the same; tourists clutter up Kyoto today, forming lines to get into the palace and its temples. I was alone then and hobbled around on my walks, supported by my canes.

One day I became lost and couldn't find my way back to the place where a jeep was waiting to pick me up. I spied a short plump Japanese and asked him in English, "Could you please tell me where I might find a taxi?"

He shook his head, not understanding those treacherous English sounds, and then nearly without accent addressed me in French, "Ah! It would be better if you could speak French."

As a disciple of Edmond Aman-Jean, he'd studied painting in Paris. We soon became friends, and he took me to meet a friend of his: a well-known and high-born Samurai artist who was, they told me, born of the imperial family. Which didn't prevent him from leanings toward alcohol and women. He lived in a very old, very beautiful house with a Zen garden of combed sand and artfully placed stones. But you could freeze there as soon as you moved any distance from the brazier, a huge and aesthetically placed blue vase full of hot ashes that warmed nothing.

Thanks to these two good companions, I came to know Kyoto well. Not the Kyoto of the tourists—such a thing hardly existed then—nor that of the occupying soldiers who all believed they could take the geishas to bed. The geishas sent their disguised servants to the soldiers, who never knew any better. My friends conducted me to an antique dealer such as I've never met before or since. He occupied a boutique near the hotel and made a gift to me of two rare and erotic prints so that he'd not have to sell them to Americans, whose manners displeased him. A one-time captain of a ship, an old military attaché in Europe, and a veteran commander of a submarine group, he had the fierce and beautiful face of a Kamakura warrior; but Japan's defeat and the bomb on Hiroshima had made a confirmed pacifist of this son of the Rising Sun.

It was he who acquainted me with a collection of letters from students who had died in the war, published by the University of Waseda. Among them were some of the last messages of the Kamikazes—the suicide pilots. The letters had been sent to their families in small white boxes which also held nail clippings and locks of hair—a sort of urn intended to be placed on the altar of their ancestors. Unmasking his old gods, the antique dealer told me that these Kamikaze pilots, almost all of them in the navy, were no longer volunteers toward the end of the war. They were unceremoniously pulled from the ranks of the worst pilots or those who'd received no more than rudimentary flight training. To make certain they'd do as they were supposed to do, they were given the oldest of the planes from which all the instruments had been stripped. They had only enough fuel for a one-way flight, and pursuit planes accompanied them to the objective before turning back.

I was able to procure that collection of letters. (I published some of them in *Paris-Presse.*) They became an essential part of my first book, *Ces Voix qui nous viennent de la mer.* [15]

One morning my Japanese friends came to find me at the hotel, and the sergeant of the guard kicked them out, calling them "yellow dogs." I left the Myako and they followed me, finding me lodgings in the off-limits section of the city—at the school for the *Maikos,* the geisha students. During the last week of my convalescence I did my best to help them with their education, and they helped me to perfect mine.

I returned to the hospital, where I was granted leave until time for my departure for France. A colonel I'd met while in the hospital invited me to accompany him to where he was stationed on an island north of Hokkaido, and where he was especially charged with train-

15. *These Voices That Come to Us From the Sea.* (Translator's note.)

ing, far from prying eyes, a new Japanese army in the art of winter combat.

Because in February of 1952, the Americans planned to thrust the Japanese into the Korean War, and were training them to that end.

I assisted in their maneuvers. There is no possibility that I could be mistaken.

Then the whole idea was abandoned. The Koreans would have viewed unhappily the return of their old occupiers, even if they were to be fighting on the same side this time. And Japan, disgusted with having lost the war, had become resolutely pacifist and wanted no part of anyone else's war. Public opinion was against the sending of any expeditionary forces to Korea—or anywhere.

It was at Hokkaido, or at Kyoto, or perhaps on the ship carrying me back to France, that the idea of a story came to me. The setting for it was among the cadre of a Korean battalion, more precisely during an attack on Heartbreak Ridge.

When I finally returned to my pigeon roost under the eaves on rue de la Montagne-Sainte-Genevieve, I had an urgent desire to write; and, on a typewriter purchased at the PX—the American army supermarket in Tokyo—I worked at it for a month. The result was *Le Sang sur les collines,* and it appeared in the collection entitled *L'Air du temps.*[16] It was a mistake.

I'd hoped for so much from it, but it was not a success. It sold fewer than two thousand copies in six years.

After a short stay at Val de Grâce, I was demobilized. I hunted up Max Corre, who asked, "And now?"

He regarded me with a different eye than previously.

"You have the makings of a good journalist. This time we don't have to rewrite your articles."

I was taken on at *Paris-Presse* as a major reporter. The title was high-sounding, but the pay was misera-

16. *The Mood of the Times.* (Translator's note.)

ble. Three months later Max called me into his office
and asked, "Tell me, wouldn't you like to go back to
Korea?"

In Korea the battles went on. Christmas drew near.
Eisenhower, elected president because he'd promised to
bring an end to the war, had come to Korea to make
his round of the army messes. I was assigned to cover
his trip. The temperature was twenty, twenty-five
degrees below zero; the icy winds blew in from Siberia.
Eisenhower, dressed in a parka, his face stiff from the
cold, was still uneasy in his role as president.

Each time he spotted me in the crowd of journalists
around him, he came over and squeezed my hand with
obvious feeling. I've never understood why.

I went to visit the French battalion, who were freezing on the hills. Their positions hadn't changed or improved. I wrote all about it for *Paris-Presse*. I was
housed in quarters reserved for members of the press
and was beginning to be accepted in that brotherhood.

Among the members were Robert Guillain, Max
Olivier-Lacamp, Giuglaris, and many others. They
explained to me what a journalist had to do in order to
make the best use, for his stories, of all the facilities
and opportunities provided by the American command.

RULE ONE: It's not at the front but at the rear—in
the camps of the press and of the staff officers—that
the most important news is to be found, news that will
make the biggest headlines.

RULE TWO: A good correspondent doesn't let himself
be taken in by every little chief who insists on talking
about himself and who makes a big to-do about his
every action. Up front, in the combat units, the correspondent will find plenty of color, but no hard information.

RULE THREE: The American press officials absolutely
require that "off the record" be respected. An announcement of a new offensive, for instance, could not
be divulged until after a prescribed period of time had

elapsed. Everything else was allowed, as was demonstrated by a pretty young woman who joined our new group and who made the special acquaintance of the general in order to get choice hints from him. She must certainly have received other things from him as well, since she later married him.

RULE FOUR: Never trust your colleagues. If they can steal a story from you, they'll do it.

For the correspondent, war took on a completely different aspect from that for the combatant. She was still just as dangerous; she was often fascinating; she showed herself in all her breadth and fullness; she showed her contradictions, her complexities; but she was also able to bring to the correspondent those moments of great pleasure: when the reporter could, for example, have a hot bath and an iced whiskey two hours after having seen and assisted in a battle where two companies of men were pinned down, harassed, unable to use their frozen weapons, and obliged even to seek shelter in order to be able to open their flies. She allowed the reporter, when he needed to clear his head, to get on any military plane and take off for Hong Kong or Japan.

There was a fabulous press gathering place in Hong Kong—The Peak—where the food, the drink, and the rooms were practically free. A Eurasian doctor, Han Suyin, had to meet correspondent M—— there before he could go off to die on the hills of Korea. From that brief encounter was born *Multiple Splendor*.

It was evident that the Americans could no longer carry off a victory in Korea because they didn't want to pull out the big gun MacArthur had asked for—the atom bomb—were no longer able to continue letting their boys be massacred.

The Chinese and the North Koreans, on their part, were locked in their positions, all their offenses ending in bloody failure.

The Communists, before accepting the fact that peace

was inevitable, sought to explain their reverses by accusing the Americans of using bacteriological warfare. Their propaganda was so well orchestrated that I was asked by my paper to see if there was any truth in it. *Paris-Presse* would not pass as a progressive newspaper.

I quote André Fontaine, who could not be accused of being a summary anti-Communist, as I had been:

> The object of that propaganda campaign has never been quite clear. It ceased abruptly on the death of Stalin, and the Communist leaders have never since made the least allusion to it. It's possible that it began as an explanation of a typhus epidemic which broke out in North Korea and in Manchuria. Very soon, in any case, the whole affair assumed the dimensions of an immense collective hallucination, carefully organized and exploited by cynical minds, mobilizing in the service of their improbable thesis the confessions extorted by torture from downed American pilots and the statements of naïve or obliging foreign observers. . . .

Because there was never a shadow of evidence that the Americans used bacteriological warfare in Korea, or even that they even contemplated doing so.

In Korea the cold war cost more than two million lives. If it had warmed up, as Stalin had wished, what would it have cost?

The world brushed perilously close to a hot war when MacArthur asked that the atom bomb be used against the Chinese, who some years later were going to become America's allies against "revisionist imperialist Russia," and who were going to fight beside American mercenaries and South Africans in Angola against Cuban and Soviet "volunteers."

In one camp, one is a "mercenary"; in the other, a "volunteer." Though they both do the same thing, always the very same thing: fight a war.

On my return from Korea I was often regarded as a mercenary. What, then, is a mercenary?

According to Larousse: "A soldier who serves a foreign government for money." And according to Littré: "Mercenary troops, foreign troops whose service one has bought—figuratively: one who can be put to whatever use one wants for money." That was never so with me. I never took the proposals of General Razmara very seriously.

I have given this definition:

> The mercenaries I've met and whose life I've sometimes shared fight between the ages of twenty and thirty years to remake the world. Then, until they reach forty, they fight for their dreams and that image of themselves they've invented. Then, if they're not already dead, they resign themselves to living as the rest of the world lives—but badly, because they never receive retirement pay—and they die in their beds of congestion or of cirrhosis. Money never interests them, and they worry very little about the opinions of their contemporaries. In this way they are different from other men.

I must add that it is often their own employers who provide them with another kind of demise, who liquidate them. As happened to the mercenaries of Carthage and to the campaigners whom du Guesclin massacred. But at least they were never required to confess at mock trials to imaginary offenses.

In my opinion, it is better to be a mercenary for the Americans than to be a volunteer for the Russians. It's a matter of self-respect, of dignity, and of aesthetics, for those who aren't fighting for a belief.

The "believers" fighting their wars scare me to death. They are inexorable; they're pure; they're pitiless. Nothing is worse than virtue.

Apropos the war in Vietnam I recently declared to a journalist, "I've always preferred Vice to Virtue, Vice when it produces the Renaissance to Virtue when it produces the Inquisition."

The journalist lopped off the second part, in order to create a more eye-catching title:

Lartéguy: "I'm in favor of Vice as opposed to Virtue" (*Le Quotidien du Médecin*).

One day at Seoul I received a telegram from my paper: "Indochina is on your way back. Stop at Saigon." I stopped—for twenty-five years. With trips back and forth, with periodic absences that lasted one or two years at those times when I was declared undesirable. But I always went back.

That country caught me by the guts and by the heart. I missed nothing that happened, not a *coup d'état*, not an assassination. I knew well the war France fought there; then that of the Americans; then that of the Vietnamese. Until the final collapse of Saigon, when I felt as though I were the one being strangled.

When I arrived in Indochina from Korea, de Lattre, eaten up by cancer, had just handed his command over to Salan, in order to return to France to die.

I didn't like de Lattre. I've already told you that— and why. Instinctively I reject those who rule either a command or a government by humiliation. But "King John" had succeeded in saving a situation that was more than compromising, following the loss of Cao Bang and of Langson. He'd lashed his men into throwing themselves back into combat. They went, furious, grinding their teeth, and swearing: "We'll show him; we'll show the idiot what we can do." They were trapped into going. When they came back, their anger evaporated; they were decorated. Once more they had fallen into the trap.

In my first paper I compared the war in Indochina with the war in Korea. In Indochina at that time men still fought men, the combatants holding a certain regard for each other, much as though they knew each other, as was sometimes the case.

In Korea masses of men were thrown against machines. What the masses lacked in weapons and in technique, they made up for by their numbers, by their discipline, by their organizational framework.

The troops of "volunteers" sent to Korea by Mao Tse-tung, more than five hundred thousand men, were mostly composed of Chiang Kai-shek's old soldiers, hastily recruited at the last minute, and not very reliable. Why had they been mobilized? The fewer of them who returned, the better for the new order. It saved work for prison and camp guards. And for the executioners.

The Chinese fascinate me and yet disconcert me by their assurance and by their brutal logic. All the sons of Heaven who've ruled China, from the Jade emperors to Mao Tse-tung, resemble one another. They are holders not so much of power as of logic.

In Vietnam, in all of Indochina, wherever the Chinese influence is counterbalanced by that of India and of the Occident, among all the peoples of mixed blood, I feel the most at ease.

I shall always remember the colors of the sky, the taste of an English bonbon in my mouth, and the morning I landed at Hanoi. I shall remember the strange feeling of *déjà vu,* of *déjà connu.* As if I'd already been there. When? In a dream? In another life? I don't believe in another life. It's the old mystery of love at first sight. You often believe that the woman who pleases you, the woman whom you are going to love, whom you love, is someone you've already met. Not one of her gestures, not one of her words surprises you. So it was with Hanoi. Among all the cities I have loved, Hanoi occupies first place.

I'm going to speak now of the war in Indochina. Without going into too much detail. But I want to do it because that war was the model, became the laboratory in which were improved—brought to near perfection— the new weapons and techniques for the wars of the future.

It would be worthwhile to study the origins of that

war. A war that never should have begun and never should have been continued. A war in which France and the United States lost more than their battles: they lost their souls.

The war in Indochina began on March 9, 1945, when the Japanese overthrew the French administration. Admiral Decoux and his party had until then maintained control of the country. The war ended thirty years later—on April 29, 1975—when Saigon fell into Communist hands.

In thirty years what mistakes there were, what chances missed, what spectacular reversals, what ludicrous and bloody marionettes danced for a few days, a few months, on that stage! What conspiracies, assassinations, bitter settlements of accounts! And what lies, punctuated by the bursting of bombs and the fire of napalm bombs!

Three million dead. Maybe more. Result: an extraordinary increase in the civilian population.

Which demonstrates the vitality of these people. While France has never recovered from the bloodletting of 1914–18.

So, on March 9, 1945, the Japanese, having no chance whatever of winning the war, or even of obtaining a peace that wasn't absolute capitulation, decided to put an end to the presence of the French in Southeast Asia. It wasn't that they had anything more against the French than against the English or the Dutch. It was only that they were white—nothing more. They surprised the French soldiers at Langson and massacred them. They crushed the French at Hue and at Hanoi and made prisoners of Decoux and his staff.

Indochina was declared independent, and rejoined the Sphere of Asiatic Co-prosperity. Bao-Dai[17] remained emperor of Annam.

17. Bao-Dai, the French puppet emperor who had collaborated with the Japanese. (Translator's note.)

But he was a prudent man, and he wrote General de Gaulle a letter from which I quote a few passages. If only the man of the speech of Brazzaville had read that letter more attentively.

> . . . You have suffered too much during four mortal years not to be able to understand that the Vietnamese people, who have twenty centuries of history behind them and a past that has often been glorious, are no longer able to bear either foreign domination or a foreign administration.

> . . . Even if you should succeed in reestablishing a French administration here, it will no longer be obeyed.

> . . . I beg you to understand that the only means of safeguarding French interests and the spiritual influence of France here is freely to recognize the independence of Vietnam, and to renounce the reestablishment here of any form of French sovereignty whatever.

> We could so easily understand each other and become friends if you would stop the pretense that you are once again to become our masters.

Bao-Dai was lazy, corrupt, and weak, but he was intelligent. He knew that France, if she wanted to return, must first recognize Vietnam's independence, even though it had been accorded by an enemy power. They could not turn the clock backwards. The Vietminh, who'd now seized all of Vietnam and was already flying the red flag from the border of China all the way to the tip of Camau, sent a memorandum to Sainteny[18] containing a list of the principal points which they proposed France agree to, as follows:

> • A parliament will be elected by universal suffrage. A French governor will exercise the functions of president until independence shall be assured to us. The president will choose a cabinet acceptable to parliament.

18. Jean Sainteny. (Translator's note.)

- Independence will be granted to Vietnam in not less than five years nor more than ten years.
- The natural resources of the country will be returned to its inhabitants after an equitable compensation has been given the present holders of them. France will profit from the resulting economic advantages.
- All the liberties proclaimed by the United Nations shall be guaranteed to the Indo-Chinese.
- The sale of opium shall be forbidden.

The Viets held all the trump cards in their hands. They could count on the support of the American secret service (the OSS), who had armed and equipped them. The service had decided to go to any lengths to prevent the French from setting their feet on Vietnamese soil again. If Roosevelt hadn't died, the French would never have returned.

As for the Americans, wrote Philippe Devillers in *Histoire de Vietnam:*

> . . . officers, journalists, all, or nearly all . . . displayed their sympathy for the Vietminh liberator of the Vietnamese people. They assured him of American support. They held out to him the bright prospects of all the advantages which would come of a collaboration with the United States. They publicly demonstrated their support.

The Japanese, even after their capitulation of August 15, 1945, would continue to aid the Vietminh and all the anti-French movements, notably the religious-political sects which have degenerated into little more than pirate gangs, such as the Binh-Xuyens,[19] or the V.N.Q.D.D.,

19. There were several such sects within the country. Three of these—the Cao-Dai, the Hoa-Hoa, and the Binh-Xuyen—had their own private armies, their own secret parties, and many thousands of followers. The Binh-Xuyen was probably the best armed and the most powerful of the groups. Under the French, who'd encouraged them partly as a means of splitting South Vietnamese sentiments, they were used on the Saigon police force. During World War II, they cooperated with both the French and the Japanese. Only after 1955 was Diem finally able to move against them and to expel them from Saigon. (Translator's note.)

the pro-Chinese nationalists. They'd have helped the devil if they could, just so long as he had slant eyes.

But the Vietminh mistrusted the Americans, who were viewed as primarily interested in moving Vietnam away from the influence of the French into the camp of Chiang Kai-shek, who'd had Communists burned in steam boilers at Canton.[20]

The Japanese were defeated, and no longer counted among the contenders. Besides, they'd revealed themselves as being of the same pattern as any other of the dangerous imperialists.

At that time, certain of the Vietminh leaders, such as Ho Chi Minh, thought that for tactical reasons and for the sake of old sentimental ties, it would be best to run for a while in double harness with France.

And de Gaulle, very badly informed as to what was happening in the Far East, offered them what? A vague statute and a plan of organization going back to that once adopted by Admiral Decoux.[21]

The plan was for a creation of an Indo-Chinese federation made up of five countries: Cochin China, Annam, Tonkin, Laos, and Cambodia. This was to be headed by a French governor general, assisted by a council from all the five countries—a false kind of government whose ministers, both French and autochthons, would be named by the governor general and would be responsible to him.

Added to this was an assembly—half French, half Indo-Chinese—whose power was limited to voting on

20. In 1927 Chiang Kai-shek sought to win over to his campaign to unify China all the conservative elements of his country and at the same time to keep Western nations neutral; so, without warning, he betrayed his Communist allies and murdered thousands of Chinese Communists in Canton and other cities. Many more had to go into hiding, Ho Chi Minh among them, and their party was broken up. (Translator's note.)
21. Admiral Jean Decoux had replaced General Catroux as governor general, having been given that post by Marshal Pétain to make certain that colonial policy conformed to that of Vichy and the reactionary French vassal state. (Translator's note.)

the budget; and the whole plan was seasoned here and there with some of those great, redundant, unfashionable formulas, like "the indestructible attachment of the indigenous populations to the civilizing mission of France."

Not once was that magic word spoken that could have straightened everything out: independence—*Doc lap*. Even if that independence had to be shelved until a much later date.

Bao-Dai and the Vietminh both asked only that the one word "independence" be uttered. General de Gaulle sent two of his best officers to Indochina: General Leclerc and Admiral Thierry d'Argenlieu. Leclerc was to be the supreme commander of all the land forces, but the admiral was to hold the title of high commissioner and of supreme commander of all three military arms.

It was out of these decisions—the one that d'Argenlieu should outrank Leclerc, and the other that *Doc lap* should not be spoken by the French—that the war in Indochina was to come into being.

Leclerc, the military man, would understand very quickly that they must deal with the Vietminh in order for peace to come. D'Argenlieu, the friar, the man of the church, would opt for war.

And it was to the latter that Charles de Gaulle would listen.

And yet!

"I've been told," wrote Philippe Devillers, "that at Nhatrang in November of 1945 a Japanese poll of the region revealed that seventy-four percent of the population remained pro-French, and that the anti-French numbered not more than fifteen percent.

" . . . But intense hatred, poison fruit of the Kempetai and of Japanese activists, had been spread by these who wanted to erect between the Whites and the Yellows in general, and between the Vietnamese and the French in particular, an impenetrable wall of mistrust and hostility in order that they themselves could control Asia better."

And on their part, the OSS and the Americans made peaceful negotiations further impossible by their support of the Vietminh against the French.[22]

Leclerc, with his thirty-five thousand men, struck wherever he could to stir up the Vietnamese as much as he could. He took Mytho and Tayminh; he occupied Vinh Long and the great rubber plantations; he smashed the encirclement of Saigon and cleared Cholon of its pirates. He reached all the way to the tip of Camau. Ten thousand Vietnamese laid down their arms. The rest were reduced to guerrilla groups, to assassination parties, to criminal outrages.

But Leclerc knew that he had lost.

He could seize the major axes—the principal routes. He could conquer the cities and towns, but he could not gain a foothold in the countryside. Despite all his tanks and all his soldiers, despite all the go-getters from France with a taste for victory, he knew he was defenseless against the guerrillas and against terrorism.

To achieve a victory, he'd have had to fight a total war—the kind of war France did not want and that he personally dreaded, because he recognized it to be full of pitfalls and temptations.

Leclerc has been called an insensitive brute. It's true that he was a disagreeable man and that he could be brutal, but he didn't cheat or lie. In his own way, he was intelligent and one of those condottieres—soldiers of for-

22. In February 1945 Ho Chi Minh traveled to the American military mission in Kunming, China, seeking aid. The Americans were nearly as eager to assure that the French not reestablish themselves in Indochina as they were to defeat the Japanese, and even though Ho's movement was Communist, the OSS supplied his guerrillas with arms and ammunition. Later, after Japan's capitulation, while the Vietminh, aided and abetted by the Americans, were taking over Vietnam, the French representatives in China, eager to return to Vietnam, could not reach there. General Wedemeyer somehow could not manage to find transportation for them. (Translator's note.)

tune—who do not bother their heads about details.[23]

His reasoning about Vietnam was that since we could not fight a total war, which France didn't want, we must therefore deal more and more with the Vietminh in the hope that they would accommodate themselves to our presence.

He advised the French government to listen to Ho Chi Minh. According to him, an underground war would exhaust the French army. That army might achieve some successes, but it would never achieve a decisive victory. Further, we'd not be able to rebuild

23. He'd once had twelve French SS brought in who had tried to escape the camp where they'd been interned. He reproached one of them for having donned the German uniform, and the man answered that Leclerc himself wore an American uniform. "In the face of that insolent attitude . . . ," Leclerc had all the twelve men shot without so much as a hearing. This was at Kalstein, Bavaria, on May 8, 1945.

In June of 1940, that same Leclerc was a captain. The following spring, in April of 1941, he was provisionally promoted to general of a brigade, but refused to draw his full salary, declaring that his advancement had been unmerited and too rapid. He satisfied himself with a colonel's pay and gave the difference to a young man of sixteen years, Louis Debeugny, who'd joined the Free French Forces to follow his father. Leclerc refused to take part in a solemn service at Brazzaville in November of 1942, given in memory of the sailors who'd died at Toulon during the scuttling of the fleet, because he felt he owed no honor to soldiers who'd preferred to sink their ships than to fight at the side of the Allies. He was a Royalist and a Gaullist and a practicing Christian, and he arrested a German priest coming out of a Mass he'd attended because the priest, a Christian, had done nothing to prevent Dachau and the other death camps.

He had a horror of politics. He was rough and rude. He expressed himself in short, curt sentences, and he didn't hesitate to deliver several blows of his cane to those Egyptian customs officers who once sought to challenge him. Leon Blum [of the French Popular Front Government] sent him to Indochina on a Commission of Inquiry. And it was later proposed that he replace d'Argenlieu in the post of high commissioner. He asked to consult with de Gaulle in his Colombey wilderness about it. De Gaulle dissuaded him, and it was de Gaulle he obeyed. De Gaulle had no desire to have his better and more faithful general replaced. It would have appeared to be a capitulation de Gaulle could be held accountable for. So Leclerc took up his post again as inspector of the North African forces. If he'd had his way, no blacks or North Africans would have been sent to fight in Indochina. He feared their political contamination. No one listened to him.

the kind of army we'd need to play an important role in Europe.

While Leclerc fought a war and pacified Cochin China, the friar d'Argenlieu became the great inquisitor. His sole concern was that of purification, of purgation. It was up to him to wash Indochina clean of the stains of its collaboration with Vichy. The Vietnamese didn't really give a damn about being cleansed. Nevertheless, he dispatched to the metropolitan emergency courts (where the purification trials were held) those administrators and officers who best knew the country, who might be able to render him the most valuable assistance, and who did their utmost for him with the means at their disposal. Men like the ship's captain Ducoroy, to whom the Vietminh delegation solemnly returned a visit in France at the time of the Fontainebleau Accords. D'Argenlieu surrounded himself with a court of civil service administrators who hung on his coattails and who dreamed only about having their privileges restored to them. And men for whom there was never any question of pronouncing the word "independence." These men were all going to depend on the French colonials and the Vietnamese figureheads, all more or less enfeoffed to Freemasonry. The whole thing was laughable.

It remained to conquer the north—Tonkin—and in that everything depended on the Chinese who were deeply entrenched there, pillaging and lining their pockets.[24]

Leclerc was of the opinion that Ho Chi Minh was the man to negotiate with because he was the strongest. Thierry d'Argenlieu, under the influence of his court,

24. In the absence of available American forces to occupy Tonkin after the Japanese collapse, the Allies had planned for Chiang Kai-shek's Nationalist armies to occupy the North. These troops, under American auspices, would, according to the American plan, keep the French from reoccupying the area. The 1945 Potsdam Conference of the United States, Russia, and England had confirmed the decision to have Chinese divisions occupy Vietnam to the 16th parallel. (Translator's note.)

felt they must recall Bao-Dai, who'd fled to Hong Kong
after his Japanese adventure and gathered around him
the mythical "third force." Hence the conflict between
the two Frenchmen. First they negotiated with Ho Chi
Minh, and on the sixth of March, after long months of
talk, Jean Sainteny[25] and Ho Chi Minh reached an accord. The French government recognized the Republic
of Vietnam as an independent state forming part of the
Indo-Chinese Federation and the French Union. The
Vietnamese government declared itself ready to welcome the French army when it arrived to take the
place of the Chinese troops.

War retreated for a spell.

If Leclerc thought about peace, Giap[26] thought about
nothing but war. He believed that a people earned its
freedom in battle; that capitalist imperialism could
only be extirpated by force—by armed confrontation,
in other words. While others were bogged down in
negotiations and diplomatic discussions, he was building his new army, assisted by Japanese officers and by
cadres from Russian and Chinese schools. He had man-
power enough. His arms, though, were defective.
They'd been purchased from Hong Kong and nationalist Chinese generals, who demanded payment for them
in gold, in hard currency, in opium.

The conference at Fontainebleau ended in the *modus
vivendi* Leclerc and Ho Chi Minh had hoped for, and
that neither Giap nor d'Argenlieu expected to respect.

When Ho Chi Minh returned to Vietnam from
France, he found his whole party ready to fight. And

---

25. Jean Sainteny led the French Gaullist representatives sent from
China to Hanoi to negotiate with Ho Chi Minh. He was the son-in-
law of a former governor general of the French colony, and he
knew Vietnam well. (Translator's note.)
26. Vo Nguyen Giap, one of Ho Chi Minh's early and two most
trusted disciples (the other being Pham Van Dong) and the man
largely responsible for vitalizing the Vietminh. His guerrilla activities during the Japanese occupation saw village after village fall
into Vietminh hands. As commander of the Vietnamese forces, it
was he who called for a national insurrection against the French
when matters came to a head at Haiphong. (Translator's note.)

Giap was war's most powerful minister. Then came the terrible incident of Haiphong, which pitted the French military security forces on the one side against the Vietnamese police and customs officers on the other, apropos a Chinese junk that was smuggling in drums of oil. The confrontation quickly blossomed into fighting in the streets and the intervention of French artillery.

In France there was no government. Once again.

Giap was convinced that the French had never renounced their plan of conquest and that the incident at Haiphong was proof of it. D'Argenlieu was convinced that Ho Chi Minh was only playing to the gallery and that the Vietnamese had never been serious in their negotiations. The incident at Haiphong was proof of it. He said in an interview: "I'm positive of my conclusions. It is henceforth impossible to deal with Ho Chi Minh."

The war could commence.

D'Argenlieu thought it would be necessary to crush the Vietminh, after which a "renewed protectorate" could be set up; while at the same time the Vietminh ordered "the total mobilization of all the material and moral forces of the country so as to intensify the fight for freedom."

There was fighting everywhere. The admiral was triumphant; more modestly, Giap was too. *Vive la guerre!*

D'Argenlieu was recalled and sent back to his monastery, and Bollaert arrived to replace him.

War underwent a name change. It was no longer a reconquest; and the expeditionary forces were no longer there to reestablish the rights of France, but to fight communism, that hydra, one of whose many heads was the Vietminh.

Bao-Dai was back. Indochina rejoined the French Union. And France paid a price. She abandoned the Republic of Cochin China, whose President Thinh committed suicide. The administration did not grant to

Bao-Dai all his rights as a true head of state, refusing him the palace at Norodom. The Emperor stayed at Dalat, where he busied himself dismounting cars, mounting girls, and hunting tigers. Officially, Vietnam was free. Why then didn't the expeditionary forces leave? They remained to defend Bao-Dai's regime against the Communists.

1949: The Communist troops of Mao Tse-tung were at the frontiers of Tonkin. Autumn 1950: The Vietminh, now with the aid of China, moved to take the offensive with thirty battalions, encircled and defeated the garrison at Cao Bang, forcing the French army to evacuate all the upper region of Tonkin, including Langson and Lao Kay.

The Vietnamese radio announced that on December 19 Ho Chi Minh would be in Hanoi . . .

Poor General Carpentier and his confederate Pignon, who'd replaced Bollaert, were sent back to France. De Lattre arrived with full civil and military powers. He smashed the Viet assault on Vinh Yen, then at Haiphong, then at Le Day.

It was a defeat for Giap, who was confined to guerrilla warfare.

There followed a few months during which de Lattre organized his court and his ceremonial, and reorganized his army; and then the disease that was eating at him obliged him in his turn to return home.

There was always one constant in the French war in Indochina: everyone was always willing to negotiate. From the very first. But always from a position of power. And it was for this reason that war took a new turn at Dien Bien Phu. The Communists and Giap could no longer consider entering into diplomatic discussions after having taken a beating.[27]

27. Leclerc, however clairvoyant he was, made the same mistake as everyone else. He asked Leon Blum to supply the expeditionary forces with the means to reinforce their safety and to reestablish the French position of power existing prior to the recent events, the aim being, apart from that, to offer the Annamites a "negotiated settlement."

When I arrived in Vietnam, there were already two Vietnams—two wars with two centers. Hanoi in the North, where a real war was being fought; and Saigon in the South, where all sorts of things were being done, where everyone was engaged in every kind of traffic, and where sometimes a war was also being waged.

I found myself in the press camp at Hanoi. The reporters were being housed in villas near the high commissioner's office. Before sheltering journalists, the villas had been used as dance halls and houses of call. Solidly entrenched there were veteran reporters Lucien Bodard, Max Clos, Bernard Ulman, and the whole A.F.P. gang, the Peloux family. There was a Mrs. Peloux and all ages of little Pelouxes, who made a living chain to carry papa's finished articles to the censor's office, always the first reports to reach there.

You can be certain there was censorship, the reverse of the kind we found in Korea. It was an idiot censorship. All the cables were stamped and okayed only after careful examination and pulling apart, but the articles sent by letter were not examined. Journalists were thought of well or badly, according to what they wrote and how they covered events, and were sometimes even returned home because of such a judgment, though it was usually possible to come to some kind of agreement with those at the top. Censorship was, after all, only a paper tiger.

The press conferences accorded us on a generally irregular basis by the Information Service provided us with what amounted to about two-thirds eyewash and one-third down-at-the-heels news. Theoretically, it was possible for us to board military planes and to go directly into the combat zones. But what a headache that was! All we required were written orders authorized by three or four services, but one of several things could happen: those whose signatures were needed could not be found; there were no available seats on the planes (there was never a place for those who'd displeased the authorities with their articles); or there was fear on the part of the signator that too much haste might appear suspicious. All so well orchestrated that if one managed to get the signatures, and if one managed to get a seat, by the time one landed, the event to be covered was generally over with and buried with a bulletin announcing victory.

Despite all this, we learned to be resourceful and to be well enough informed, largely because everyone had accounts to settle with everyone else: the generals one with the other; the army with the administration or with the secret services; the Vietnamese with the metropolitans; Bao-Dai with the high commissioner. The various military branches were all jealous of one another—the air force, the navy, the colonials, the parachutists. The civilian aviators who worked for the army were always ready to open their big mouths for a drink or for a girl, and their information was usually reliable, for it was they who flew over the hot spots and the attack posts.

After we had assembled our information from all our sources, there remained, of course, the task of picking through the heap of gossip and tittle-tattle to winnow our hard news.

Colonel Gardes, our camp commander, swore to me one day that they were able to get more out of reading the dispatches of the journalists (especially those not permitted to go through) than they could from all the agents the services maintained to provide them with information.

And gratuitously, at that!—as stated that native of Aveyron who enriched himself throughout the entire Indochina war.

Our relations with the members of the military were complex, made up of a mixture of peevishness, of mistrust, of fascination, and of friendship. The Expeditionary Corps felt itself to be lost, all but forgotten at the end of the world, where it had to fight a "dirty war," as some newspapers were calling it.

They were professional soldiers serving no real purpose there. All they could do was to go on obeying a government, a generally socialist government, that had landed them in that unholy predicament.

News from France was a long time reaching them, and the only real lifelines connecting these exiles to their homes were not the official ones; they were—the press. You can imagine how our articles were devoured! The greatest arguments or dressing-downs ended in the bistros of Hanoi, where friendships were born. Military men showed up there furious, denying one or another victory. Or, obliged to obey the stupidest of directives, they wanted to cry on our shoulders. They usually preferred novices like myself to the big wheels, especially if we were, as I was, more or less one of their own.

Some generals didn't hesitate at all to use the press for their own purposes, for their personal publicity. That sometimes worked (de Lattre), but it also miscarried lamentably in other instances, as with Salan and Navarre.[28]

Example:

A certain general had just arrived to take command, and imagined that the date should go down in history. He invited the press to be with him at the mopping up of a particular operation.

They were all taken to a mountaintop which overlooked a valley. A large tent was set up, equipped with maps and battle plans. The general gave a summary description of his plan of action. There were whiskey and *petits fours*. And down below, a village.

"According to our information," said the general, "that area is solidly held by the Viets. We'll 'negotiate' with them."

While the ice cubes were rattling in the glasses, a

28. General Henri Navarre, who made several serious miscalculations at Dien Bien Phu that proved fatal for the French and gave victory to the Vietminh. (Translator's note.)

signal started the tanks, the 105 cannons, and the 81 mortars pounding the village in question. A beautiful spectacle. All hell broke loose! Everything was in flames. The ground troops were ready to go in and finish the attack, when suddenly there burst from one of the smoking ruins a French adjutant, who roared, "Stop, you bunch of idiots! What the hell are you doing to my partisans?"

For several months the whole region had already been won over. The general had been mistaken about the village. He'd "negotiated" very badly.

That's what could be called a *"bavure."*[29] There were many of them. Wars are made up of *bavures*.

When journalists find themselves in situations where no censorship constricts them, the world can read about a My Lai. And an entire country can be sickened by a war.

My Lai and Watergate—the causes of the loss of Saigon and the abandonment of South Vietnam by America.

I've already told you that the war in Indochina, that fought by the French, despite all its horrors, despite all its *bavures,* perhaps thanks to its "artisinal" nature, its small scale, had not yet become that cold and inhuman monster, that insensible robot animated by computers, which would come into being at the time of the American war there.

Nor was it that kind of confrontation between two armies completely unknown to each other, as was the case in Korea.

In Indochina, before the Americans, everyone knew one another, so to speak, and the scales of war weighed heaviest on the side of the man who had war most under his control, who kept it from turning into genocide, who kept it from getting out of hand.

---

29. There seems to be no good English translation for this. Nothing quite says it, but fuck-up or blot or black mark give us a weak hint of the author's intention. (Translator's note.)

There was no lack of *bavures*. Nor of the massacre of
civilians: 150 Europeans and Eurasian men, women,
and children were horribly mutilated in the city of
Heyraud, and as many others disappeared around the
port of Saigon. On the nineteenth of December at
Hanoi, there was a massacre of the Vietnamese, and
not only of armed Vietnamese. Caught in the fire of
the navy and the artillery at Haiphong: 6,000 dead according to the army, 1,500 according to the navy—
their figures never agreed—and 30,000 according to
Communist propaganda, which frankly exaggerated.
Communists didn't give a damn about figures, about
real arithmetic. These were merely a concept of the
bourgeoisie. Figures were only of value to them if they
gave impact to their propaganda. Propaganda: still another of the many faces of war. And all that, all those
deaths, whatever the true number, was for the sake of
saving face, for the sake of the prerogatives of some
customs officials, for a mere nine tons of contraband
salt.

The Viets were ready for that battle, because all
their roads were mined and all the rooftops held their
snipers. They profited from the occasion by seizing the
airfield at Cat-Bi, which was later taken from them.

None of this kept the representatives of both sides
from meeting with each other between engagements
and gravely discussing how they might bring the war
to an end. Many times. Those times when war held
back a little. But she always managed to hold sway
again. Always.

I want to tell you two stories to demonstrate to you
that if the war in Indochina then was sometimes hard,
sometimes pitiless, she at least never had the inhuman
character she later took on. Because people knew one
another, because they often spoke the same language,
because they'd lived side by side for so long, had a history of direct or indirect contacts one with another. Because between the Vietnamese and the French there

was such an effective bond of love that even their hatred sometimes resembled love, a disappointed love.
They'd been able to understand each other, to come to
an agreement together. Everything that happened had
come about because that one word, *Doc lap,* had not
been uttered in time, perhaps neither side understanding the vital significance of it until after Dien Bien
Phu and the collapse of the myth of "Associated
States."

The first of the two stories was told to me. The second I witnessed myself. The one is about a little girl,
the other about a twenty-year-old sergeant.

In 1947 or 1948, a Vietminh battalion attacked a
plantation in the Terres Rouges region. The time of the
attack had been admirably chosen. The Viets were extremely well informed. Always. The planters, their
wives, and their children were all gathered at the club,
a large, brightly lighted building. There were a bar and
a swimming pool. The waiters were attentive and discreet. The whiskey and soda and the gin and tonic
were always perfectly measured and chilled. I know the
club, having been invited there myself on several occasions. People are rather snobbish in the Terres Rouges,
and there was a lot of hand kissing, and *nya-nya-nya*
drivel spoken from the back of the throat in a very refined way: "What play is being shown in Paris now?"
"Neuilly has become positively *unlivable,* my dear. Far
too noisy."

The great rubber plantations of Cochin China, especially those along the Cambodian border, were all in
the Viet zone, and they were to remain so until the end
of the war. The planters eventually managed to reach
agreements with the occupiers, but at the time of
which I speak, it wasn't yet so. So the Viets, determined to make their case comprehensible to the Parisian bankers who controlled the plantations, and decided to strike a forceful blow.

On the night of the attack, there was, as I've said, a
party at the club. For what occasion? A birthday per-

haps, a promotion, or simply because they wanted to
try to dispel the fear and the sense of danger that
prowled the green shadows of the rubber trees. Dinner
jackets and evening gowns. No one was armed, and the
guards slept or partied themselves.

The attack was brutal. Bursts of machine-gun fire,
grenades, Molotov cocktails. The club burned, along
with a number of other buildings. Red stains spread on
white shirt fronts, and evening dresses served as
shrouds.

When the Viets left, stock was taken of the damage
done. It was not a pretty sight. And a little girl nine
years old was missing. They numbered her among the
dead. No one would hear of her again until the conclu-
sion of the Geneva Conference in July of 1954, when
the Communist troops of South Vietnam, by virtue of
the accord, moved north with their weapons and baggage. Or some, not all—only the regular army units
that everyone knew. The others went to earth, waiting
for that day when they could come out of hiding and
become the Vietcong.

The Vietminh commander who'd headed the attack
on the club was tough as leather and totally lacking in
sentiment. Machine-gunning unarmed civilians posed
no problem to his conscience whatever. It was all part
of his war, an all-out war, a total war, which, since it
served the right to independence, imposed no restrictions at all. He found the little French girl who'd escaped from the club wandering lost among the rubber
trees and half crazy with terror. He took her with him,
probably at first with the idea of holding her hostage
and exchanging her for some rice, some money, some
badly needed weapons. The abduction of hostages was
common in Vietnam. But he'd just lost his own daughter of the same age, and he became attached to this little foreigner. Soon he no longer thought of exchanging
her for anything. She lived with him for six years, in
his wilderness, a part of his life. He raised her as he
would have his own child; she never left his side, and

she became a true Viet. One who walked barefoot; who could live on a bowl of rice, a few swallows of water, a sip of tea; who could spend whole nights in the forests. She knew how to use a knife, a machine gun, a grenade; knew how to creep through the trees without making a sound, how to burrow herself into a hiding place. She went with him to all his meetings. Vietnamese became her language.

On her part she grew attached to her Vietnamese father. It had been a long, long time since she'd been his prisoner, this little Viet with the fair skin and blond hair whose ancestors had fought in the crusades and whose parents were so proud of their title.

When the commander was able to return north to Hanoi, when he realized he'd no longer be able to keep the girl with him, that he'd never be allowed to, he decided to return "his daughter" to her true parents. His heart broke, and so did hers.

She was fifteen years old. A real young panther. She was sent to a convent in France—a fine one, naturally—Our Lady of Zion or Our Lady of the Birds, or some such thing. Where she could be taught correct French, not that of the *nha-guês:* "I not know you. You much big. *Con.*"[30] Where she could be taught good manners as well. She knew only how to use chopsticks and to eat with the rice bowl, holding the bowl up to her nose so she could push the rice into her mouth. She blew her nose with her fingers, refused to wear shoes, jogged along toed in like a duck, as though under the weight of a yoke with a basket on each side. On her blouse was the effigy of Ho Chi Minh. She was sly, suspicious, closed in, a caged animal ready for the slaughter.

She lost no time at all in crossing a good sister at the convent, who boxed her ears soundly to make a

---

30. Not easily translatable in the same common or vulgar sense the author must mean: idiot, clot, cunt, etc. It can mean all of these. (Translator's note.)

proper young lady of her. With the loud cry of *"Ho Chi Minh Muon-Nam"* (Ten thousand years of life to President Ho!), she decked the good sister with a judo throw.

I don't guarantee the end of that story. The friend who told it to me is not lacking in imagination.

Another time I followed an operation in that zone with an old war buddy I'd found.

We uncovered the command post of a Viet chief. In a bookcase made of old crates there were a dozen or so French books. Not the whodunits, but Zola, Victor Hugo, Balzac, and Saint-Exupéry. My friend smashed everything else he could lay his hands on, but not the books, saying to me, "He can go to hell, le Nhoc. But all the same, I can't destroy his books."

The adventure of the little sergeant happened in December of 1952. I'd just landed from Korea. Thirty kilometers from Hanoi is Khê-Sat, a large town surrounded by rice fields. There were many Catholics there, and to accommodate them a huge cathedral, whose framework was made entirely out of the scrap metal of the great ferris wheel that had given Parisians so much delight in 1900.

A Spanish priest had bought the heap of iron, had found the means to have it shipped, probably without cost to himself, and to turn it into a church. He'd made it yet uglier by filling it with those horribly painted statues of the Latin American style. Uglier even than Saint-Sulpice used to be before the makers of devotional objects were influenced by the new look.

I'd climbed to the clock tower of the church with an information officer. He loaned me his binoculars and pointed out to me an old military post in the distance, a kind of grayish protuberance the same color as the rice fields before the paddies pushed out their tender green shoots.

"Dô Mi," he told me. "That post is held by a sergeant twenty years old, who commands two sections of native auxiliary troops. He's been surrounded by the enemy

there for nine months. Now the commander has decided to mount an operation to rescue him. You'll be
able to see it through with us."

I repeat that Khê-Sat is thirty kilometers from
Hanoi. Dô Mi is four or five kilometers from Khê-Sat.
At that time a post could be encircled and cut off for
months at a time that close to the capital of the North.
De Lattre, who never did understand that war very
well, who was only able to take occasional advantage of
the mistakes Giap made, had believed it was possible to
defend the Red River Delta by erecting concrete fortifications—the "de Lattre line," a sieve through which
the Viets passed to re-form themselves behind the line.
Proof of that was the encircled post I speak of.

Besides that, bazookas quickly rendered the fortifications useless. For me, having just arrived from Korea,
all this was very new. In Korea, at least, we could see
better what was going on. Everyone had his place,
friend as well as enemy. And they kept their places. In
Indochina everyone and everything was all mixed up
together, and this required that another kind of war be
fought, political as well as military. The kind of war
where intelligence and the need to utter that damned
word "independence" mattered above everything else.

But to return to Dô Mi. It happened after all to be
not so small an affair. It became necessary to augment
the battery of artillery, the tank squad, and the attack
battalion with a company of engineers, which had to
completely rebuild the dike that served as a road and
that the Viets had blown up in a dozen places.

The artillery began to pound the village from the
right. They "negotiated" with it, as the saying goes.
And very well at that. The roaring flames licked the
green trunks of the palm trees, while the straw roofs of
the houses collapsed in a rain of sparks. The Viets had
it coming to them certainly, but not the civilians. It
was difficult, impossible to separate them, and it's primarily in this that war is so strong and capable. She'll
dirty the hands of anyone who gets mixed up with her.

I'm taking advantage of this story to describe to you a little of how an operation of this sort is mounted, with the intervention of a mobile group. Cement block-houses and mobile groups: the two big conceptions of de Lattre.[31]

At Dô Mi the bursts of fire followed in close succession, the grenades bursting very near our jeep. It wasn't the Viets (the two companies of auxiliary troops had vanished into the rice fields), but the attack unit that cleaned up the village before raking it out. You negotiate, you clean up, you rake out. War disguised as a gardener.

We finally reached the post: an old building of moldy brick, which must have been built a century before, when Francis Garnier conquered the Delta. There was a great square courtyard piled with bundles of weapons and cases of ammunition, with cages of chickens, and even a black pig tied to a bamboo tree, all the baggage of the new commander of the garrison, this time a Vietnamese cadet.

The old commander, a sergeant, shook his head as he watched everything being brought in. He indicated the cadet to me. "The poor kid," he said. "He's had it. But for all that, he doesn't act nervous. Still, with the Viets you can't tell; you have to get to know them. They laugh when they're sad, and pull long faces like this when they're enjoying themselves hugely."

The sergeant had a thin face, a childlike smile. He appeared very fragile. But he'd held out for nine months with soldiers whose language he didn't know. Twenty years old, he looked more like sixteen or seventeen. I listened to his account, the first, the official one.

"Everything was quiet for about three months. We made our regular patrols in the villages, we were

31. A mobile unit, under the command of a colonel or a lieutenant colonel, comprises:
  one command company
  three battalions.

rarely fired upon, and the leading citizens made long
speeches to us, bowing politely, their hands joined.
Then there were long conversations, not one word of
which I understood. I returned their courtesy. Since I
was incapable of making up conversation, I recited long
passages from things I'd learned at school: 'The Fox
and the Crow,' anything at all. They didn't understand
what I said, either, but they were satisfied. Then the
Viets stationed two companies—at least two hundred
guns—in the two towns to the east and southwest of
us. As soon as our patrols left the post, their guns
opened up, and all my supplies, which came by way of
Khê-Sat, fell into their hands. The Viet captain who
commanded these units sent me the following letter—
look, I've kept it. You can read it. It's in French."

Monsieur le chef de poste.

The Captain of Tu Doi 30 [Tu Doi company] sends you
greetings and wishes to inform you that he has taken all
your supplies [there followed a list of the supplies taken]
valued at about 10,000 piastres. He encloses this receipt.

[Stamped with the seal of Tu Doi 30]

N.B. If you're not satisfied with this accounting, you
have only to come forward with thirty riflemen, and I
shall come to meet you with an equal number of men.

With my regards.

I gave the letter back to the sergeant, who carefully
folded it and returned it to his pocket. He was obviously
keeping it. A souvenir?
"And then?"
The sergeant hesitated. "I didn't go. If I had, it
would have been the end of Dô Mi. After that we
had no further contact with the village. We retired
within our four walls and lived to ourselves. Nothing
to eat but a little rice, tea, and canned monkey meat,
which we had to use sparingly. Our only supplies
came to us by parachute, but the weather was nearly

always cloudy, and the containers often fell off to the side of our post into the hands of the Viets. We couldn't relax for a minute. There weren't any real attacks against us, but we were subjected to harassment, to small thrusts, making our lives impossible. There were about four weeks of that, and then the Viets set up a loudspeaker system. They'd start by firing several rounds at us, forcing us to dash for the battlements to defend ourselves, and then the sales talks would begin. First in French: 'You, Sergeant Untel, you who come from a family of miners from the north of your country, you son of the proletariat, what are you fighting for here? Surrender. You'll be treated fairly and sent back to France.' Then in Vietnamese for my partisans. One of my corporals translated for me: 'Cut off your sergeant's head and go home. Go back to your wives and children. All we want from you are your weapons and the Frenchman.' My auxiliaries were the first to give in. They had wives and children in the villages held by the Viets. They could hear the pleas and sobs of their families over the loudspeakers. They gave me their guns and they left. I understood why. All that was left to me was a handful of regulars, Vietnamese too, but they hadn't given in. Perhaps because they liked me, or perhaps because they expected no real compassion from the Viets. Also, they had no one of their own in the area. The loudspeakers never stopped their bawling out of their slogans, their threats, and their promises, interspersed with Vietnamese and French songs. If you hadn't come, I'd have cracked."

The sergeant was given a medal and the *Croix de guerre* T.O.E.[32] with Palm. He returned to Khê-Sat with us.

Something didn't ring quite true in that story. Someone little more than a boy held out for nine months in that rotten corner of hell, surrounded by rice fields and

32. *Théâtre d'opérations extérieures:* Foreign Service. (Translator's note.)

mud, the sole white man in the middle of yellow men, and completely encircled by Vietminhs. I hardly mention the climate: the constant drizzles, the suffocating heat, the humidity of that tropical hothouse. Impossible circumstances. I couldn't let my sergeant go, and, after having plied him with several drinks, attempted to get him to open up to me. It wasn't too difficult. He had a great need to talk with a fellow Frenchman, and by my bribery I finally learned the truth.

The Viet captain who spoke and wrote such good French and the sergeant, isolated in the midst of his partisans, suffered one as much as the other from the solitude. They were both there because they'd been ordered there, and neither was particularly anxious to fight.

The Viet had learned his history of France from the same books as the sergeant—Mallet and Isaac. The sergeant had answered the captain's letter in which the latter had proposed they meet, each with thirty men, in the lists—as in the Middle Ages of Pleörmel, when thirty Bretons faced thirty Englishmen. "Beaumanoir drinks your blood." The reply simply stated that the sergeant had no real confidence in the word of the Vietminh; otherwise he'd have gone.

The captain was indignant, and they continued to send letters back and forth, at first to abuse each other, then gradually to speak of other things.

The garrison had to get its supply of drinking water at a place located outside their post, a water source also used by the Viets as well as the inhabitants of the villages.

The Viets and the French partisans managed not to go for their water at the same time of day. It was a tacit agreement between the captain and the sergeant. This amicable arrangement lasted three months. As simple soldiers they went further, exchanging chickens for ducks, boxes of rations for rice. The rations were left at the watering spot and the rice picked up.

One day the two men, the captain and the sergeant,

found themselves face to face. They hesitated. Neither would fire. There was a slight gesture of the hand, as with me and my Fritz in the Vosges, and each returned to his own side. Soon they began to exchange books, sending them by their usual intermediaries. The Viet had studied at the Lycée in Hanoi, and the little sergeant had been conscripted because he'd failed his final exam.

I personally believe they went still further—that they must have met each other over a lukewarm beer at the Chinaman's place in town, or quietly in the evening to speak of their families or of the books they both loved. The sergeant never acknowledged this to me. It only seems logical to me that it should have happened thus. Just as it's logical that the captain was denounced, relieved of his command, and replaced by one of those Viets with the soul of an inquisitor who'd instigated the harassment over the loudspeakers. The captain had told the sergeant everything about himself, had told him all he knew, and his own use of the loudspeakers had been to speak to the sergeant of his parents, of the place where he'd lived, of the problems he'd faced.

A very strange war, wouldn't you agree?

I wrote an article about the official version of the story. The other, at that time, wouldn't have been understood. The article appeared in *Paris-Presse*. Kessel's brother read it, hastily wrote a scenario around it, and sold it to a producer. Some years later I was asked to write an adaptation of said scenario, which had only been a reproduction of my article.

I applied myself and came up with a fair piece of work not too far from the truth. But the Minister of National Defense, at the reading of my script, refused to furnish, with or without cost, those things the producer needed to make a picture: soldiers, weapons, munitions. His motives? I'd made the regular adjutant a drunkard; and the fictional lieutenant who commanded the partisans, a reservist of mixed blood, was more intelligent than his regular colleague and had contacts with the Viet chieftain, who also presented problems.

My adaptation ended up in the trash can. Léo Joannon later took it, located the story in Camargue Delta, and it became *Fort du fou*, a bit of conventional tripe easier to swallow.

I know only one film that perfectly reflects the ambience of the war in Indochina, *La 317ième Section*, by Pierre Schoendorffer.

And nothing better depicts what it was like behind the lines, in a city like Saigon, than *Hoa Binh*, by Raoul Coutard. I can't help it that they're both my friends; that, as I have, they've been tainted by the "yellow sickness," and that Indochina remains for them a paradise lost.

Temporary understandings such as that illustrated in the story of the little sergeant had nothing to do with treason. And they weren't at all incompatible with the very hard confrontations that could follow afterwards. Nor with physical or moral torture, with extortion, with the kidnapping and rape both sides engaged in, the Viets more than our side, because that kind of subversive war, revolutionary war, almost certainly ensures that torture must take place. Everything in that kind of war depends on intelligence, and there aren't many ways to obtain it.

Here is where war is the most disgusting. By her very logic, by an ineluctable chain of events, she leads men who are by no means beasts, who are quite the contrary, into the commission of acts that will mark them for life.

The real inquisitor—he who has the faith, who is convinced that his cause is a just one and that every means which forwards that cause is justifiable—he, I believe, will find very little to worry his conscience. The victor is able to believe in a possible absolution for his crimes. Never the vanquished; not, certainly, he who goes on fighting and no longer knows very well why.

The French didn't engage much in the practice of torture in Indochina, for in the military there were still those traditions that expressly forbade certain practices.

They left the Vietnamese to deal with the assassination committees as best they could. It was their baby, and for them it posed no particular problem. Torture was part of their history. It had been common practice at the time of the Emperors Lê and Nguyen. Some pedants of the law were even specialists in the methods of torture, were real connoisseurs. Far too important to soil their own hands with the filthy business, they directed the torturers, advised them how to play the game.

In the questioning of a suspect, many means were available: cold pincers, red-hot pincers, the torment of the hundred knives, or of the hundred wounds, crushing the fingers between two boards. And if the suspect was obstinate, there was the excision of the nose, amputation of a foot, castration, and slow death.

Witnesses who turned a suspect in were themselves put to the question and beaten with rattan canes or the cat-o-nine-tails. There was also the plain cangue,[33] the pillory, or the heavy cangue fastened to the feet with iron chains.

The problem of torture was especially acute in Algeria when the French army found itself alone there, without any auxiliary aid, to face the Algerian rebellion.

For the sake of greater effectiveness, to achieve some kind of victory after so many defeats, to fight the enemy with his own weapons, and to profit from all that was learned in the camps of the Vietminh, certain elements of the French army practiced what was called "operational" torture. It took place even in the special units such as the D.O.P.

---

33. The cangue is a wooden framework, usually several feet square, fastened about the neck as a portable pillory. (Translator's note.)

I never permitted any torture, though I have to acknowledge that this point of conscience never confronted me as it so dramatically did my comrades in Algeria; but I really think that even were I driven to the wall, I would be physically incapable of inflicting torture, come what may.

I would like to see torture universally condemned. I would like us all to stop speaking of good (useful) or bad (useless) torture as of good or bad wars. Torture practiced by revolutionaries is as bad as that practiced by counterrevolutionaries. The same can be said of war.

Or else we should all stop lying. Let's frankly cry: *"Vive la guerre, vive la torture* — provided it is leftist."

Happily we're finally commencing to grow indignant over such torture as is practiced in the Soviet Union, where it has become a science in the psychiatric asylums of the K.G.B. and is systemized in the country's Gulags, used on all those who do not comprehend the beauties of the Communist paradise. But we took our time to become indignant. We had to wait until 1975.

The only solution: make it unlawful on both sides to practice torture. But, then, why can't we do as much with war itself? That would be difficult in the extreme when one notes that the Russians and the Americans can't even come to a simple agreement to limit only certain atomic weapons!

But let's return to Indochina and to that interminable war, which was to leave its mark first on the French army and then on the American army. As we look at it we become aware of just how much was asked of the soldiers of the expeditionary forces and to what degree they were made fools of. At the end, abandoned and insulted, they no longer knew at all why they were there. The war never stopped changing about.

1946–1947: They came to reconquer an ancient colony fifteen thousand kilometers from home, to defend the Terres Rouges plantations, the cement factories of Nam Binh, the coal fields of Tonkin, and the banking privileges of the Bank of Indochina.

1947–1950: During this period they fought for the Associated States; for Bao-Dai, who'd been gathered up in a Hong Kong gambling den and brought back to lead the newly formed Empire; and for the piastre! But especially for the anachronistic privileges of a colonial administration that refused to let go and of a wealthy Vietnamese bourgeoisie that made up the whole of the political caste.

From 1951 to 1954, they were there to contain the Communist thrust in Southeast Asia. With American dough, American armaments, and their own blood.

Something had to come out of it all, though.

It was during this last period that I was to meet Bigeard. I'd accompanied the young Brigade General Cogny on an operation in which he'd gone to check on the dependability of one of the three sectors of Tonkin. He was a courageous giant, intelligent and ambitious, and for whom any action was permitted. He was one of the best stallions in de Lattre's stable, and de Lattre was the only one from whom he would accept the bit. He was already balking under Salan, who'd come to replace "King John." He would later be worse under Navarre at Dien Bien Phu, and their quarrel would poison the whole atmosphere. A windfall for the journalists, because Cogny had learned from his old patron how to deal with the press. Navarre was less clever and would alienate the press.

The delta in the area of Nam Dinh is particularly inhospitable, with the water, the mud, and the little islands of villages protected by their impenetrable hedges.

A battalion of parachutists had received orders to take one of those villages, which had been transformed into a fortress by the Vietminh.

A slim silhouette atop a knoll, his microphone in his hand: the unit's commander. He was giving voice directions to his companies, who worked there in front of him and whom he moved about like pieces on a chessboard. It was an impeccable maneuver. Everything looked perfectly timed, as though the parachutists had a dozen times practiced the operation on long-familiar terrain. A well-run war like that becomes an art, a ballet, after which the dancers, when they fall, do not get up again.

Cogny, a graduate of l'Ecole Polytechnique and of the War College, was hard on those officers who came up through the ranks. According to him, it was better for them to remain executants. But of the commander of that parachute unit, he said to me, "That major, who was still a sergeant in 1940, is Marcel Bigeard. He barely passed his elementary exams, but he has an inborn talent for maneuvers. Look at that demonstration. And no casualties. Or nearly none. He could be given a regiment, a division, and I'm convinced he could cope just as well. In combat. Not at the rear."

"What'll he become, general?"

"A colonel. No more. Napoleon would have made him a field marshal. Because he's lucky. Do you know what Napoleon called luck? That mysterious sixth sense, intuition, which in war counts for more than brains. War has other criteria than civilian life does, than even a professional army does. I've seen the phenomenon I speak of in action, and I know what I'm talking about. He'll get another citation, but he'll go no further than five bands."

That year I spent Christmas in the fortified camp of Na San.

Na San had been a successful rehearsal of Dien Bien Phu, had been a victory gained through luck and the mistakes of the enemy, but one that, because we tried to repeat it fourteen months later at Dien Bien Phu, would cost us dearly.

I arrived over the Na San Basin in an old Dakota. The air was like a bowl of milk, and we had to wait to land until the haze dissipated. Before the big offensive of the Vietminh in the Haute Region, it was only a makeshift airfield, a grassy runway where meandering buffalo had to be chased away before a plane could set

down. One auxiliary company of natives guarded it. A
month after the offensive, fifteen thousand men were
stationed there with their rolling stock, their weapons,
their cannon, their fuel depots, and their generating
sets. A radio beacon guided the seventy planes a day
that landed there.

General Gilles, a parachutist, commanded the position. He surged up out of a hole in the ground and considered me with his one eye and that half-innocent fe-
rocity which was characteristic of him.

He was squat, and his shoulders were rounded
because of their highly developed musculature. He had
the bloated face of a condottiere and the gait of a peasant. He was dressed in odd bits of uniform and was covered with earth and dust, the only new thing on him
being his two shiny stars, which he'd just received.
Gilles didn't like journalists, and he grumbled at me,
"So, when the battle's done, when the danger is over,
you come sniffing around the war? Get the hell out of
here!"

Luckily, his adjutant surfaced after him—a lively
Gascon, whose bush hat tipped to one side gave him
the look of a musketeer. All he needed was the plume.
It was Colonel Ducourneau, whom I'd known when he
was captain of the commandos. He said to the general,
"He's one of my old lieutenants. I'm not familiar with
Lartéguy, but I know Osty. I'll keep him with me."

For his own reason, different from those of his chief,
Ducourneau also couldn't stand reporters. He claimed
they all wrote like pigs in a language that only vaguely
had anything to do with French, and that out of pure
laziness they never got their information where they
should get it. They did damn little and got their tips in
the bistros of Hanoi, where they drank hugely. His
bugbear was Lucien Bodard.

Neither Gilles, a shrewd creature of war, not
Ducourneau, one of the army's most brilliant officers,
felt easy in his mind about Na San. Sitting there in
that amphitheater of mountains in that badly put to-

gether hedgehog of fortifications was not calculated to reassure them.

I spent the night with Ducourneau in one of the forward blockhouses, where we partied among his parachutists with lukewarm champagne.

"We're going to be lucky here," he said. "Very lucky. If we only have the balls to grasp the chance we have."

General Gilles and Colonel Ducourneau each in turn later refused to take command at Dien Bien Phu. After Na San, they understood the danger.

At midnight, while Ducourneau, who had a prodigious memory and an even more astonishing educational background, was reciting Montaigne from memory, the Vietminh attacked.

Flares lit up the sky, and the countryside all around us took on the hues of plaster. There were heavy blows of mortars and machine-gun blasts and exploding rockets. Then nothing more, except the moans of a wounded man in the barbed wire.

The Viets had only come to test the position, to see if its defenders were still there.

The French had "broken the back" of the Communist thrust, but it had obviously not been destroyed.

General Salan later said, "An infantry such as that [the Viets], which can bind up its own wounds and rise again six months later with the same ardor, is an incomparable instrument of combat."

That autumn the Viets were masters of all the high valley of the Red River; and the 308th, the elite division, made a surprise attack on Ngia Lo, gaining the middle valley of the Black River. The 316th joined up with the 308th and all the middle region was in the hands of the Communists, who could then descend toward Hanoi.

It was for this reason that Na San was improvised, the French hastily setting up their fortified camp for use as a simple base from which they could launch commando raids against the Communists.

Every hill became a base, with the artillery in the

middle. One after the other, the 308th, the 312th, and
the 316th launched their attacks, violent and brutal
ones, especially those of the first and second of December. The waves of their auxiliaries, armed only with
bengelores and grenades, threw themselves onto the
barbed wire to break through it. Trained for three
months in this kind of combat, they had as their sole
function the clearing of a path for the regular units so
that they'd not suffer too many losses. The auxiliaries
were drunk on choum, someone told me, even on drugs.
But in my opinion they'd been conditioned by incessant
propaganda. And by knowing they couldn't retreat, because behind them were the political commissars who'd
drummed into them how very bad it was to run away,
who would blow their brains out if they took it into
their heads to do so. They threw themselves forward in
small groups, carrying their explosive charges in front
of them on the end of long bamboo poles. Absolutely
contemptuous of death.

When you have no choice, it's better to die while attacking than while running away.

After my meeting with Ducourneau, I celebrated
Christmas with the legion at one of the bases, the P.A.
26, which held one battalion of the Third Regiment of
the Legion. They'd been attacked by the regiment of the
Viet 316th Division and by another regiment of the
308th, and the engagement had been particularly hard.
I made my way over the slopes of the mountains, using
the zigzag trenches to get around the networks of barbed
wire. I was accompanied by the stale, nauseating odor of
badly buried bodies who'd fallen near the position. Bits
of flesh and pieces of uniforms still hung on the barbed
wire. They belonged to those volunteers who'd jumped
with their explosive charges and who'd been pulverized.
The three waves of them got no farther than the barbed
wire networks, were unable to breach them. Tirelessly,
the machine guns mowed them down, and the barbed
wire became weighted with whole clusters of their bodies. Then it was the turn of Giap's soldiers to attack.

"One of the best infantries in the world," the Legion commander who'd invited me told me admiringly of the 316th. "Better than the Russians," said the German Legionnaires who'd fought both of them; better than the SS against whom I'd fought.

Firing all their weapons at once, supported by their mortars and bazookas, they attacked without cease all night long. At our base, the Vietminh 174th Regiment alone left three hundred dead. More than that number of volunteers died.

What a strange Christmas it was in that encampment of blond gypsies with naked torsos who spoke every language, mostly German. Under the hot sun they dragged back to camp the trees they'd just cut, trimmed them, and decorated them with paper streamers to make Christmas trees. They set the tables for the Christmas dinner, covering them with opened parachutes and green boughs.

To the donkey used in their festivities they gave a large pan of wine, feeling somehow obscurely that he'd behaved so well during the battle, he deserved some reward. Completely drunk, the donkey collapsed on the tent where four noncoms were playing cards. Soon the area was turned into an immense crêche, and everyone sang *"Stille Nacht."*

To bring myself back to reality, I also recall the black muzzles of the machine guns and the F.M.s that poked out of the holes in the fortifications, the mortars ready to fire. And everywhere the odor of badly buried bodies.

The commander proposed a toast:

"To Forget" (Major Forget).

Everyone raised his glass.

That same battalion of the Legion, the Third of the Third Regiment, had been completely destroyed at Cao Bang by the Vietminh 174th, and its chief, Major Forget, killed.

It had been re-formed at Sidi-bel-Abbes, and Forget's best friend, the chief who'd raised his glass, had taken command of it.

In its turn, the Vietminh 174th was massacred at Na San, the base held by the new Third Battalion.

I'd have found it perfectly natural if the commander had raised his glass to the Vietminh 174th. And if the other side had done as much for the Third. But the new rules of war prohibited it. We'd returned to the "religious" wars.

The smoke of the brush fires hung in the air, which had grown purer and sweeter with the coming cool of night. The blue of the distant mountains turned to mauve. A cannon began to fire at long intervals, as though for conscience' sake.

Ducourneau, who'd come to find me, touched me on the shoulder. "Our last night at Na San," he said to me. "Tomorrow it will become an operational base, and we'll be leaving. Another battle will begin. We're going to take the offensive. Two Vietminh regiments are waiting for us at Co Noi a few kilometers away."

At Co Noi the battle was extremely fierce, which went to prove that the Viets hadn't lost their mordancy.

Giap learned a lot from the beating he'd taken and was never again to make the same mistakes. He wrote a criticism of himself in the borrowed jargon of the Soviet and French P.C.[34]

> It is subjectivism that causes one to underestimate the enemy, to fall into overconfidence, and that leads to a superficial bureaucracy. Evidently we showed a great deal of fervor, gave the appearance of having nothing to fear from the enemy. In point of fact, it was more a question on our part of leanings to the right, of negativism, which blinded us to the extreme cruelty and ferocity of the enemy, which blunted our hatred of the adversary, and caused us to flag in our vigilance.

A criticism that the French generals would have done well to direct at themselves, only in the language of Descartes and Montaigne to please Ducourneau.

34. Command Post. (Translator's note.)

The evacuation of Na San went forward without hindrance, a genuine miracle which we turned into a victory. More simply, the Viets were licking their wounds and rebuilding their decimated divisions, repeating over and over to themselves the mistakes they'd made, so they wouldn't make them again.

We'd lost the whole of Thailand. Our faithful ally, Laos, was threatened on one side from the Plain of Jarres, and every day an announcement was made of the fall of Luang Prabang. All we held was Lai Chou, where the Black River met the Pavie Trail and Nam Lai. But we didn't hold it for long. I hurried there after I left Na San. An acrobatic landing at the bottom of a cuvette between two smooth mountain walls more than a thousand meters high and vertical.

The pilot didn't even cut his gas, and after having let go his cargo of barbed wire and cases of ammunition, he took off. According to him, the spot was too risky, in danger of falling from one hour to the next. It wasn't defendable.

The Black River, clear and transparent, encircled the town and then lost itself in the blue valleys.

I saw something astonishing there: great big colonels, fat colonels, officers of the commissary, digging trenches, filling sandbags, making ready the shelters. In the heavy heat of the dog days and under the amused regard of two white Thais (the Thais are distinguished according to the color of their wives' bodices: red, black, white, etc.), they worked, two long thin ropes, two lianas, swinging freely down from their large hats of braided straw.

Furious, the colonels sent me elsewhere. They gave me a jeep and a driver to take me to the Claveau Pass, which defended the access to Lai Chou and was where the action was expected.

The driver was a French North African infantryman who drove at top speed along a narrow winding mountain trail at the very edge of steep cliffs. I asked him, "Where are the Viets?"

"Askoun!"

He let go of the wheel to spread his arms. "Every-where. The Viets are everywhere."

We very nearly were. He took the wheel again a hair before we'd have descended back upon Lai Chou like a glide plane.

At the pass the jungle was being burned to clear the field of battle. When he saw me, the commanding offi-cer who held the position began to fume: "Another one of the idiots sent me by the general staff. What are they saying in Hanoi?"

"That nothing is happening here. That everything is quiet in Thailand."

"In that case, since nothing is happening, right? and because we don't know what to do with ourselves, we spend all this leisure time we have burning forests. Just like the Meos.[35] When planting season comes, we'll all be able to plant rice in the cleared land and then harvest it a few months later. Except that our Meos have all disappeared. Shit!"

In the evening after dinner, I was invited to a game of bridge in one of the blockhouses. In Hanoi they'd said that nothing was happening. So when nothing is happening, you play bridge. I've never played another game like that one, nor heard such whimsical bidding. And during every hand, the dummy, except when I was dummy, popped outside to see what was going on and returned with a long face to take his place.

Finally they had had enough of the comedy and let fall their cards.

"Do you know what day this is?" the commanding of-ficer asked me. "It's the birthday of Ho Chi Minh, and to celebrate it the Viets are going to take Lai Chou. They already dominate all our positions. Their assault troops are in place and ready. Good night, Monsieur journalist. You'll be able, if you're lucky enough to get out, to write a report on the Vietminh camps."

35. One of the various ethnic groups of the Haute Region. (Transla-tor's note.)

A brutal awakening three hours later. Mortars exploding, long bursts of machine-gun fire, shorter ones from the F.M.s. A green flare hung in the sky.

The battle drew near, making its entrance with the dance of grapeshot and grenades.

After twenty minutes it was over, and the Viets took off. No one has every understood why. In Lai Chou there was only one cannon, two fat commissary colonels who didn't know how to fire it, fifty or so supply soldiers, some Thai partisans who'd already decided not to fight, and four hundred weary and demoralized French North African infantrymen to hold the pass.

I asked a master sergeant who'd gone back to town with me, "Why are you fighting?"

He answered me in words that could as well have been in the mouths of the whole army in Indochina: "Because it's in my contract and I'm being paid for it. And then, I like it here."

Before returning to Paris I was entitled, according to custom, to an interview with the commander-in-chief, General Salan. Salan was not comfortable with the press. He'd stepped into the command formerly held by the virtuoso publicity seeker de Lattre, but he was of an altogether different stamp. He hadn't de Lattre's gift of presence, his key formula for wooing the press. Nor was he the stage manager de Lattre had been, who had sometimes foundered in that kind of incredibly bad acting that came to be known as the "theater of Marigny."

Raoul Salan was one of those secretive and taciturn Southerners found in the regions of Languedoc, a land impregnated with Protestants and practicing Cathars.

He was a moody man given to pondering the imponderables, a man of long silences, of meditation. He was also timid and hid behind his panoply of decorations, which hung almost to his waist, much like those of a Soviet marshal. People attributed to him distinguished vices, strange practices, mysterious contacts. They claimed he converted to Buddhism, that he was a friend of Ho Chi Minh, that he and Giap understood each other.

His surname: the Mandarin.

As a mandarin and having spent most of his career in the Far East, he understood the problems of the Asiatic mind—understood the finesse, but also the indecision. He never made mistakes; he let things happen and then intervened just in time to prevent a catastrophe.

He was necessarily an optimist, and he gave me a panoramic view of the situation in Indochina as he saw it, with enough gloomy touches so that later he couldn't be charged with having been *too* optimistic.

He was an astonishing personality. Not at all liked by the soldiers with whom he had no personal contact, esteemed by a few initiates, he turned in upon himself and his own secrets, which were said to be innumerable and sinister.

Without getting his own feet wet, without interfering, he let his subordinates under his disenchanted but attentive eye make a new kind of war. They were to furnish me with the characters for *Les Centurions*.

In 1951 there was created the G.C.M.A. (*groupes de commandos mixtes aéroportés*), small units of partisans recruited from Haute Region minorities traditionally hostile to the Vietminh (and to all the Vietnamese) and organized by French officers and noncoms.

They'd at last decided to put into practice those theories of Wingate and of Chapman, all those things we'd learned in the C.L.I. that would bring war up to date, make it modern: political action united with military action, daring and economical action.

The development of the G.C.M.A. naturally ran into its share of problems. They needed men and radio sets, small groups capable of living and functioning for months at a time in the jungle. Hence the intensive and specialized training of groups of autochthons who could speak and understand all the different dialects and recognize one another's costumes.

All this only happened after Na San, when it was believed we'd found the secret of blunting Giap's attacks by the use of aeroterrestrial bases. To defend these bases effectively, the bases needed eyes and ears in the countryside, needed information on all that the enemy was doing. Above all, the enemy could never be allowed to feel at ease, to feel at home in those big, empty, and abandoned spaces he occupied: he had to be disquieted, alarmed by guerrillas wherever he went, whatever he did; his supplies had to be constantly menaced and his communications cut. The G.C.M.A. could do all that.

They began by immediately changing the name to G.M.I. *(groupement mixte d'intervention)*, a common practice in the army. You change the name and you're convinced that'll make things happen.

Then the new service was given the means to operate, which they'd lacked before. At the time of the fall of Dien Bien Phu, those partisans, numbering about fifteen thousand men, were massed at a distance around the fortified city. Or at least there was pay for that many men, and supplies and ammunition for that many were parachuted to them. It's possible there weren't quite that many.

Badly used, or not used at all, they weren't outstandingly successful; but all the same, they so alarmed the Viets at Dien Bien Phu that several battalions were sent out just to try to rout them out.

They were recruited from among the mosaic of ethnic peoples of the Haute Region: Thais under Deo Van Long, an old Chinese pirate's son whom they made chief of a confederation; Miongs; and especially Meos.

It's of these last that I'd like to speak, because they were the hardiest and most dependable of the underground, the ones who held out the longest. And for having believed the promises first of the French and then of the Americans, they are now dying of starvation and disease in Thailand in this year of 1976, which according to the Chinese calendar is the Year of the

Dragon and of great upheavals. And so will pass from the face of the earth one of those peoples most dedicated to liberty.

No one really knows where the Meos came from. From the south of China? From the Aral Sea? From Lake Baikal? They call themselves the sons of the Great Dog.

In legendary times, in the time of the Jade Emperor, a dragon devastated China. Unable to subdue it, the son of Heaven promised half his royal kingdom and his daughter's hand in marriage to the one who could get rid of the dragon for him.

The dog Meo killed the dragon and went to demand his promised reward. He got the girl. That was no problem. But upon the advice of his counselors, the Emperor, who hadn't determined precisely how he was to divide his kingdom in half, granted to the slayer of the dragon only all that part of the kingdom which was located on the far side of the clouds.

In memory of their ancestor, the Meos wear a heavy silver collar and live in the mountains apart from other people. Convinced that laws would only be used against them, they can't stand laws. Their only crops are rice, which they grow in the cleared area of the forests, and opium, which they sell and themselves use in moderation. Occasionally they'll use tobacco and medicines, letting their children smoke, too, when they have colds. No one has ever known intoxication among them, one more mystery to all those who are able to get close to them.

They never market their opium themselves. The Thais of the valleys or the Laotians who are a branch of the Thais, the Lao Thais, gather together by villages at harvest time, get up a subscription, and convert their money into silver. Then some of them meet the Meos halfway up the mountain slope, where the exchange of money and opium takes place. The Meos cannot tolerate going down into the valleys, where they feel ill at ease, prisoners.

Life continued like this for them until war dragged them down into her whirlpool. Thereafter their successive protectors accepted the responsibility for selling their opium. The G.C.M.A., a para-official organism dependent upon the Expeditionary Corps, took it upon themselves to sell the opium to get funds and weapons for themselves and to help their friends the Meos.

In 1954 I returned from the Meos' mountains in a plane chartered by the army and crammed full of opium. In their turn, the American special forces and the CIA which came after us took over the task of transporting and selling the Meos' opium in Thailand.

In his memoirs[36] General Salan wrote:

These Montagnards [the Meos] grow their poppies and easily turn themselves around in the direction of anyone who'll help them dispose of their opium. Information which reaches me indicates that the Vietminh find this a favorable moment to approach the Meos and to offer to sell their opium for them. . . . In the present circumstances, we need the Meos, and our G.C.M.A. Service asks me to take the opium for ourselves. Moreover, we presently lack sufficient money to create in those mountains an underground that will serve us. I've made it the responsibility of one Tou By, a chief who is known to the Meos, to transfer the opium to a destination in Cholon. The G.C.M.A. Service guarantees the transportation of the opium by plane. [The plane in which, by the greatest chance, I'd embarked—a Nord Atlas.] There at Cholon, General Bai-Vien [the head of the Binh-Xuyens and of Saigon's fraternity of thieves, and an associate of Bao-Dai] takes the business into his hands and regulates the selling price of the opium. With the money he receives, Tou By places thousands of armed men at our disposal.

Unhappily the transport isn't made with the necessary discretion, and some reporters have learned of the affair. . . . There's no way I can explain to the press all the reasons that moved me. . . .

At the time of the governor generals, such opium trans-

36. *Fin d'un empire (end of an empire),* T.II (Les Presses de la Cité).

ports were often made, whether for the benefit of the political parties or for society's needs.

Excellent animal breeders, the Meos adore their little
long-haired horses so much that they take them into
their miserable huts with them. When you're in the
hut of the Meos at night, by the light of the small fire
that burns between two stones in the middle of the
room you can see the luminous eyes of the horses shining in the gloom.

The Meos resemble the Tibetan Sherpas, and they
may even have the same origin. They're squat, with
enormous leg calves, have pushed-in faces, and go about
barefoot but wearing unbelievably filthy leggings. The
women wear beautiful silver jewelry on their cast-
metal breastplates.

Men and women alike are able to carry great weights
for days and nights at a time in their back baskets. And
their scouts don't pick their way back and forth up the
mountains, but choose a line straight up the face of the
steepest slope and forge ahead.

They've always lived apart from other people, as I've
said, in small family units, some of the families united
by a vague line of parentage. And even then their huts
are widely separated one from the other.

No great importance is attached to fidelity on the
part of their wives, although one of them who called
himself a chief but exercised little authority explained
to me that they cover their wives in noisy jewelry for
the same reason they bell their sheep—to know where
they are. He had two or three wives, but they could
leave, return, disappear, without his being really
alarmed.

They are unstintingly hospitable, and they hold liberty above all else. One morning a Meo looked at his
wife and his children and decided he'd seen enough of
them, that they could get along very well without him.
He took off for six months, a year. No one asked him a
thing. He went from mountain to mountain, from Meo

hut to Meo hut, where he was given food and drink, a pull on the bamboo pipe; and if he felt like having a girl and the girl was willing, he took her. Then one fine day he disappeared from his new haunts to return home—or to go elsewhere.

The Meos didn't like the people of the valley, the Thais, who always sought to best them in their opium dealings. It was worse with the Vietminh and their allies, the Pathet Lao, who were even more foreign to them, who sought to meddle in their affairs, to forbid them their perpetual revelries, to regulate their cultivation of the poppy, to assemble them, to impose leaders and cadres upon them so as to initiate them into the ways of Ho Chi Minh.

Some French officers and noncoms were parachuted down to them with weapons and radio posts. Those sent into that insane venture were all young men between twenty and twenty-two years old, completely freewheeling, as nonconformist as the Meos, and upon whom discipline weighed heavily. They were wholeheartedly welcomed. The Meos quickly learned how to use the modern weapons and to operate the radios. A whole year after the Geneva Armistice, the underground Meos were still fighting the Viets. Because they wanted to and despite orders, because they'd found their field of combat: for liberty, true liberty, their liberty.

When the Viets captured them, they decapitated them with sabers. One of my friends was among them.

When the French left Indochina, the American Secret Service took the Meos in hand. The better part of them, under the orders of Van Pao, the son of Tou By, were organized by the Special Forces, the Green Berets, and in the north of Laos and on the Plain of Jarres they kept up an incessant guerrilla warfare against the Vietminh and their satellites, the Pathet Lao.

What remains of them today? Thirty thousand of them fled into Thailand after the fall of Saigon and after the Communists of Hanoi and their Soviet coun-

selors took over Laos. Eight thousand of them still
fight in the mountains. Abandoned by everyone, as
much by the French who launched them into this venture as by the Americans who took them over and
promised them never to let them down. They are closed
in in the region of Nong Khai, dying of hunger and disease, without medicine or food supplies, in danger of
being turned over by the Thais to the Communists,
who've decided to exterminate them.

And with them thirty-five thousand white, red, and
black Thais of the region of Lai Chou, who fled to Laos
after the city was taken, swimming the Mekong to get
there, leaving in small groups under the guns of the
Pathets and the Viets.

War's fallen!

War likes to simplify things. She doesn't just dream
of gigantic confrontations, of dehumanized armies coming to resemble each other. All those who are different,
who are colorful, who give savor to the world, the minorities with their customs and their folklore, all must
be destroyed in her big bloody tracks. War is an idiot.
She knows nothing of nuances.

The creation of the underground was the first step
toward another kind of conflict.

The second came about through the parachutists,
who, unable to do otherwise, abandoned the principal
lines of advance and attack and plunged deep into the
jungles. They realized they could survive there with
the help of the partisans. Or even without it. Victims
of an error of the high command, Bigeard's battalion
parachuted into Tu Le in the Haute Region to hold a
difficult-to-defend position dominated by two mountain
peaks. The battalion was to support the garrison of
Ngia Lo, which had been attacked by the 308th. Ngia
Lo's garrison had fallen at the first wave, and Bigeard's
men found themselves alone, seven hundred men facing ten thousand. The weather reports were unfavor-

able, and there was no hope at all of support from the air.

Bigeard received an order to fall back to the Black River. He refused. That would have meant throwing themselves into the waiting arms of the Viets. Instead, Bigeard and his men occupied the two peaks, broke up three assaults upon their positions, and disappeared into the jungle, abandoning their wounded, amounting to nearly a quarter of the battalion, to the care of the chaplain. Bigeard was later severely reproached for his action, "because such a thing is just not done." But if they'd had to bear the wounded with them on stretchers, four men to every one wounded, the battalion would barely have crawled along, could not have fought at all, would have been annihilated.

Once in the jungle, instead of just slipping away and escaping, they laid ambushes for the Viets where they were least expected. Instinctively rediscovering the rules of that kind of jungle combat, they maneuvered brilliantly. Already the majority of them went barefoot, and they jettisoned their heavy parachute packs and everything else that wasn't absolutely essential to their equipment.

The column reached the small post of Muong Chen, held by an adjutant and several of his partisans. It was an even worse position than Tu Le. Here the five hundred parachutists faced the entire 312th Division, ten thousand fresh men who'd not yet been engaged. While the tiny sacrificed garrison made as much noise as possible to give the impression that the battalion remained with them, Bigeard and his men withdrew into the night.

Once again into the jungle. But it was the jungle that protected the French. Twelve hours of march without halt, of march over steep slopes, through passes overgrown with elephant weed, and along nonexistent trails. Muong Chen was destroyed, and the adjutant, Peyrol, who'd defended the post, himself took to the jungle with his partisans. The jungle is neutral: she shelters those who are not afraid of her. The march continued in silence, the much faster "commando" march they'd now learned.

The next day they crossed the Black River on rafts— after a week in the jungle without sleep.

Bigeard not only brought back five hundred out of seven hundred of his parachutists, all in good condition, after escaping the encirclement of two of the best Vietminh divisions, but further, on his passage through the jungle, he roused up three hundred Thai partisans who followed him.

Even the adjutant (Peyrol) in his turn was able finally to return to the French lines, going all the way by way of the jungle, where the Viets, like the Japanese in Burma, were never at their ease, where they maneuvered badly and repeatedly let themselves be surprised.

Bigeard himself told me that his success had been due to two things: he'd lived two years in the Haute Region, commanding a Thai battalion, and the physical training of his men was remarkable. Even when they were at ease, every day they were made to do fifteen kilometers of commando march at a fast pace with all their arms, all of this interspersed with firing practice.

Tu Le was celebrated at one and the same time as an unusual exploit and as a necessary instruction. If only we had followed it! If we were to support the underground, we needed to create jungle units as the English had done, the kind of war to be fought not having really changed at all. We couldn't win. But we'd have come out of the war honorably, without Dien Bien Phu and with infinitely fewer losses.

We began to understand the war when it was already too late.

We continued in our way out of pure laziness and for lack of imagination, always hoping to negotiate "from a position of force," caught in the toils of a war we shouldn't have made. When an occasion presented itself to make peace, no one knew how to seize it.

As in 1949, when the Communists lined up along North Vietnam's border.

I well remember the story of an old French chief administrator, Lallemand, one he'd told me in Hanoi, that deserted city the French hadn't yet totally evacuated and the Viets hadn't yet entered. It was on the fifth of September, 1954, during the course of a strange dinner I gave to celebrate my birthday. My table guests were Lallemand; Tran Van Lai, who was the Viet authority in the city; Commander Gardes; and Helen Xoung, who'd been variously Madame General, Madame Governor, Madame Admiral, Madame Emperor, and with whom Bernard de Lattre had spent his last night before going home to die.

Lallemand, of Decoux's old crowd, told me he had kept up his friendship with the other side, and in 1949 Tran Van Lai had contacted him on Ho Chi Minh's orders.

With the Chinese standing on their border, the Viets were seized with panic: the old ancestral fear of the Chinese who'd occupied their land over the centuries. And Mao's soldiers were Chinese above everything else—more than they were Communists—and thought of Tonkin as a lost province of theirs, as in the minds of Chiang Kai-shek's troops the territory belonged to them, Chiang Kai-shek having been practically assured by the Americans that Tonkin would pass under their influence.

Sio Wen, the chief of the secret service section of the army of occupation of the Kuomintang,[37] now served as political representative attached to Mao's troops.

All of this made the Viets anxious, and their leaders proposed an accord with France: the cessation of hostilities and independence, but independence within the fold of the French Union and allowing for the maintenance of a certain number of units of the French Expeditionary Corps along the frontier of China.

37. The main political party of the Republic of China, founded by Sun Yat Sen in 1911, and after 1925 led by Chiang Kai-shek. (Translator's note.)

Lallemand told me he'd sent the proposal on to Pignon. But the business dragged out. To accept the proposal would have meant dropping Bao-Dai, to whom our high commissioner was so greatly attached. Then, it was generally felt that the propositions were too vague, and we let the opportunity for peace escape us.

Ho Chi Minh, like Giap, was an occidental Communist. Shaped by the French Communist party, he'd participated in the Congress at Tours. He always experienced an instinctive defiance vis-à-vis Mao and his methods, and he felt that Mao's actions betrayed him as the son of Heaven, the heir of the great Emperors, for whom Vietnam was a colony peopled with outcasts from great China.

Ho Chi Minh returned to the charge and made us other peace offers. In November of 1953, for example, through the instrumentality of a Swedish journalist, Löfgren of *L'Expressen*. But his conditions were imprecise. Through other sources it was known that Giap, who didn't want peace, who'd never let himself hope for it, had prepared extensive military operations for 1953–54. He had, in fact, already communicated his plans to the Military Committee, plans that culminated in Dien Bien Phu.

Ho Chi Minh's maneuvers were by this time psychological. That hadn't been true in 1949.

In any case, it would have been impossible to respond to that offer of peace made to Lallemand, even if our high command had wanted to. There was no French government behind them. For a month Versailles had been occupied with the election of a president who represented nothing and had no power.

Then everyone had gone on vacation.

In France the New Year intermission in the Chambers is sacred, like the month of August. The world could blow up in the meantime, but they would leave on vacation.

We return now to Dien Bien Phu, though I'll not

dwell long on the subject. So many books have already appeared, attacking or defending the principle of that base so far from our lines, at the extreme limit of the range of our aviation. But our politicians said we had to defend Laos at all costs, that single state of the ancient Indo-Chinese Federation that had remained loyal to us.

It was believed that if Laos collapsed, the same thing would happen to Cambodia. Then Thailand would follow, and in a relatively short time the Communists would be masters of Southeast Asia.

General Navarre, another one, had been sent to Tonkin to make peace, not war, but peace on the condition, of course, that he also reestablish our affairs there and that he negotiate from a position of force. He wore the hat of ambassador, Ambassador Dejean being one of those cultured, ineffectual diplomats who could drown in a glass of water.

> In the French camp it was the combination of the disadvantageous location of the battle site and of the absence of intervention by American combat aviation that brought about the fall of Dien Bien Phu, while in the opposite camp it was their acceptance of the huge numbers of sacrifices that would be necessary and the increased Chinese aid that brought them success.[38]

Be that as it may, we didn't have to go to Dien Bien Phu.

But good sense is that quality least provided for in what is called the art of war, which is more often than not only an *a posteriori* explanation of vast and totally disorganized quarrels.

38. For those interested in the causes of defeat at Dien Bien Phu and in the unfolding of the battle, I recommend the book *Pourquoi Dien Bien Phu?*, by Pierre Recolle (Flamarion), from which the above quote is taken.

In my opinion the best accounts of the subject are *Nous etions à Dien Bien Phu,* by Jean Pouget; *J' étais médecin à Dien Bien Phu,* by Grauwin; and *Dien Bien Phu,* by Colonel Langlades.

We were finally able to come to an understanding of each other at Geneva after the fall of Dien Bien Phu, which earned the worthy Pleven a couple of slaps across the face beneath the Arc de Triomphe,[39] and the loss of fifteen thousand soldiers from the best battalions of the Expeditionary Corps.

I hung around Hanoi and Vietri for a long time waiting for the release of the prisoners. Time dragged. How it dragged! One fine day the Vietminh authorities, to demonstrate their spirit of cooperation, let it be known they were inviting two journalists to accompany them on a tour so that these reporters could give on-the-spot accounts of the life of one of the major units of the People's Army. All the reporters in Tonkin wanted to go. The Americans were the most anxious, especially those among them who, when the Americans took over from us, were revealed to be top secret agents. Not having been hired by the K.G.B. to do so, I'm not going to give their names. That would make it awkward for them, particularly for those who became keen "liberals" on the American political scene. A kind of lottery had to be set up to pick the two journalists who would go. I won, along with a friend from the A.F.P. But since there is no such thing as chance in the communist world, I'd very probably have been chosen in any case.

At Vietri they put us on a sampan—at the bottom of the hold, so we'd not be able to recognize the route we took. That way we did not have to be blindfolded. I spent what seemed an interminable length of time there among the smells of old oil and rotten fish. It was enough to make one vomit. As soon as we debarked, we came upon the camp of a division at full strength, the 304th, which had become famous at Dien Bien Phu. We had tea under a lance pennon, tea that tasted like dishwater, and cigarettes that tasted like hay. We stared at

39. In an interview with an officer on the incident at the Arc de Triomphe, I asked him why Pleven had been the one to be humiliated, and he answered me, "Because he was there, because he was big, and because he had a head that attracted blows."

one another. No one knew what to say. We and they had come from different planets altogether. We were invited to dinner, our host being Commander Hoang Yen, who was in charge of all the publications of the People's Army and was considered to be one of the foremost writers of North Vietnam.

We were installed in a large straw hut lit by small oil lamps, simple wicks stuck into pieces of broken bottles. Close by flowed the river Claire. In the distance was what remained of a ruined church, its bell tower truncated.

We had an excellent European dinner of game and fresh-water fish, all of it served on dishes of the National Navy. The Viets had salvaged chinaware and table silver from a small building they'd wiped out.

The wine was excellent, the atmosphere relaxed, and the war far away.

Hoang had a fine head like that of a Vietnamese curé, attentive, prepossessing, his eyes shining with Marxist charity and love behind steel-rimmed glasses. All that was missing was the habit. But in place of the cross, there hung upon his chest, covered in greenish material, a curious insignia—that of the "New Culture," a lathe surmounted by a red star that lighted the world. This New Culture movement which had been started in the midst of war had as its objective to rid the Vietnamese of their old culture—that which had come from the Occident, "decadent, rotten, that which called up all the lowest instincts in people."

Across from me was Lieutenant Pham Tinga, a veritable encyclopedia, an electronic memory. Two plaits hung down on each side of his homely face; nature hadn't corrupted the machine with beauty. He was Hoang's walking dictionary. Officially he was his interpreter.

We spoke to one another about literature, in order to avoid ticklish subjects. Both of them, the lieutenant and the commander, had read everything, even the

classics—the better to condemn our best authors. Even
Malraux, for whom the good Hoang seemed to have a
secret and unpardonable attraction—despite the
"adventurism" of Malraux.

Then everything was spoiled by the damned wine we
drank. Our hosts had long ago grown unused to drinking wine, and it went to their heads. Soon their good
manners disappeared, their friendly attentions to us,
their toasts: "to peace between our peoples and a better
mutual understanding."

War came to join us at our table with her atrocious
parade of villages destroyed by our napalm and artillery, her cortege of the dead, the mutilated, the tortured, as they were recounted to us. War breathed her
hate all around us—or, rather, she tore masks away.

Where did Racine and Victor Hugo, Zola and Balzac
go? Instead, I had thrown in my face all the atrocities
of the Expeditionary Corps. I very much wanted to remind them of their *own* atrocities, that this war was
growing out of the mud, the shit, and the blood spewed
out by *both* sides. But I prudently kept my mouth shut,
because I also wanted very much to return to Hanoi.

Lieutenant Pham Tinga told me how his father had
been killed under torture at the hands of police agents,
"those Vietnamese mercenaries of colonialism." An officer, who until then had pretended to ignore us
Frenchmen, told us how all his family had been
crushed by bombs dropped by the B-26s.

Then, fully satisfied by what she'd accomplished, war
got up from our table and walked out on the mess
she'd made. Surface calm returned. We took up the
amenities again. But the Vietnamese avoided wine and
stuck to water and tea.

We smoked together, and then we were invited to
view a performance of songs and dances by a company
of the division. We were on an immense meadow
whose limits it was impossible to see in the night; a
huge crowd of people was all around us, mostly soldiers, but also civilians—men, women, and chil-

dren—seated on the ground, attentive, well behaved, collected.

The wind tossed the blue curtain of the stage. The platform was high, well lighted, able to be seen from a great distance.

There were dances, and there were songs, and then more dances. There was the dance of the coolies setting up the cannons on the hills around Dien Bien Phu, and, with backs bent, of their discharging the guns with the firing cords. Soldiers mimed a dance of agrarian reform, and four young Vietnamese girls, dressed in the Thai costume of white bodices and long skirts, performed for us the dance of the butterflies coming by the thousands to welcome the valorous soldiers of the People's Army.

All of it was touching enough in a way, despite the clang and clank of the tambourines and the whang of the violins and tinny pianos.

And the thousands of soldiers, so calm, so disciplined!

It is of him, of the Viet, of the complete soldier, that I'm going to speak to you now, and of the influence he's had on our soldiers, on us centurions of battles won and wars lost, and on all the other armies of the revolutionary Third World.

Then I'm going to speak to you of another soldier, his opposite, but one as good as he, one who even outclasses him—the Israeli. We could never turn out another army like that of the Vietminh, but if we should one day want to build an effective army, we'd do well to copy the Israeli model. If, of course, we could give our soldiers analogous motivations.

After the French left North Vietnam, I remained with the Viets. The next year I went back to them again, for no other reason than to study, to comprehend, and to get as close as I could to that extraordinary soldier, that Martian.

Let me introduce you to war's best servant, the Vietnamese infantryman, the *bô doi*.

A *bô doi* is fabricated out of a certain number of ingredients:

• A fervent nationalism that could double for the fervor of imperialism: the belief that the Vietnamese nation will come to play a great role not only in Vietnam, but in Indochina, which will one day also be Vietnamese (Laos-Cambodia), and in all of Southeast Asia, which will come under its influence (Thailand, Malaysia). They act out of a certainty of their superiority, which they carefully endeavor to conceal beneath a pretense of graciousness and every kind of reassuring declaration.

• Hatred of the occupiers of their land, of the whites and all who serve them, a hatred methodically fostered and kept alive by recalling and making use of all the mistakes of the ancient French colonizers, later the Americans. And even when their mistakes are slight, they are always baptized "crimes."

• An underlying racism everywhere. The white man's greatest sacrilege is to have sexual contacts with Vietnamese women, unless the individual is serving Vietnamese interests. From the day the Viets entered Hanoi, I never again saw a single one of my "little allies." They risked concentration camp if they were found with a *Tay* (a pejorative word for a white). For the sake of Viet propaganda, every atrocity in the form of punishment not only could but *had to* be used to fit the crime of the hated violation of the Vietnamese by the white interloper.

• That which I call "Boy Scoutism." The majority of those people responsible then for Vietnam's youth had been formed in the schools of the cadres of Admiral Decoux, trained there according to the principles of the national revolution, a training perfectly suited to their temperament. They always remained profoundly marked by it.

Hence that side of them praising "Work-Family-Country," that affectation of devotion to duty, of graciousness, of camaraderie. It it were possible they'd have made more blind people, just in order to be able to help them across the streets. And there is that manner of reprimand they have for those who do not behave quite as well as they should, calling them "little brother" or "little sister," chiding them gently, sweetly, helping them to understand just how serious their mistakes are, even should those mistakes be mere peccadillos. Helping them to see that repeated peccadillos can be harmful to the war effort, therefore to the people, therefore that they are really grave sins. And sinners are sent to shovel coal in the mines of Hon Gay.

Ta Quang Buu, Co-Minister of Defense, was Commissioner General of Scouting under Decoux.

• The fight against Evil, which is everywhere, many-sided, forever springing up again out of its own ashes. Evil is negligence, laziness, gossip, gluttony, a taste for play or for girls. The *bô doi* must reform himself and must help others to do the same, must denounce himself (self-criticism) and denounce others (revolutionary vigilance).

• Total submission to his chiefs, which, though, doesn't exclude criticism of them for their good, but on the condition that those chiefs first give the signal that criticism is now welcome. Because nothing is ever improvised, not even repentance.

The quality of the *bô doi* and his value in combat depend on the masterly blending of these ingredients.

The one most responsible for this explosive cocktail and the one who set it off was Nguyen Van Giap. He himself was shaped by hatred, and he had some reasons for it. His wife had died in a French prison.

Was he a Communist? Maybe. A Marxist? Marxism was for Giap a better tactic than any other, and it gave one absolution for one's actions—since good conscience in the world danced then to the tune of Moscow's violins. Now Moscow isn't Marx, but Ivan the Terrible, Peter the Great, and Stalin, the pitiless conquerors. Nationalistic, Nietzchean, mad with power, Giap created fear, even in Ho Chi Minh.

He read everything of the great military authors.

Clausewitz and Napoleon were his masters.

He quoted Clausewitz all over the field of battle: "The objective of war is the annihilation of the adversary. There are no limits to the violence that may be used to that end. . . . War is only an extension of politics, with the use of different means to achieve the desired goal."

He applied Napoleon's theories to his own situations: What does it matter if one is the weakest in an armed conflict, even throughout the whole length of a battle, if one can manage to be the strongest at the time and place of decision?

To that end he organized everything. He broke new ground, made innovations. He worked out his plays on two boards, the political and the military.

For his military plan he wanted an army that could destroy a post as well by corrupting it as by blowing it up with bazooka fire; a corps of soldiers who could become at once active propaganda groups, implanted guerrillas, and then, when necessary, could regroup themselves to confront a large military unit and defeat it in classical combat.

The foundation or base of the army is the nest, a Chinese inspiration; it is a cell of three men, one of whom is obliged to belong to the party.

The *bô doi* live closely with one another, helping one another, enthusiastic together, but also keeping watch over one another. The regulations state that "if a man goes anywhere at all, the other members of the nest must know where within the next half hour."

Solitude? It's bad for him. Isolated, a combatant might dream of peace and lose his keenness, his punch.

A set number of nests—three—make up an assault group; four nests equipped with two automatic weapons comprise a firing group.

Two firing groups, two assault groups, and a command group with one or two intelligence nests make up a section of twenty-five men.

The company is made up of three combat sections and one command section of intelligence and political action.

The regiment enjoys a huge autonomy, being a kind of small division:

• Three battalions of three combat companies.

• One heavy company of six recoilless cannons.

• One signal company.

• One company responsible for the protection of those in command.

And, most important of all:

• A company of recruits.

• The famous Trinh Sat, the company responsible for intelligence and political action.

The pursuit of very detailed information on the disposition of French troops and on their habits was consigned to special units designated by the term Trinh Sat and which constituted the most original formation of the Vietminh battle corps. They were made up of a set number of cells of three specialists in intelligence, each of whom acted at one time as a simple scout and at another time as a spy, to observe the enemy's defensive systems, to disclose his movements, to listen to rumors, to seize his documents, and finally to provoke desertion among the colored soldiers, or again to capture a prisoner. . . .

No single offensive action, not so much as an ambush, was set in motion without the prior gathering together of precise documentation. . . . This was, in fact, assembled and set forth in the greatest detail, and any initiative taken by the commissioned and noncommissioned officers was minimal, probably because the iron discipline imposed upon them was incompatible with freedom of action, and also because all their instruction had a rigid and even schematic character. . . . Whenever an unforeseen incident introduced itself during the course of combat, the cadres were at a loss, and nearly never did they know how, nor did they dare try, to improvise a variant of the fixed maneuver.[40]

40. Pierre Recolle, *Pourquoi Dien Bein Phu?*

In the Israeli army, on the other hand, improvisation was the rule, each element being allowed to play an important role, if not always a decisive one, without referring to a superior echelon. The Israeli victory on the Golan Heights was due exclusively to the qualities of the individual soldier, to his free will, his liberty, his imagination.

But to return to our *bô doi*.

His political indoctrination is total in every echelon. He's the fly caught in the spider's web; his threads are held by the commissioner.

The role of these political commissioners extends infinitely further than that of their Soviet homologues. Not only do they control the doctrinal purity of everyone, of everyone's loyalty, and teach the Communist catechism, but they keep watch over relationships among the civilian population and the morality of the *bô doi*. Read morality in its narrowest sense, its most puritanical sense: the prohibition of sexual relations, or even simple romantic involvements. There are many women in the People's Army, especially in the Trinh Sat. And love is the enemy of war. That's well known. Hence the slogan "Make love, not war." The Viets reverse the slogan. The political commissioner is the grand inquisitor endowed with formidable powers. During long autocritical sessions, one must publicly confess his sins, sins against the Communist doctrine, against the flesh, against the spirit.

The stake is always near, always lit. On his knees, hands tied behind his back, the sinner receives a bullet in the nape of his neck, after having recounted all his sins with humility and demanded not his pardon but his just punishment.

The *bô doi* whom I discovered at Dien Bien Phu and whom I later saw again was admirable, terrifying, war's best machine.

But his soul had been stolen from him, and that's what crippled him.

The selection of men and the formation of cadres

were very different from that of other armies.

The men recognized as being most capable of becoming leaders first had to prove themselves in the ranks—had to serve their novitiate, if you prefer. They were put to the test very much as they would have been in a religious order. They were accepted into the group, and then they were sent out into camp monasteries, where they followed courses of instruction, did their probationary training. These courses were short and frequent. The men were taught war, how to use a weapon, how to maneuver a section of men, how to capture a post. But above all, they were required to submit to a daily self-examination which followed every study session, every exercise. They were put on and kept on their mettle by the awarding of "good and bad marks": by praise or by public blame.

They were taught to detect and uncover in others, but also in themselves, every trace of sin, of weakness, of doubt, and immediately to confess to the Reverend Comrade Commissioner, in order to be reprimanded, chastised. *1984* became obsolete.

And the war became sacerdotal.

During the whole of the French war, when Giap's army was at its best, the soldier, the officer, and the commissioner worked with an inhuman tenacity, worked like moles digging out underground villages beneath the real villages, planting rice by day, making war at night, organizing committees and subcommittees, organizations of young women, of old women, of widows, of dyspeptic old men, and of boys six and seven years old.

They rarely slept, were underfed; they seemed at the end of their strength, but somewhere they always found the strength to continue.

All of us were struck by their physical appearance: ascetic face, large eyes, a loose, floating, and noiseless walk.

During the course of my visit to the 304th Division, one of the men described for me the day-to-day life of an officer, the same as that of a *bô doi.*

"We always changed our locations at night, moving
in long, silent lines. We were trained to make no sound
whatever, to secure our canteens and weapons by wrap-
ping them in rags. In order not to get lost and not to be
seen, we each fastened tiny transparent paper cages on
our backs, in each of which was a firefly. We followed
their tiny glow. I've known soldiers who kept the same
firefly alive three nights in a row. They were so happy
when they succeeded. To escape encirclement, it has
sometimes happened that we've had to march for twenty-five nights, with our only nourishment being rolls of
rice packed like sausages, which every combatant carried around his chest, plus a few herbs, a little dried
fish. At the end of such a march I had the feeling that I
was a phantom, half or fully asleep, that I merely
followed my mechanical twin, who marched and paused
alone."

The Vietminh reminded me of those student bookworms who, by dint of hard work, by their tena-
ciousness, win all the prizes and honors, even though
they're less talented than the other pupils.

Confronting them were the children of the rich (beggars when compared to the Americans who took up the
war from them)—our soldiers—who also departed on
combat operations by night, but in trucks, and who
launched their attacks, and who sometimes succeeded
in drawing up beautiful balance sheets (that sinister
phrase which has come to replace the word "victory" in
the jargon of war). And who then returned to their
base without having really sought to exploit that
success—which must be done—with an explanation to
the populace of why they were there and how it was
they'd won without having real superior strength: had
won because they were *right*.

Pute borgne! [41] War in that arena became harder to

41. Not readily translatable and not used in polite company, the
phrase literally can mean either a blind whore, a one-eyed one, or a
disreputable one. An approximate expletive might well be son of a
bitch. (Translator's note.)

satisfy. She tolerated no weakness, no respite. It became more than a question of taking a hill or lifting an assault on a village. She penetrated deep within you and installed herself there, freezing your heart and clouding your mind.

But, diligent and earnest, the green ants, the bookworms of the Vietminh, meticulously went on with their war. They knew why they were fighting. *Doc lap:* independence.

We, on the other hand, fought for Bao-Dai and the corps of civil service administrators, for the metropolitan mandarins who wanted to retain their comforts and their privileges.

The *bô doi* weren't really better soldiers than those twenty thousand of ours who actually fought the war. Because there were never more than twenty thousand parachutists, Legionnaires, and a few battalions of infantry elite or a few marine commandos who fought, and who were used for everything. All for the one hundred thousand others who were in Tonkin, who guarded the bridges, napped in their offices, remained secure within their posts.

But every one of the Viets did everything, did it willingly, equally, enthusiastically, or, when not enthusiastically, at least with thorough resignation to having to do it; regulars, regionals, women who carried munitions in their baskets under a bed of rice, children, all became liaison agents. They sometimes made mistakes, but they corrected them, criticized themselves tirelessly, and tirelessly they'd start all over again.

The *bô doi* became notetakers in the extreme. All of them we met threw themselves on us with pencil and notebook in hand to interrogate us under the overall direction of the interpreter. "Name? What do you do, and what do you think of peace? Of the armistice? Of the Vietnamese people? Of section 5 and of the declaration of Ho Chi Minh on the status of foreigners living in the territory of the People's Republic?"

Simple soldiers!

But when we questioned them in turn, they answered with a formula pulled out of their catechism. Whenever we wanted to delve a little deeper, to get a personal opinion from them on even the most innocuous subjects, the phonograph broke down, and they began to repeat over and over, this time in a voice gone shrill, the same idiot slogans, slogans that had nothing to do with what had been asked of them.

And the interpreter or the soldier took on the prim nose-in-the-air look of a spinster passing a urinal from which exits a man still doing up his fly.

"You are insulting the People's Army." Or "the people," depending on the circumstances.

All the Vietminh, from the simple *bô doi* to the commander of a regiment or of a division, were fixed into the narrowest formalism. The least departure from ritual immediately became a sacrilege, an insult to the people.

I have seen how among a group of prisoners a wrong phrase could cause huge problems for the prisoner under question. One should never say the Vietminh, but the People's Government of the Republic of Vietnam. Especially forbidden was to add North Vietnam. That was taken to have a malign intention. I understood immediately. The Geneva Accords were barely signed before the Viets thought of little more than recovering the South.

They were sticklers for all the bureaucratic priorities and precedences, while at the same time it was impossible to get them to say who their bureaucrats were, what their ranks were, or their functions. A genuine puzzle. They were nothing, no one, but by the grace of the people they were everything. The people, that distant and indeterminate divinity they'd baptized by that name.

In my first encounters with them I believed they mistrusted us, that they were overtaken with acute spy mania. It was more serious than that. They really had nothing to say to us but their slogans. Everything else was deeply buried, covered over inside themselves.

Their life was limited to the party and to the army, all mixed up in the same organization. For seven years some of them had been conducting a clandestine war and carrying on the work of intense propaganda. They'd lived in ruined mountain villages among the Thos or among other small clans to whom they were foreigners. Or they'd lived in the Delta, forced to bury themselves in the middle of a populace that wasn't always happy to acquiesce, that rebelled against their demands, and that needed to be persuaded by propaganda and sometimes by terrorism.

There they were reduced to living among themselves in a politico-military community, intransigent, rigorous, strongly hierarchical. At fixed hours they were subject to the call to "prayer" to Marx, to Lenin, and to Ho, who was the Holy Spirit of the Trinity.

They needed all their strength to survive, to resist the effects of the night marches, the murderous combats. And afterwards they had to devote themselves to the indoctrination of the masses.

No one in the entire cadre, neither the *bô doi* nor the officer, any longer had the strength or the desire to question the system in which they were obliged to live. They accepted it all, swallowed everything whole, all the categorical imperatives and the ready-made definitions.

"Make the motions and you'll believe," Pascal said. And you'll believe all the better if you fast and mortify the flesh, said the founders of the great monastic orders. The Viets made all the motions so well, repeated them so many, many times, that they secreted their faith; and then they went beyond it, became inhabitants of another planet, strangers to the world of humans, to their weaknesses but also to their greatness.

"Man is a changeable and diverse animal," said Montaigne.

"No," answered Giap, mad with pride and inhumanity, "he is an instrument of the party and must be like a cadaver in the hands of his superiors."

"Perinde ac Cadaver," said the Jesuits, those "enemies of man" who raised me and whose stamp I found on the Viets.

The *bô doi* all came to resemble one another, floating along in their too-large uniforms cut Chinese style. All with the faces of old and tired children. There was no spontaneity left in them, but their reward was that they also had no problems to deal with. Because to every problem they responded with the correct dialectic solution.

They'd become serious, slightly condescending, like all those who are in possession of the absolute truth. They carried a nun's smile, which signified nothing, on their faces.

I was fascinated. One doesn't meet Martians every day.

There was a Soviet journalist, the correspondent for *Isvestia,* whom I met at Hanoi and who said to me, "How can you put up with them? How can you waste your time trying to understand them? They've become crazy. Pride and chastity have gone to their heads. They're even more bloody annoying to us who are on their side than to you who are on the other side. You have the weakness of a colonialist for a mistress you've kept for a long time, who has cuckolded you, and whom you'll always love."

Of that generation of monk soldiers of Dien Bien Phu, few were going to survive. The American war was going to exterminate them. Saigon would be captured by baby faces sixteen or seventeen years old who wouldn't be part of the Order, who would only have been recruited by the Order's survivors.

I recognized them immediately, my Viets, first by their age, and then by their deeply marked faces, their vaguely smiling masks.

No longer was there a large number of men in the Order. Nothing remained but an elite, an aristocracy. But they continued to lead their people and to dream of an immense empire they'd build to stand up to China, whom they feared less than before, thanks to aid from the Soviets, who needed them for their own grand designs.

I remember a story I'd like to tell you, one of my first exercises in reeducation. The French had evacuated Hanoi, and my fellow reporters had done me a dirty turn by naming me as the one responsible for the press camp.

The French army had left us an old jeep which must have seen campaigns in Africa and in France before coming to Tonkin. Still, it had four wheels, a motor, and it rolled. I'd inherited it.

Hanoi was deserted, without a single vehicle. The Vietminh troops were concentrated on the outskirts of the city. During the last days of evacuation the city had been one great hustle and bustle, with traffic blocks, blasts of horns, the whistles of the traffic police. Now I was alone with my jeep, as I'd been in Paris in 1944, and I wanted to reexperience the same adventure. Always that same need for exorcism.

I rode through all the streets where so many times I'd gotten soused, had sworn, had raged, this time going the wrong way on one-way streets.

A police whistle! A Viet. I stopped. It was a woman soldier. She wouldn't have been bad looking if it weren't for those two braids hanging sadly down each side of her helmet, that too-large military uniform, and that offended air of an assistant schoolmistress who'd just nabbed a dirty brat in the act of stealing some jam.

In heavily accented French she said to me, "You've been going the wrong way on a one-way street. That's against the regulations."

I answered, "What does it matter? This morning mine is the only vehicle in Hanoi."

Continuing in that precise voice, moralizing, sermonizing: "It matters very much. You have insulted the Vietnamese people by refusing to respect the laws decreed by the People's Democratic Republic."

"I didn't want to insult anyone, but simply to go from one place to another by the most direct route."

"By going the wrong way."

The woman climbed into the jeep beside me and made me retrace the entire route back to my point of departure, this time going the right way.

"I hope," she concluded, "that this has been a profitable lesson for you for the future."

And she signaled me to take off.

I'd forgotten that I was no longer the victor but the vanquished, that I'd just landed in a world where every whim was forbidden, where every unusual action could be taken as an insult, a provocation.

In the minds of the Vietminh we French had to become more dispassionate about our defeat in order to see ourselves as more than the vanquished—as the guilty.

In the prison camps, the Viets applied themselves diligently, persistently, to making all those who'd fought against them aware of their culpability. In their colonialistic, imperialistic war, the French had sinned against God and the Vietnamese people. They had to repent. But first they had to be brought to a full consciousness of their fault.

They especially applied themselves to the officers, who in their eyes were the representatives of a caste, defenders of a particular society by their birth into a particular class. The Viets could not be mistaken about this subject: their usual oversimplification kept them on what they saw as the path of truth. The French officers were thus stained with original sin, and they could only be cleansed of it, absolved, by a new baptism: adherence to the theses of the party.

The methods they employed were appalling: hunger and humiliation as a means of persuasion, of obtaining the necessary repentance. At the same time, their quest for approbation from their enemy was pathetic. And disquieting! As if they weren't very sure of their faith.

The Vietminh commissioners failed to indoctrinate those soldiers of ours who had no ideological problems, those beasts of war. But they seriously marked the real Christians among the prisoners, those whose religion constantly calls into question the world's standards. They marked, too, the ancients of the Resistance who'd long wondered what they were doing fighting in that bear pit. They disturbed the balance of the most civilized, the most fragile, those whom I called "crystal warriors," and who let themselves fall into the dialectical trap.

Some of the officers who'd been taken prisoner at Cao Bang had been in the Viet prison camps four years. Those who survived pulled themselves through by recognizing and dubbing "the political fiction of camp #1."

In wanting to do too much, the Viets often arrived at an opposite result. They inoculated men against a temptation to communism. The communism of the Vietminh, not that of the Russians, for whom communism had ceased to be a religion and had become a system. Death!

But I was in no danger! I was no longer a Christian, and I never could believe in original sin.

But you'll find all that in *Les Centurions*.

I loved the Vietnamese. I was sensitive to both their good qualities and their shortcomings. I was always tempted to be their accomplice, to help them in their crazy undertakings. And they were talented. They did have good points. They were a treasure to me. But though I loved them, it was never to the point of renouncing my own country, even when it was wrong. And it was wrong in Vietnam.

People will say to you that the Vietnamese are double-dealers, hypocrites, thieves, racists, and arrogant. They're all of that for those who don't understand them, who don't feel for them.

They're very sensitive to the image you gain of them,

and they try to conform to the worst image as well as
to the best. They're very plastic. They're not as self-as-
sured as the Chinese, who are so sure of themselves
that they don't feel the least need to justify themselves
to anyone. The Chinese are so conscious of their
superiority, of their antiquity, of their valor: feelings
fostered and maintained during four thousand years of
civilization from the Chang emperors to Mao Tse-tung.

One can be friends with a Chinese on an equal foot-
ing. Friendships are exchanged and understandings
reached based on equal strength. With a Vietnamese
it's more complicated, as it is to be friends with a
woman or a skittish adolescent. If you have a Vietnamese boy in your household employ, you know he's going
to steal from you. It's a rule. But he must do it right
under your nose and without your noticing to increase
the pleasure of it. If you should catch him in the act, it
only proves that you're more wicked than he, that
you've merely won the first round, and that he's waiting for his turn. He can't understand that if you're
honorable you'd have anything to do with a louse, a
guttersnipe, a thief. He wants to fleece you—just a little—to amuse himself—a lot.

With your Chinese cook, you enter into a kind of
agreement. You say to him in effect "Let's understand
each other. How much do you intend to take me for?"

He gives you a figure, twenty percent on all the
household purchases. You bargain with each other, you
understand each other, and you settle on fifteen percent. He sticks to that and doesn't steal a sou more
than that if you on your part respect certain rules and
don't cause him to lose face.

If I hold any reservations about the Vietnamese, it
would be with regard to the Vietnamese women.
They're beautiful, especially in the South—slim and
willowy, and they have beautiful skin, always fresh.
But they're cerebral, not erotic; far less erotic than
the Cambodian women, the Laotian women, the
women of Thailand. The Vietnamese prostitutes are

the most frigid, the most common, the worst scolds of any I've known in the world, as if they need to exaggerate everything, even their worst qualities. While you're making love, they're thinking about catching flies. But when the head and the heart can manage to strike a happy balance, when the two can work as a pair, the Vietnamese woman can become an extraordinary companion. But she can't refrain long from bringing up insane schemes, lunatic transactions, money. Not out of greed, but for sport.

Between the Vietnamese and the French—I'm speaking only of that period I know about personally, from 1950—that genuine barrier caused by racism did not exist. It had existed formerly, but war had removed it. The one time when she's done something that wasn't bad!

The French who'd been called to spend a long time in Indochina generally had female companions with whom they lived and whom some of them married.

They felt themselves to have been abandoned, especially the common soldiers and those ruined children of war, the Legionnaires; so they found refuge and tenderness with the women of the country.

It sometimes ended badly.

It was after Dien Bien Phu. On the long promenade bordering the beach at Nhatrang, small shops were set up which sold soda and Chinese soup; all of them were lit by oil lamps. Across from them was the sea, and out on the sea was that continuous line of fire that sometimes disappeared behind a wave: fishermen working by lantern light.

An improbable truck running on its wheel rims and covered over with a roof of plaited bamboo drew up and huffed to a stop, out of wind. A Frenchman in his thirties got out, face emaciated and overgrown with beard, dressed like a peasant, shod in wooden shoes. Then came a Vietnamese woman, frail and graceful, and three children in whom flowed the mixture of the two bloods.

With a few boards and some pieces of canvas, they set up a stall like the others. The shelf was covered with bottles of soda and beer, while on a fire made of wood charcoal the woman prepared a bouillon from beef bones, the base of all Chinese soup, either *pho* or *my*.

They told us their story. He was a veteran of the Expeditionary Corps, which had been demobilized, and he'd come to know her when he had been stationed there. They'd saved money and had started a small farm on a hillside. They'd cleared the ground and plowed it themselves, and they'd done fairly well growing tea and coffee. Until the Vietminh came. The Communists didn't like that kind of union. It disturbed their simplistic conception of relations between whites and yellows. Difficulties for the pair began immediately. Heavy duties and land taxes were imposed on them. After the Viets came the partisans of Diem, the band of his brother Ngo Dinh Can, the madman of Hue, who used the same tactics but with even more brutality than the Viets.

The farm was burned. The Frenchman and the Vietnamese woman and their children fled in the old truck, which reminded me oddly of that in *The Grapes of Wrath*. But this family no longer fought back. They were too tired, too sickened, and could think of little more than survival.

The Vietminh reestablished the old racial barrier. To fit what design? Because they were convinced that hate made better fighters, that hate would win wars.

They were wrong. Giap should have read his history more carefully. The victorious people, those who achieved their grand design, took an immediate position above hatred and above racism.

I've always thought that the Nazis lost their war for the same reason Alexander won his—he wanted to know nothing of that thing called racism and obliged his associates to marry the women of the countries they conquered.

Between the Americans and the Vietnamese, racism

played a large role. Of course there were exceptions: among the outcasts that are journalists, or those other outcasts of the American army, the Green Berets.

I'd have been willing to marry a Vietnamese woman. The thought of having Eurasian children would by no means have prevented me—on the condition that the children be raised in France, certainly the least racist country in the world. In Asia the Eurasians, the half-castes, fall between two stools, between two races. Uncomfortable.

I admire the toughness, the courage, the sense of organization, the efficiency of the Vietminh. But I found sinister his refusal to let any softness into his life. Still, could he have done otherwise? Used other methods to fight on two fronts, against the French and the Americans and against the lassitude of the populace? Thirty years of war!

In the face of the war, amazing people sometimes rose up in the Far East, an area prodigal with its amazing people. In them mingled trickery, naïveté, lies, sincerity. Half kings and half clowns, they once in a while managed to hold back the course of the war. Perhaps because it amused them to do so.

Such a one was Sihanouk, and I have to speak of him in the past, because he no longer counts for anything.

While war raged in Vietnam and became a clever game to the initiates in Laos, Cambodia remained a peaceful sanctuary. One had only to go a hundred or so kilometers, a few minutes by plane, to leave Vietnam, a devastated country, its rice fields plowed by bombs, its forests defoliated and ruined, its cities overrun with sacks of sand and with barbed wire, to reach the land of beautiful temples luxuriating in the midst of lush green and the bright orange splashes of the monks of the "Little Vehicle,"[42] of the *samlos* pedaling their bi-

42. The Hinayana. (Translator's note.)

zarre tricycles, of peaceful cafés and the Hotel Royale,
and of Angkor, where the tourists flocked.

Over this kingdom reigned a small restless person,
round as a partridge, with a falsetto voice and a mass
of ideas, notions, opinions that collided and crashed at
each moment like billiard balls; more talkative than
Fidel Castro, but less of a braggart, less crafty and
naïve: Monseignor Comrade Prince Norodom Sihanouk,
chief of state and head of the only political party, who
was himself dethroned to make room for his mother.

At one and the same time he was the kingdom's foremost film maker, foremost saxophonist, foremost journalist, foremost football player. He went in for everything. And he gossiped about everything, especially
about those things and people he didn't dare look too
closely at or that he had to pretend to be ignoring. Although in his way he was democratic, he found it quite
normal that his ministers walked four paces in front of
him, their foreheads bent to the dust—ministers whom
he beat when he was dissatisfied with them and whom
he called every kind of name.

He told anyone who would listen to him that nothing
could prevent Cambodia from one day falling into the
Communist camp because of the accumulated stupidities of the Americans in Asia. He was right. All he
wanted was that it be put off just as long as possible,
adding that it would after all not be so bad if the
Khmers became Communist. There he was wrong. The
Khmer Communists were to be the maddest, the most
atrocious, the bloodiest of all the Communists.

For that reason—to hold off the inevitable—he'd
chosen China as an ally over Moscow, for China alone
could protect his country against North Vietnam, ally
of the Soviets, whose territorial greed was appalling.

With Sihanouk at least one was never bored. On a trip
to Phnom Penh I asked to see him, at great risk, for I
had no way of knowing where he stood at the moment in
his tumultuous relations with the members of the press,
whom he sometimes cajoled, at other times detested.

The day I saw him was one of his good days. He received me in the garden of his palace.

"Ah, my dear master," he said to me.

(Fortunately he was one of the few to give me that bizarre title which equates a writer with a notary.)

He shook his head vigorously while his eyes rolled like ball bearings.

"It's annoying. I swore I would never, *never* give another interview to reporters."

He was visibly pained, a condition brought on by the nervousness he suffered each time he returned from Grasse, where he took a slimming course under the direction of Dr. Pathé. He'd gone into his little act with me, because it was only when he was performing that he could forget his distress and that restlessness which made him so voracious. At that time he believed that the CIA was going to do away with him as they had Diem in Vietnam. Diem, his old enemy, whom he'd begun to lament soon after having decreed "three days' festivities" to celebrate his death.

Suddenly his face lit up. "I'm going to give you a press conference."

He summoned his two customary attendants: the heavy Barrett, veteran of the Foreign Legion (in which he'd sought refuge on a number of occasions) and head of the newspaper *Réalités cambodgiennes,* which people called *"Irréalités";* and Meyer, who'd once been a secret agent in the Binh-Xuyens, the pirates of Cholon's arroyo,[43] and who went on from there to become Peking's eye in Cambodia. The one was heavy, the other thin; the one ceremonious, the

43. The Binh-Xuyens have been mentioned in an earlier note. Cholon was an old Chinese trading port, and during the Japanese occupation a man called Le Van Vien or Bay Vien organized this band of pirates, who collected taxes on all traffic to and from the city. In 1948 the French gave recognition to the gang in return for certain favors. (Translator's note.)

other grave; the one operated on guesswork, the other on knowledge.

We were at a large table, with Sihanouk between his two "chandeliers" and me opposite him. It was noon, and the heat was frightful. Sihanouk couldn't remain still. He banged his fist violently on the table.

"It's finished," he said to me.

I asked, "What's finished, Monseignor? Your patience with the Americans and their perpetual intrigues?"

He looked at me, astonished. "No. My son has just gotten another girl pregnant. He thinks I'm going to pay for it as I usually do, but I'm not going to pay. It's finished! He's big enough now to be careful. I have to take care of everything in this country! I have nothing but incompetents around me, or thieves. Everyone dips into the coffers. They engage in illegal traffic. Even the queen, *ma chère*, with her shady deals in pharmaceutical products. When I tell her that what she's doing is wrong, she calls me an idiot, tells me I'm not careful enough with money, that she has to think of my future and put money aside for me. I don't need money. If things go wrong for me one day, I'll become a monk. I'll shave my head and eat rice. Rice is very good with dried fish. Aren't you thirsty? We'll drink some champagne. Champagne would be good, wouldn't it?"

And while we were waiting for the bottle to come, he told me the gossip of the city. About the ambassador from France "who tells everyone he loves Cambodia . . . but it's the little girls of Cambodia he really loves. He has them taken to Mother Nam,[44] you know."

And so it continued. Everyone came under the fire of his tittle-tattle, and he was especially fond of stories like the above.

---

44. Mother Nam was an honorable madame who gave courses in . . . deportment to her very young pensioners and nursed them on bottles of Coca-Cola. Several notable guests in her house helped her from time to time in her task and were able to uncover for her particularly apt students.

The champagne was finally brought to us, lukewarm
and too sweet. A poor courtier, I made a face. It made
him angry.

"My champagne isn't good enough for you?"

"Pah!"

"Nevertheless, it's French. So! No more imports of
champagne. Do away with champagne in all of
Cambodia. So! My champagne isn't any good!"

That was the day, after he'd read an article that displeased him in the *Philadelphia Sun* or in one of the
local rags of the same kind—he read all the papers—
that on his own authority he devalued the dollar for
the American tourists who were wandering about in
the ruins of Angkor with their cameras.

They were to learn about it when they paid their
hotel bills.

There were moments when he navigated his ship of
state in complete delirium. He made me think of the
little king of Slogow. An insufferable, spoiled brat!

When he was in the mood to play the role of film
maker, he arranged a film festival. As chairman of the
panel of judges, he awarded himself all the prizes. He
made crazy films in which he played the parts of his
family, his ministers, his court, his army. He composed
French songs in the style of a young French dressmaker,
which he sang in his falsetto voice, accompanying himself between verses on the saxophone. And it wouldn't
do at all for anyone to laugh. In fact, I fell out with him
for having criticized his saxophone playing. We made up
later—I told him I wanted to—when he came to move
into a villa he'd purchased next to where I stayed in
Mougins. I told him I'd exaggerated, that his playing
wasn't as bad as I'd said, that I had no ear at all for good
music.

He often addressed his people on the radio for five or
six hours running and without notes, and he was capable of speaking both absolute poppycock and great good
sense. He had a genuine human contact with his Cambodians; he was the first ruler who appeared to be really

interested in them. He's been known to toss rolls of
fabric out to them from a flying helicopter. They
expected anything and everything from him, and his
fine little Khmers adored him for it.

Sihanouk had one obsession: to keep his country out
of war. That he succeeded for so long was an astonishing acrobatic feat. He was not Communist, nor pro-Chinese, nor anti-American, and he had a weakness for
France. He'd found the means to enrich his Khmers
and to make Phnom Penh, a small sleepy village on
the Mekong, into a real capital. He did it by setting all
the other countries in competition against one another,
letting the Americans build his roads, the Russians a
hospital, the Chinese a factory, the French another
hospital; and he had the largest stadium in Southeast
Asia built through a great public works enterprise for
which he forgot to pay.

He held out as long as he could. But one day war had
had enough. Sihanouk had ceased to amuse her. Her
black cloud spread all over the land, and the famous
gentle smile of the Khmers became a grimace. Corruption, which had been kept within decent limits, grew to
gigantic proportions under Lon Nol, and all limits to
atrocities were removed. Do you remember certain
news photos of that period: the hearts of their enemies
being eaten raw, heads lopped off and massed into
heaps?

Ethnologists who know everything will tell you that
the answer lies in anthropography. That it was all just
ritual. That one eats the heart of the valorous enemy
in order to gain his courage. It was a mark of esteem of
sorts.

It's true that the good little Khmers were gentle-
people, so much so that the war didn't make them completely mad.

They were a very old people who, when the French
arrived in Cochin China in the nineteenth century,
were themselves being devoured on one side by the
Vietnamese and on the other by Thailand.

I went back to a war-devastated Cambodia after the Americans and the South Vietnamese had invaded her in April of 1970. I was searching for seventeen journalists who'd disappeared without a trace, all within a few days and all from the same place.

They were French, American, Japanese, German, Austrian. No one had found a single one of them, not even their bodies. But I know they're dead. How? Why? I don't know. The only hypothesis I can come up with, and one to which I cling because it fits the situation, because it proceeds from a certain logic, and because it's worthy of war and her obscenities, is this:

You must remember that at that time, after the Americans and the South Vietnamese had entered Cambodia, Radio Hanoi had broadcast a series of communiqués asserting that the Americans were guilty of savage aggression in Cambodia—unjustified aggression, since the North Vietnamese had no troops in Cambodia.

That was a lie. The North Vietnamese occupied two provinces along the northern frontier through which passed the famous Ho Chi Minh trail, Mondolkiri and Rattanaki, which they'd already decided not to give up and in which they'd already established their administration—all of which sent Sihanouk into a rage.

Imagine, in this context, seventeen journalists with their cameras and movie apparatus coming upon divisions of Vietminh regulars moving around in Cambodian territory and then returning to their forest hideouts. Those journalists could be left-wing or they could be right-wing; there before them were thirty or forty thousand men, regulars with all their paraphernalia, who weren't, by their own words, supposed to be there, proof of a flagrant lie. Whatever the journalists' politics, they'd *have* to speak of what they'd seen. So the Viets went into a panic. They couldn't have it known that they'd lied—good revolutionaries can't do that. They have to be believed. If their word is in doubt, they're finished. They did away with the seventeen journalists. There, to my mind, is the only possible explanation. If anyone can propose another one to me, I'm more than ready to welcome it.

The war in Cambodia unrolled in total confusion. It was an insane and bloody orgy.

Everyone lied. First the Viets and then the Khmers, who were still their friends. The Cambodians began by wanting to do as everyone else did. They ended by outstripping everyone else in their lies, adding their own touches.

For example, I came across a Cambodian official of one degree or another of ordinariness and asked him, "May I go to Angkor?"

"Certainly you may go to Angkor!" he told me, not wanting to lose face by admitting that the regime he served, Lon Nol's Republic, had lost the sacred city and that the red flag waved over its ruins.

Precisely such a thing as that may have happened to the journalists to let them get so close to the Communists.

That official at the Office of Information, a little captain whose name has been buried in my unconsciousness, went even further when I indicated a certain cynicism about Angkor. He granted me a travel permit that would allow me to go by air to Siemreap, the airfield at Angkor. The plane awaited me as promised and took me to Siemreap.

The plane landed me and my photographic equipment and then took off immediately. I think it was the last plane to land there. And there we were—a friend and I—wandering around a dead, deserted city, barely missing the selling out of Seimreap. We were taken for the first of the returning tourists, but two swallows don't make a spring, nor two pseudo-tourists a peace.

We were able to reach the temples. Everything was tranquil. The only people who remained were two Frenchmen: Groslier, the conservator, and Boublé of *L'Ecole française* of the Far East. After showing us all around the ruins, Boublé asked us what nut had sent us there. Angkor was under North Vietnamese control. In other words, we were there with all our equipment in the very midst of the Viets. All the employees of the "Conservation of the Temples" were originally from Vietnam, and there could be Viets among them. We wouldn't know one from the other, the non-Communist from the Communist. The ruins were full of refugees who did their cooking in the middle of the galleries of Angkor Wat and of Angkor Tom and who hammered nails (to hang their clothes) into the beautiful and marvelous apsaras.[45] No North Vietnamese was going to forbid them, either. The history of Angkor wasn't theirs, and they had no monuments.

It was impossible to learn anything about the traffic in statues through Thailand engaged in by the Viets and the Khmers.

And as for the death of Puyssesseau, it was due to one of those *bavures* of war I've mentioned. The Khmers mistook the zoom of his television camera for a gun and his sound engineer for an imperialist spy guiding an aviation bombardment.

The Khmers fired several bursts, and Puyssesseau lay dead. Dead in the ruins of Angkor! A fine finish for a journalist who had nothing with which to defend himself and his memories of a prestigious past against the new barbarians but his ridiculous weapons: a pen and a camera.

We had to return to Phnom Penh. But there were no more planes to be had. Siemreap was encircled by Communists who threatened the airport. Siemreap's garrison dozed, and the colonel who commanded it and whose siesta we'd disturbed asking for a plane wanted to throw us in jail. It was hard to know what to do. When I looked around at the mess the Cambodian

---

45. Apsaras–in Hindu mythology, a supernatural female being, either the mistress of a soul in paradise or a succubus; also the representation of such a being. (Translator's note.)

army's Information Service had gotten us into, I sought
a way to get out of there by any means. In the marketplace we finally found a collective taxi loaded with
women, children, chickens, and ducks, which was preparing to leave for Battambang. We took off. Every
four or five kilometers the taxi stopped, the driver got
out, disappeared behind a hut to take a drink or to urinate, then returned to us, and we left again. Later I
learned that we'd crossed a zone controlled by the
North Vietnamese and the Khmers rouges. Each time
the driver had halted, he'd shown his travel permit to
a guard and had paid various duties. Hence the exorbi-
tant cost of our transport.

The trials of that poor country were not over. The
victory of the Khmers rouges was to find expression in
one of the greatest, most tragic, wastes of history. War
offered up a fine festival! One, two million Cambodians,
no one knows exactly, torn from their cities and towns
and thrust into the country without food, with nothing
at all. All the signs of civilized consumption were
destroyed: refrigerators, Mercedes (they'd abounded),
air conditioners. Hospitals were closed. The defenders
of back-to-the-land, the disciples of Jean-Jacques Rousseau, went crazy. The main themes of our ecological
left were applied to the letter: a million shot, dispersed,
their bodies all along the roads. And we were made to
understand that it was only the beginning. The huge
retrograde wind of history had begun to blow, and it
carried death with it. Something to meditate on.

Everyone sought refuge at the French embassy,
where the vice-consul did what he could, poor man!

We saw the small parade of seven members of the
Soviet embassy, who'd believed things would be different for them, led away in handcuffs, kicked in the behind as they went. They'd been hunted down like fleas.
The Khmers rouges had forced the embassy doors with
bazooka rounds. The Khmers were pro-Peking and
against the deviationist imperialists of the Kremlin.

Didn't the Russians know that?

In Laos problems were at first never very serious. Even the war took on more the air of light opera.

The Laotians have a taste for the tranquil life and for settling matters among themselves, *à la Laotian.* They'd found a way to have a pacifist king who liked to work in his garden and play the flute—nothing but classical music. That enraged Sihanouk, who jealously asked me, "Well? Does he, too, play badly?"

The king was the best of men, and one who moreover governed nothing. He was flanked by a number of princes who did everything: Souvanna Phouma, who favored neutrality and France; his half-brother Souphanouvong, who favored Hanoi and the "peace of the people," but an armed peace; Bou Noum, who'd always been shabbily treated by us, even during the resistance against Japan, who'd been allowed to fall, and who flirted with the Americans.

The Laotians believed they were secure on all their borders. Naïve!

Laos was the Southeast Asian country the least prepared in every way for war. In military art as in politics they applied at every echelon the famous *Bo Pe Nhamg,* which means that everything will always take care of itself if one just does nothing.

The last time I went through Vientiane in June of 1975, everything had *not* taken care of itself.

Laos had never been conquered, annexed, colonized. She'd *given* herself to France because the envoy extraordinary to Laos had such a wonderful face that the Laotians couldn't resist him and wanted nothing so much as to please him.

His name was Pavie. He was Norman, a telegraph installer by profession, a gentleman. In all his life he'd never carried a weapon, saying that since men were essentially good, guns served no purpose. His was a fantastic story, the finest one of our colonial folklore.

Pavie was putting together a telephone system near Phnom Penh, when one day he heard some natives speaking in a harmonious language unfamiliar to him.

Pavie had a musical ear and was able to learn all the dialects with a disconcerting facility. Now he asked himself who these people were he'd heard speaking. They were not Khmers, nor Chinese, nor Vietnamese of any kind. He then interrogated a Cambodian, who told him, "They come from the north, very high up, in the land of great rivers and great waterfalls."

Pavie was one of those people so pure in heart that they are full of self-confidence, and he immediately went to Hanoi's governor general to ask him for a leave of absence and for information on how he could go through to the "north." That personage was fascinated by the naïveté, the beautiful manner, the noble beard, the half-child, half-man air of the installer of telephone lines, and so he accepted absolutely that he really did want to try his luck, seek adventure.

And so Pavie left on his heart's search. The Laotians he'd met at Phnom Penh went with him as guides. He crossed rivers, went far up others, untiring. When he reached Laos, he could already speak the language.

One day he saw a Laotian foundering in some rapids and saved him. The man was a minor local king, and Pavie had made himself a friend. He continued on his way, doing good everywhere, giving good counsel. In addition, he found favor with all the women, for he was good to look at and had a proud manner that attracted them. He resembled the painter Courbet.

The Laotians, who no longer knew which way to turn and who had all sorts of trouble with their neighbors, with the Burmese pirates, with the Chinese pirates, with their racial brothers from Thailand, said to themselves, "If all the French are like Pavie, why don't we ask France to come and defend us and to take us in charge?"

At the end of a year and a half, the vigorous bearded giant reappeared in Hanoi, his sack on his back, his color ruddy and fresh, his calves round and sturdy from walking. He carried a proposal of alliance in which the various kings of Laos asked for the protection of France. He had to be stopped! He was still in passage, he said, still obsessed by his dream of going ever farther northward, on foot, to draw close to and to love everyone, to gather in for us . . . Yunnan? To stop him, they made him an ambassador to Thailand. Which only goes to prove yet once more that the best way to neutralize a man of character is to enter him in the diplomatic service.

He's told his own story—in blank verse. He retired to his homeland in Normandy, where he holds a kind of court frequented by Lyautey, Savorgnan de Brazza, the father of Foucould, all of whom became his disciples. Because of him we could have found ourselves head of an immense empire, and we failed. A catastrophe! Think of it: an addition of eighty million Yunnanese!

We felt comfortable in Laos, at home, among friends. Everything was an excuse for a fête, parties, girls *(phousaos)*. We'd engaged ourselves at Dien Bien Phu partly to keep the North Vietnamese out of Laos. The strategic plan was absurd; the sentimental plan I can comprehend. Then the Americans came, and Laos became a place of tilting contests among spies, all the secret double agents, triple or quadruple agents. And weaving in and out of it all the oppressive odor of opium.

In Laos I was invited to accompany one of Prince Souvanna's counselors, an unimposing little Frenchman who gave the impression of being nothing at all. In reality, he was one of our foremost agents (P'tit Ricq in *Les Tambours de bronze*)[46] in an important operation of psychological warfare. It was essential in the grand scheme of things to rebuild the confidence of the gallant Laotian people after the thrashing we'd taken at Dien Bien Phu.

Psychological warfare as it was waged in Laos was enough to reconcile one forever to that kind of activity.

46. *The Bronze Drums.* (Translator's note.)

Everywhere else there is outright and rank swindling
of the public, and loud propaganda spiels over loudspeakers, when that propaganda isn't delivered with
boots in the rear. Here propaganda material was a
Baby Pathé 8-mm movie projector which operated by
means of an automobile battery and projected small
films of the Cathedral of Chartres, of Notre-Dame of
Paris, of the wheat fields of Beauce. Lunatic and surre-
alistic! The propaganda personnel were some eminent
members of the royal Laotian army armed with guitars
and mandolins. Proudly we left on our mission, though
a little late—nine o'clock instead of five o'clock—in a
truck with an asthmatic motor. At noon we made our
first stop, which was prolonged by a siesta, then by a
little *boun*.[47] Our valiant warriors went in search of
chickens; the neighboring villagers came; there was
dancing; there was eating; there was music; and the
aforementioned films were shown, with tent canvas for
a screen. Everyone was happy and began snoring on
the spot.

The next day—I always wake up early, as you know
—I roused the others and asked, "When do we leave?"

"Let us sleep in peace," the propagandists said to me.
"There's no fire."

We took off about ten-thirty, and at noon we stopped
again in a little village. A meal, a prolonged siesta, a
little *boun*. We ate; we danced with the *phousaos;* we
drank rather a lot; we slept; we left. Soon the truck refused to roll, and the Baby Pathé broke down. There
were only the guitars and the mandolins left to go the
distance. In the end we abandoned the truck and the
projector, and we piled our things into a buffalo cart,
and softly, peacefully, bumpily, we made our way up
the trail toward Luang Prabang. Every evening was a
fête. We went on from *boun* to *boun* during I don't
know how many days. Time had ceased to exist: the
one sure sign of happiness.

47. Presumably a party of sorts. (Translator's note.)

Once we halted near a monastery. I was obliged to forcibly defend my virtue against the little Buddhist monks who grabbed for my fly and showed me their behinds. These monasteries were veritable temples of sodomy! What a sacrilege! And meanwhile, the girls of the country were beautiful, merry, welcoming, and the least inhibited of any in the world.

Try swimming naked in a river and you would be sure to have a dozen *phousaos* lining the river and eyeing you carefully to see if they could discover how well you were made.

The Laotian women are like the Tahitian women, the *phousaos* like the vahines, always with a flower behind the ear. But they're simpler, prettier, and lacking that susceptibility to sickness of the Polynesians. To make war in such a country is a crime against happiness! I no longer know in what *boun* our psychological operation came to a halt, nor if we ever lifted morale, whatever that may be, but all my life I'll remember that trip outside space and time. Very far from the war.

Press correspondents often pay their own kind of tribute to war, themselves triggering or urging confrontations, as they did in the case of the various sects of South Vietnam.

The function of the journalist is to follow the course of events and report on them. And if there should be no events to report? It's bad to have nothing to send to your newspaper or your wire service. They're very apt to forget you. While something is happening for you to cover, you triumph; you're king, you're needed, you're cajoled. When nothing is happening, you're only a poor mendicant who begs for tips at official dinners, where you're seated at the lower end of the table, no one quite daring to stick you all the way in the kitchen.

War between the sects could have broken out in any one of a number of ways, but it would probably have been far less murderous if the journalists hadn't gotten mixed up in it. We precipitated the movement to open

war; we threw oil on the fire; we cut the ground out
from under all those who contemplated certain complicated transactions to settle their differences—where everyone would have been swindled and everyone would
have profited. Diem, who was then in power and supported by the Americans, had the piastres he needed to
buy off the heads of the sects, that incongruous and picturesque clique, and there the whole affair would have
ended.

Much later, in *Rois mendiants*,[48] I wrote about the
journalist-spectator who sets himself up as an actor or
as a judge in the events he writes about, who mounts
the stage and then can no longer control the demons
his participation has let loose. That the theme stayed
with me so long is an indication of how much I reflected on the role of the journalist in that war of the
sects. (Look, too, at what happened in Watergate,
where the press helped sacrifice to American puritanism and hypocrisy a real head of state—that he may
have been a swindler besides is not being argued; can
one be a head of state without being one?—and who
was then replaced by an ectoplasm. Thus began the de-
cline of America and the heavy-handed Soviet stran-
glehold on the world.)

But back to our sects. There were three: the Cao-Dai,
the Hoa-Hoa, the Bihn-Xuyen, all part of that esoteric
world of Cochin China. The Japanese used them
against the French during the time of Admiral Decoux;
the Vietminh tried to attach them to themselves by
killing off their chiefs and winning over their troops.
Check. Then the French services used them against the
Viets.

Our secret services took these illuminées, these primitive beings, these pirates, and made them colonels and
generals. Their noncoms became captains. The services
distributed arms among them, and gave them uniforms
and shoulder braids as well. The military doesn't like

48. *Beggar Kings*. (Translator's note.)

to work in a fog. Its members want to know exactly and at all times just what to make or believe of the person who has just come to speak to or deal with them, without having to go to all the bother of an investigation into his merit or level of influence. The uniform will tell.

Thus it was that the good Tran Van Soai, absolutely illiterate and an ex-stoker of a steam boiler, found himself general. But he was given only one star, something unheard of in the French army, where the least important brigadier wore two.

And it was thus that the private armies of the sects were born and that the Saigon police, the famous *Sûreté*, came to trust and work with the same bands they'd always fought, the Binh-Xuyen pirates. The Binh-Xuyens, whose leader had a buffalo thief for a father and who began his own career assassinating a rickshaw cyclist for three piastres. He had a truly astonishing face: unsmiling, inscrutable. He distrusted everyone and spent long hours in the company of some deer which were part of his personal menagerie. People claimed it also contained a tiger which was his only friend.

Then Ngo Dinh came to power. And with him came his shadow, his Père Joseph, the brains of the family, Ngo Dinh Nhu. Nhu was an old Chartist, a disciple of Emmanuel Mounier, and he soon sought to impose Christian Personalism[49] on Vietnam. By force and by denouncements.

The Ngos were as fervent Catholics as the Viets were fervent Marxists, and they were Catholics in the same way the Viets were Communists: they were nationalists above all, wanting to disencumber their country of one hundred years of French occupation. And they wanted no more of the sects, of their private armies in the pay of Bao-Dai and his French spies, and of their chiefs disguised as officers.

---

49. A modern philosophical movement locating ultimate value and reality in persons, human or divine. (Translator's note.)

Diem was virtuous. He'd never come near a woman sexually. He was a virgin chief of state. He'd even wanted to be a priest and made frequent retreats in monasteries. The head of the family was Monseignor Ngo Dinh Tuc, archbishop of Hue, the cradle of the family.

Diem wanted to reunite Vietnam as much as the Viets wanted to, and he'd refused to sign the Geneva Accords so dear to the hearts of the French. He wanted to form a national army and was convinced that the sects could only return the country to the Middle Ages. More police under the control of shady characters, more brothels, more hole-in-the-wall taxi-girls, more drugs, everything to offend his respectable puritanism and his American protectors, one of whom was Cardinal Spellman.

The Binh-Xuyens, who controlled the Sûreté and who were protected and fattened by Bao-Dai, and the French secret service under the command of Savani, in whose employ they were, were all tactless and lacking in good judgment. The chief, Bai Vien, had set up a giant brothel in his fief of Cholon. It held three thousand women of every origin and of all ages and was the warrior's repose for an entire army corps. It was a confusedly constructed city that resembled nothing so much as bad pasteboard; paints that shrieked inharmoniously at each other covered the little houses where the women welcomed their clients; neon signs blazed; loudspeakers blared. It was a gross fair honoring the god of sex.

Not to mention the dunghills that abounded: the gambling dens where the coolie bet his few hard-won piastres and would later die of some old *dross*[50] or of heroin sold to him by Bai Vien, the "friend of the people."

In the name of virtue, Diem launched his official war

---

50. Residue left in an opium pipe—"green mud." (Translator's note.)

against the sects, his agents first seeking to divide
them. It was relatively easy. His protectors and advisors having finally read him a lecture, Bai Vien promised to make amends and decided, as a starter, to close
le Grand Monde, suiting his decision with a thunderous
declaration: "In order to win the fight for peace, we are
cleaning out the vestiges of a rotten regime which has
been paralyzing our efforts in the nation's cause."

What a sense of humor! At least the advisor that
drafted the message had a sense of humor. Dry humor.

Le Grand Monde was located in la rue des Marines.
You could find everything there, even at three in the
morning: a girl, a boy, a transvestite would serve you
a Szechwan duck basted in several glasses of cognac,
tailor you a pair of pants, or buy you a shirt. You
could dance yourself to exhaustion with a Chinese, Malaysian, Thai, or Vietnamese taxi-girl for ten piastres
an hour. But you had to dance with the girl of your
choice—were she to stand for long in front of the bar,
she'd lose esteem and be embarrassed. To keep her
with you longer, in private, without music, would cost
you a great deal more.

Le Grand Monde was before everything else a Temple of Joy. It was built in the shelter of a great ochre
wall, high as a prison's, and at the entrance to it you
were searched from head to foot by both the *Sûreté*—
with their green berets and their Colts at their sides—
and by the Binh-Xuyens—with their rackets and other
schemes. Inside were immense gaming halls crowded
with thousands of people: the contemptuous taxi-girl
next to the coolie who pulled his crumpled piastres
from a dirty handkerchief, the elegant white-haired
Vietnamese woman dressed in silk and brocade next to
the *amah* with the betel-reddened teeth.

The raffle wheels clacked and numbers were shouted
out, while perched on high chairs, like referees at a
tennis match, other Binh-Xuyens kept watch over everything, machine guns across their legs.

One table, where bowls and roulette were played,

was reserved for heavy stakes, and here could be found the wealthy Chinese and European merchants in evening dress. If one went out to a formal dinner, the evening had to include a tour of *le Grand Monde*.

And now our Bai Vien, touched by grace, had denied himself one of his main sources of profit, wrested in fierce combat from the Chinese gang who ran the brothels and casinos in Hong Kong! Won by kidnapping and assassinating various leaders of that honorable corporation.

Still, don't waste too much pity on the chief pirate— pardon me, General Le Van Vien. He went on opening clandestine gambling houses everywhere and, no longer under anyone's control, took the liberty of making a gift of a small percentage of his profits to his imperial benefactor and friend.[51]

Nothing availed him, however, despite that demonstration of goodwill and even though he set himself up as a patron of a number of leagues of virtue. For instance, now, if he took the daughters of refugees, it was not to make them prostitutes or taxi-girls, but to dress them in white, put green berets on their heads, and use them as traffic police.

Diem wanted his skin. He began, as I've said, several operations against the sects, during which his agents strove by every means available to divide them. Which wasn't too difficult, all their leaders hating each other, jealous of one another, and believing more in the great god Piastre than in all of their bizarre divinities.

Suddenly Diem stopped everything. On their side, the sects ceased to agitate. Everyone waited. What had happened? Nobody knew anything. Our happy cohort of journalists saw themselves frustrated with their "big story," after having announced that South Vietnam was in for a bloody war. I was taking a few days' peaceful vacation in my native Lozère and thought it better to return at once to South Vietnam.

51. Bao-Dai. (Translator's note.)

One after the other, my colleagues sought out the sect chieftains and said to them, "You're doing nothing? Inaction is very dangerous for you right now. It can only serve Diem, who is going to use the time to buy off your troops. Already Trinh Minh The has gone over to the other side with all his weapons and equipment. Ba Cut isn't sure what he'll do. Not to mention Tran Van Soai, who can be bought with a handful of piastres and that second star he wants so badly."

And the same thing for the other side, except that one had to sing a slightly different tune. These were not ruffians, but distinguished persons, descendants of the great mandarins, men who'd studied political science, though they were all as suspicious, as devious, as cruel as their opponents. And they were colonels out of our schools who still hoped to move up to general, one of them being Big Minh, who for forty-eight hours was the last president of South Vietnam.

To them the journalists said, "You're letting your best opportunity pass. If you don't act now, the sects, aided by the French, will strengthen themselves yet further. And Bao-Dai, their protector, will be on your doorstep. An entire army will follow him. The Americans, deceived by your inaction, won't lift a finger to stop it. All that will be left to you will be to leave for Paris and open Vietnamese restaurants. There are already too many of them. It's no longer a profitable business."

They agitated so much that civil war did indeed break out. The two sides began again to glare defiantly at each other; they insulted each other in the small newspapers, each trying to be one up on the other. Each side once again took the initiative. Teletypers were overloaded with copy, when only the day before, they'd had nothing at all to send.

I asked one of my friends, an old Minister of National Defense, to find me a quiet and unobtrusive place to stay. Not a hotel, but a small pad where, far from prying eyes, I could receive those people I knew to be always crammed full of secrets and tips, but who avoided places such as the Continental and the Majestic like the plague. He found me the ideal place, next to the bridge in Y where the Binh-Xuyens made their general quarters. As night fell, there were a few bursts of fire, a few huts went up in flames. Then quiet returned to the night, and I went to bed. At six o'clock in the morning, I was rudely awakened by an infernal crackling. The whole house was on the point of exploding; everything snapped and crackled. I found myself in a cloud of plaster; pieces of wood from the walls flew across the room in bursts; bullets whined over my bed. I threw myself to the floor and stretched flat, not daring to lift my head. I spent several interminable hours in that position, half asphyxiated by the dust. My pad had been well chosen—smack between the National army and the Binh-Xuyens! Everyone out there was shooting back and forth through my walls, my thin, thin walls of simple wood and plaster partitions! They had to get me out of that hornet's nest with an armored car.

The war of the sects caused thousands of deaths, especially among the civilians. Entire districts were burned, with all their men, women, and children. Their little wooden houses exploded like boxes of matches.

In the middle of this crazy world were the French detachments, who tried to see that the treaty which never really existed was respected. Meanwhile, at Camp Chamson the old patron of the shock commandos, General Gambiez, fretted and fidgeted. He wanted to roll out his cannons and fire on the presidential palace. Fortunately General Ely, who always managed to let a contretemps serve him and who was for Diem, virtue, and lawfulness, intervened and forbade him.

We'd done a good job, made a fine hash of everything!

The affair concluded with a victory for the National army. Diem was solidly implanted in power and proclaimed the Republic. The French were chased out, and they let it happen, happy to leave. The Americans rushed into the breach to take their place.

The second war of Vietnam was ready to begin.

I wrote a story about the war of the sects, *Les Ames errantes,* [52] which, with *La Ville étranglee,* [53] became *Le Mal jaune.* [54]

I was sure that the Vietminh would never accept the cutting up of their country into two parts. They were too nationalistic for that.

Now, in their turn, the Americans fell into the trap of trying to make them see the light and were unable to carry it off. It could only have been done by waging a Communist kind of war, total war, where each combatant became in turn a propagandist, an amateur organizer of diverse organizations, and conducted himself with the civilian populace like a monk-soldier: chaste, brotherly, inexorable. They would also have had to speak the language, know the country and its customs, and have a taste for asceticism, all contrary to the temperament of our Yankees, to their conception of existence, to the kind of army they had.

The French were infinitely closer to the Vietnamese, had been installed in their country for over a hundred years, and they had failed. *They* could do nothing else, short of blowing everything up, of smashing North Vietnam, of bombing the dikes of the Red River and drowning millions of Tonkinese. Which they didn't dare do. In short, they couldn't have hoped for a victory.

In 1960 Henry Cabot Lodge, an eminent member of Boston high society, became ambassador to Vietnam. The Cabots, they say, speak only to the Lodges, and the Lodges only to God. Now, since God is more often than not mute as a clam, they were reduced to remaining

---

52. *The Wandering People.* (Translator's note.)
53. *The Strangled* [or Restricted] *City.* (Translator's note.)
54. *The Yellow Sickness.* (Translator's note.)

among themselves and failed to notice that while they'd closed themselves off, the world had changed.

We could not envisage a member of that caste understanding Vietnam and all her strangeness and complexity.

Diem and his brother Ngo had just been assassinated by those ambitious generals whom the two murdered men had started on their careers and who'd been pushed into murder by their American advisors. It was even a colonel of the CIA who'd made all the detailed plans for the putsch. I knew him well. We frequented the same restaurant, *L'Amiral,* and both preferred its bordeaux to its burgundy.

Cabot Lodge presided over the operation, but—he claimed to me, and I believe him—he did everything in his power to save the lives of the two brothers by proposing to them that they go into hiding until they could seek refuge in the United States or in any other country that suited them. They refused. They had all kinds of faults, but they were courageous men, proud men, and they were sincere Nationalists. They couldn't tolerate owing their lives to those who'd brought them down.

The motive behind the assassination: the Ngos, exasperated by the perpetual intrusions of their American advisors into their affairs, had contacted Hanoi through an intermediary, the ambassador from France.

It's my opinion, regardless of what anyone else may say to the contrary, that what they did was no more than blackmail, pushed to its extreme limits by Ngo Dinh Nhu, who paid for it with his life. It was contrary to the education of the Ngos, to their temperament, to their past, to their religion, to deal with the devil: Ho Chi Minh. They were simply seeking to loosen the vise the Americans had on them, to keep their country from drowning in the flood of dollars.

Cabot asked Bernard Fall, a Franco-American journalist and a university professor, and me to talk to some American generals and members of some related

services about Vietnam. In essence what we told them
was this:

"Be careful; this war isn't going to be easy. Get over
the notion that the French are as stupid as you think
they are. They fought well and intelligently, often cou-
rageously. They held trump cards you don't hold and
often played those cards with sympathy against the
Vietnamese, sympathy based on long cohabitation,
whereas you are coming here with preconceived ideas,
based on your successes in Europe, in the Pacific, and
even in Korea. You seem to suppose that France's defeat was because she was the colonizer. In reality it was
due to her hesitations and shifts, to her inability to
choose and maintain a political stance. The French government had only one idea—negotiate—but the conditions for negotiation were never the same as those of
the Vietminh. The Viets are remarkable soldiers, and
their political organization is at all times subordinated
to the exigencies of their struggle: to have an immense
army where an entire people is formed into brigades.
You said that the Ngo family is a bad lot. It's true. You
said that the democracy you're going to establish here,
after the elimination of the Ngos, will propel the people
to take part in the contest for freedom. False! The kind
of democracy you propose to the Vietnamese is yours. It
won't work for them! Finally, France fought this whole
unpopular war with professional soldiers. Above all, do
not use recruits. And you have to forget your wealth in
this war. You have to make it a war of the poor. You
have to ask infinitely more of men than the material.
And you must see to it that your fighting man knows
the reasons for your intervention here, reasons that
touch him personally, in order for him to be able to accept the sacrifices demanded of him."

We talked into a void, reduced to playing a role of Cas-
sandra. We battered our heads against a stone wall of
the certitude of the general staff and its experts: those
naïve experts who believed that because they could handle figures, they could understand human beings.

Here then were the American masters of Vietnam. They placed a junta of generals at the head of the country, and then they changed it about. First it was Khanh and then it was Ky; it was Big Minh and then Little Minh; one waltz after another, until they reached Thieu, more serious than the others.

The American troops landed in force. (The effective force sent to Vietnam was more than five hundred thousand men.) Another war began, that of material, of gadgets, of laser bombs, of huge bombing raids, everything directed by computers.

War took on a new disguise. There she was in the white coat of a laboratory technician or in the fireproof suit of those specialists trying out new weapons in the California deserts, or passing as a distinguished gentleman, a diplomat, a university professor.

She took on the face of Ambassador Colby, who later became the number one man of the CIA. If one didn't know his duties and his history, he could have been taken for a competent civil-service functionary of a certain rank, whose life passed between the pages of his ledgers and dossiers.

He fought the war in the middle of an air-conditioned office located near a large base next to the airport of Tan Son Nhut. He ruled over several computers, which each day made him up pacification maps colored in green, in yellow, in violet, in red. False maps, because his computers worked only on false information.

War also took on the face of the pilots of those giant eight-engined bombers, the B-56s, whose bombing raids were regulated by softly purring computers in the armored caves of Thailand or on the island of Guam.

War was the corruption that was made of Saigon, of Da Nang, and of all that zone of small and large American bases, trading centers where sellers of girls and drugs, pillagers for the PX, deserters and their accomplices could indulge themselves to their heart's content.

War was those summary executions, sometimes by night and sometimes by day, all the rotten tricks, the rampant misery in which war shows her true face: repulsive, horrible. She stank of putrifying flesh, piles of filth, and she danced in the bars where thousands swarmed to the sound of mad rock music.

I've written about all that in *Un Million Dollars le Viet* and in the *Voyage au bout de la guerre.*[55] I'll not take it up again here.

I will relate three stories told to me then, the first by a madame who ran a Thai massage parlor.

She told me, "You see, the GI was so afraid of contracting a venereal disease that he didn't dare kiss a girl. So I had several small cubicles made in my establishment where he could go to be caressed by a girl. It didn't take long—ten minutes a session—and off he went, happy again. My masseuses were students and civil-service wives who earned more in a few days than their husbands did in a month."

The second was Hélène, a beautiful Sino-Vietnamese who also ran a public bar. Gone now were the plush days in Tonkin when she'd entertained with General Linarés at her side, and she'd gone through a very bad period; but she came out of it by picking up the admiral who commanded the American fleet. We reminisced about the old days: about Hong Kong when she'd lived there with Bao-Dai, all the time, though, having to work as a dance hostess, because funds were forever low at the end of the month.

She told me, "One day he arrived with a valise stuffed with dollars the French had given him in exchange for his return to Indochina. He was completely satisfied with the arrangement. I told him to give back the money.

" 'What in the world for?' Bao-Dai asked, puffing.

" 'Because when one is an emperor, one asks for

---

55. The first title is clear; the second is *Voyage to the Bottom of the War.* (Translator's note.)

more than that. And not in a valise. In a bank.'

"Lartéguy, I just can't manage to stand the Americans, however much I've knocked around. Saigon has become such a sad place, it's enough to make you cry. There was a time when we could have a good time here. But look at things today. Sure, the girls have never earned so many piastres, so many dollars, but they're bored stiff. In the bars with their clients they're still successful, but that's it. What are they to say to the Ricains?[56] They don't know three words of English, and they've forgotten their French. They're satisfied to find the commander, the colonel, with whom they can set up housekeeping and who will pay them with the house, the car, the clothes, leaving it all to them when he goes back home. Look at that one over there. She's still attending the *lycée,* and every night she's out on the street earning money from the Americans, sent there by her parents.

"Do you remember Hanoi? How different it was then? When de Lattre had me sent to Hong Kong because he found my conduct scandalous? Bernard [de Lattre] said to me: 'My father doesn't give a damn that the troop commander of Tonkin has a mistress. But he was shocked that Linarés had an affair with you. Very funny coming from him. Linarés is a gentleman, not a bourgeois, and if my father has his way, he's not going to set a mistress up in a villa on the shore of Petit Lac so he can spend his siestas with her.' "

General Do Cao Tri, commander of the southern front and of the troops in Cambodia and whom I knew when he was a captain in the parachutists of the French army, said to me, furiously, "I'm general of an army corps, but I had more power when I was a captain in the French Expeditionary Corps. Now they[57] dole out to me my measure of fuel every day, the amount I receive being decided by an American non-

56. Americans. (Translator's note.)
57. The Americans. (Translator's note.)

com to whom I must account for it. I haven't even the right to give an order to an American sergeant. When I was a parachute captain and had to call in my adjutant, a French lieutenant, he stood at attention in front of me. Outside of duty we spoke to each other in the familiar. In the French army I was never treated as though I were inferior because I had slant eyes, but now I'm not even allowed into the Yankee noncoms' mess. It's intolerable."

We French committed our share of errors in Indochina, the most serious being our willingness to continue a war we knew we'd lost. Even if we'd won a victory, the same result would have been arrived at: we'd have accorded independence to Indochina within the framework of the French union, an independence that would have collapsed immediately, as it did in Black Africa, for example. Eighty-three thousand dead for nothing, and a few promotions among the young Saint-Cyriens.

The Americans did worse than we. The gravest error they made, in my opinion, was to send the conscript to Vietnam. The draftee asked himself what he was doing there so far from home. How could you explain it to him? The Americans, theoretically opposed to colonialism, criticized the French for their attachment to an old-fashioned structure, for having refused the people the right to decide for themselves. When they took the place of the French, they set up and supported freakish governments of little roistering generals, after first having gotten rid of the government of Diem, the only government that had been able to bring about a certain order, a certain solidity in the land, the one government that wasn't corrupt and that, through the use of some of the tactics of the Viets, had achieved some important results.

It was difficult in the extreme to make the little GI understand what his role was supposed to be, to inculcate in him in all his insularity the notion of his international responsibilities, to explain to him that the containment of communism in the world must be accomplished precisely on that peninsula, to him who frankly hadn't the least interest in strategy.

Not only didn't he understand, but he was bored to tears. He drove the giant bulldozers, the "scrapers" that leveled the hills, the planes that flew at Mach 2, 5. He got his water from the Philippines, his food supplies from the United States, his frozen meat from Australia or New Zealand. He drew his pay. But he didn't like the girls of the country, not really, nor the Chinese soup, nor the salt-water crab, nor the war, nor the country.

Only thirty thousand men, supported by fantastic logistics, did the actual fighting. The others lived to themselves in the army bases, brooding over their resentments, now knowing what to do when their duty was over. They were ripe for a new kind of assault made upon them in the form of "schnouf." And war was transformed into a widespread traffic in drugs.

On that subject it's enough to read the interview Chou En Lai gave to Heykall, the Egyptian editor-in-chief of *Al Ahram:* "The Americans had their helicopters, their B-56s, their napalm, and their delayed action bombs. Against them we used one weapon still better: drugs."

The use of drugs had begun to spread throughout the American army between 1966 and 1967. By 1970 it could be found everywhere: in the marketplaces of Saigon, around all the military bases, in all the bars where the girls hung out. There was no need to ask for it. It was offered to you.

In 1951 in Soul Alley, a hot quarter of Saigon, I was able to buy a capsule of 254 grams of heroin for seven hundred piastres, less than two dollars. I had it analyzed. It was ninety-five percent pure. Its price in New York, Los Angeles, or Detroit, for the same quantity but cut fifty percent by lactose or something else like it, would have been one hundred dollars—fifty times more![58]

58. For more on the subject see *Voyage au bout de la guerre* (Presses de la Cité).

The flow of drugs was made along diverse routes: the Chinese traffic across Laos; Vietminh agents who supplied the wholesalers; the South Vietnamese air force in collaboration with certain police, who made a pretty penny on their deals.

The Communists already controlled a part of the poppy of the Golden Triangle, that of Xieng Khouang. They'd pushed it into the Haute Region, and, at least before the quarrel between Hanoi and Peking, the Chinese had given them the necessary supplies to grow their crops. Before the opium was delivered in the form of heroin, it was refined in China, in North Vietnam, and in small forest laboratories.

Opium is a weak drug that acts very slowly and requires, in order to be smoked, a great deal of leisure time and complicated equipment. The GIs didn't want to bother with subtle pleasures. They preferred to "shoot"—the main line, the quick jolt. A dozen or so needles of heroin hooked him. Hooked him for good, and barring a miracle, he'd end up swelling the multitudes of half-starved addicts wandering in Central Park or in Needle Park; and because he was cut off from his old source, he'd kill to get the necessary dollars to pay for his habit.

War had refined her art of ignominy. She never lacks in imagination.

The third Indo-Chinese war, that of the Vietnamese of the North against those of the South, without direct foreign intervention, would end badly for the Southerners.

I witnessed the agony and the death of Saigon and the birth of another city, Ho Chi Minh–grad, as prudish as the other one was immoderate in its excesses, as boring as the other was gay, despite all its squalor and miseries.[59]

Why that brutal defeat that no one had anticipated, not even the Communists?

59. *Adieu à Saigon* (Presses de la Cité).

Because the South Vietnamese were somnambulists, and President Thieu kept them that way. They obstinately continued to believe that the Americans would keep their promises and not let them fall. But all of America had finally had enough of the war. They no longer had a president, and their political commitments were only of value so long as they remained useful.

Because the South Vietnamese never ceased to hope for a miracle, for the arrival of a providential individual to save them. But it was difficult to find a Joan of Arc among the bar girls on the rue Catinet. As for him who took hold, or tried to, turn after turn for Joffre, Pétain, and de Gaulle, the brave, old, half-blind dyspeptic who pulled himself along on canes, President Huong, it was hard to imagine him mobilizing Saigon's taxis for a new miracle of the Marne, or turning his capital into a new Verdun, or going to Paris to launch a new appeal on the eighteenth of June.

Because Thieu was an incompetent who dismissed out of jealousy all the military men with an understanding of tactics or strategy, Thieu who knew nothing of these things. He also dismissed those who showed any strength of character, for fear they'd not be able to revert to their baser selves.

Because the country was corrupt to the core, and the army, while it still had a few excellent units, was no longer effectively commanded by anyone.

Because the fear of communism is a negative feeling, and if it's going to be opposed at all, it must be by another belief. People don't generally murder for ease or money.

Because, finally, everyone was fed up with the war, in the North as well as in the South. Except that in the South, where the political structure had collapsed, its powers discredited, where everyone followed his own inclinations and acted accordingly, people grew discouraged and gave up. It was impossible for those in the North to give up and to walk away from an army already staffed by the old, the survivors of battles, and the monk-soldiers of Giap.

The Vietnamese thought they would at last come to know peace. They were wrong.

War had developed a taste for Indochina. She needs its customs and its faithful servants as seed ground. She is preparing there for the great confrontation that will be her apotheosis, when Russia and China face each other off, first by one or another people interposed by each, by various liberation movements in these hands or those. Then directly, dragging the rest of the planet into her murderous insanity.

I watched her place her pieces on the chessboard. On the Chinese side: Cambodia, Burma, Thailand, Malaysia, Singapore, North Laos, the minorities of the Haute Region (the Meos, Man, Thos, Thais), North Korea, and Pakistan. On the Russian side: Vietnam, North Laos, India, Bengladesh.

Pacifists bleat—the unbearable bleating of sheep being led to the slaughter. Diplomats look for compromises that satisfy only their own puerile vanity; men of state can no longer even govern themselves; missile-guiding satellites encircle the earth in numbers. One is tempted to paraphrase the Apocalypse: "Soon the fourth seal will be broken and the fourth horse will appear. It is red." Who rides him? Our old acquaintance, war, war to whom the mission has been given to banish peace from the earth, to allow the world's people to massacre each other.

In Algeria there was another face of war. First she took a new name: peace-keeping operation. As if the police and the C.R.S.[60] were going to be enough to make or keep the peace.

I followed its evolution from 1954 to 1962, without having abandoned Indochina. I couldn't have, because

60. *Compagnies républicaines de sécurité:* state security police, or riot police. (Translator's note.)

you don't walk out on war. It's a true liaison. I moved
from one battlefield to the next, from an amphibious
marine operation in the Plain of Joncs to the rounding
up of Fellaghas in the Aurès or Nemenchas.

The rebellion in Algeria was ignited simultaneously
all over the country on November 1, 1954, in what was
called the *"Toussaint rouge."*[61] At 1:15 P.M., from the
west to the east, the rebellion made itself known. Fires
were set at Guillis; a car was attacked at Cassagne, one
at Oranais; at Mitidja there were several demolition
explosions and assassination attempts; at Boufarik an
agricultural cooperative was burned with great loss.
Three bombs went off in Algiers; plane hangars and
cork depots were burned at Bordj and Menaïel; police
were attacked with hand grenades at Tigziert and at
Tizi-Ouzou; telephone lines were cut at Azaga. One
dead at Tizi Reniff; at Batna the commander and three
soldiers were killed; three dead at Khenchela; at Biskra
the post was blown up. In all there were eight dead,
and damage in the hundreds of millions of dollars.

The rebellion was organized and mounted in a very
masterly manner, and the French, who thought of
Messali Hadj as worthless and ineffective, were taken
completely by surprise.

A rebellion? It was no rebellion; it was war. But in
Algeria no one had yet become aware of it, neither
Governor General Léonard, nor the commander of the
troops, General Cherrières. Even less aware of it were
the people, *"les français de souche,"*[62] as they say there,
even if that blood is Maltese, Spanish, or Jewish. They
said to themselves: "All right, the situation became a
little heated, perhaps. The French army will quickly
stamp out the resistance of those few outlaws. Just as
they did in Setif in 1945. A sharp rap on the knuckles
is all that's needed."

The mention of Setif reminded me of something.

61. Red Halloween. (Translator's note.)
62. Those of French stock or blood. (Translator's note.)

Contrary to what has been said, that revolt was also long and well prepared, however much it miscarried—which it may have done because its promised outside support did not arrive.

When I was in commando training for the Far East at Djidjelli, our exercises required us to prepare large quantities of explosives. In order to guard our stores more easily, we placed them in old Phoenician tombs. One day we discovered that our explosives were disappearing, and we prepared a trap. We hid several bundles of TNT under old, rusty cans of conserved food. They were connected to each other by invisible wires that stretched to the entrances of the tombs. Should a thief come, the resultant explosion would wound him badly enough to oblige him to go to the hospital for care, unless he wished to die of gaseous gangrene or tetanus. At the hospital he would be apprehended.

It was the brainchild of our English instructors and was widely used in counterguerrilla warfare.

The thieves returned. The explosive pack went off, they were wounded, and the police soon had them in hand. They weren't fishermen who only wanted to bring in their catch without tiring themselves by setting off underwater charges. They were Kabyles, one a chemist, I believe, who already belonged to an organization engaged in stocking arms and sabotage materials. They were preparing for Setif two years in advance.

When I arrived in Algiers, the first large groups of rebels were already established in Aurès, which was for a long time to be the center of the rebellion. The French had begun their operations of rounding up, locking up, and cleaning up.

I came across Colonel Ducourneau. He commanded a brigade of parachutists of the 25th Civil Defense which had come from Pau. From the Minister of the Interior, then François Mitterand, he'd received the order to put down the rebellion immediately and not to spare the means. "The rebellion must be crushed absolutely."

Ducourneau was skeptical. He'd had experience in Indochina and knew that it wasn't as easy as the minister imagined. A rebellion of "uncontrolled elements" could quickly catch fire and become a revolution of a people seeking their independence. We talked together about it, squatting before an open fire where our cans of rations warmed.

"Algeria is France" proclaimed the newspapers. It's true there were a million French colonists in Algeria, but it wasn't France. Contrary to the way I felt in Indochina, I never felt really comfortable there.

The city of Algiers, though, is beautiful, all white and rising in great tiers around the bay. At the top are the Moorish villas; and from the balcony of the Saint-Raphael, overrun with bougainvillaea, you can watch the dance of the sea below. Close to the port and in the small streets around the Casbah there hangs the heavy odor of frying, of shish kebab, of anisette.

At Bab-el-Qued they speak an especially flavorful language, full of surprises. It only takes getting a little used to the accent. The girls and boys are beautiful, bronzed children of the sun and the sea. I loved to see them on the sidewalks of rue Michelet, coming out of the schools and the universities, performing their ballet of seduction before a critical and attentive audience of other girls and boys on the terraces of the *Otomatic* and of the *Cafeteria.*

I knew the rough-hewn colonists, inured to hardship, clinging to their land in the very midst of the rebellion. You couldn't help but admire them, despite their pigheadedness about wanting nothing to change and their boastfulness, which probably served to hide their distress.

But Algiers wasn't my kind of city. She was a middle-class burgher's wife from Lille, self-satisfied, puritanical, stuffy, inhospitable, whose sole criterion was money and who'd settled with all her northern prejudices of France on the southern soil of the Mediterranean.

Very soon I was disquieted by the direction the "maintenance of order" was taking. I followed some of the operations; I hung around the army messes; I sometimes ventured to mingle with the general staff. I found some old friends, and we tirelessly compared the two wars, the one in Indochina which was still going on, but without the French, and the one in Algeria which was just beginning.

They said to me, those veterans of the Vietminh prison camps, those survivors of Dien Bien Phu, of Cai Bang, or of *"opération Atlante,"* that it was still all the same war, that we should especially try to profit from our experiences in order not to make the same old mistakes all over again, and that, regrettably, the old Army of Africa could understand none of this. It remained a prisoner of Epinal's pictures: of Arab raiding parties and fantasies, of the service hat of père Bugeaud, and of the red coat of Bournagel!

We'd failed in Indochina because we didn't say the magic word *Doc lap*—independence—in time.

How do you say independence in Arabic? *Istiglal?*

In our remote possession in the Far East, five thousand kilometers from the mother country, thirty thousand whites settled in to stay in Vietnam, in Laos, in Cambodia, among a local population of thirty million inhabitants. These were countries with a fabulous history going back to the beginning of recorded time, countries of highly civilized populations, not enslaved to a retrograde religion like Islam.

And still the magic word stuck in our throats.

In Algeria the *Pieds-noirs,* the repatriated Algerians, numbered a million. They were the descendants of the soldiers of Bugeaud, of the Communards,[63] of Alsatians chased from their homeland, all mixed up with the Spanish, the Maltese, the Italians. Among eight million Arabs. The Arabs were a weak nation, not yet formed into a united people, a nation still in "the ob-

63. The Communists of 1871. (Translator's note.)

scure ages of Mahgreb," as Gautier wrote of them. One of their leaders, Ferhat Abbas, vainly searched for a history among the ruins and the cemeteries of his country. The only history there was Roman, or Turkish. The Arabs, the real Arabs, the Arabs of Yemen, had galloped swiftly past on their horses and were gone, and they'd numbered hardly more than a few thousand.

Algeria was less than an hour from France by plane, and she was organized into departments like the mother country.

Were we going to lose Algeria for a word? Independence! So difficult to pronounce, still more difficult to allow. And what if, while we hesitate, people should find another word?

The *Pieds-noirs,* huddled around their monuments to the dead, could hope for help only from the army, and the army had no liking for them, the rancor going back a long time. The *Pieds-noirs* had considered it an honor to fight for France in Tunisia, in Italy, in Provence, in Alsace, and they'd lost many of their sons. They'd certainly earned the right to our recognition and to be defended.

But they forgot that alongside their sons had fought and died the sons of Moroccans, of Tunisians, and especially of Algerians, who were all now in the other camp, but who also had the right to be recognized by France. Sergeant-major Ben Bella had won his military medal at Monte Cassino.

Inextricable! War had carefully shuffled the cards.

The resentment harbored by the army against the colonists went back, as I said, a long time. The love of the colonists for the army is very recent.

Immediately after the conquest of Algeria, Bugeaud created "Arab Bureaus," which were entrusted to those officers who spoke the language and whose responsibility it was to defend the local inhabitants against land spoliation, especially when the lands were held jointly and belonged to collectives such as the native tribes.

He even married some of his officers to the daughters of the great tents or to the daughters of high Turkish officials, the better to implant his men in the country.

A friend of mine is a descendant of the union of one of those captains to a daughter of the Bey of Constantine. He had a right to say "the oldest family of the Algerian *Pieds-noirs.*"

In order to seize these lands and to achieve the suppression of the Arab Bureaus, the major colonists became antimilitarists, Freemasons, and radicals. They achieved their goal—they suppressed the Arab Bureaus and seized the lands, as they also seized the property and possessions of the large religious communities, the Staouéli Trappists, for example, at the moment of the separation of Church and State. The seizure was in the name of the lay Republic and was compulsory.

The army hadn't forgiven them, nor had the Arabs whose lands they took. Nor had a certain church.

The political situation was this: to the east, Tunisia was independent; to the west, Morocco was going to become so (in 1955 with the return of Mohammed V), as all of Black Africa south of Maghreb already was.

And then we come to the French army, returning defeated from Indochina to be given the mission "to establish order" in Algeria.

I've already spoken of the pernicious role de Lattre played when, for his own pleasure and to obtain a better performance in the field, he created his famous field marshals. Then he stirred up their rivalries, he flattered them, he stroked them, he exiled them from his court and later recalled them, making all of them touchy and suspicious, bitter rivals. This phenomenon was repeated in Algeria, particularly in the elite corps. But King John at least controlled his colonels. After his departure, there was no one left to command them.

In the parachute units, for example—in the blue berets of the metropolitan units, the red berets of the colonials, and the Green Berets of the Legion—each

commander made his regiment or his battalion his own
"boutique." In order to hold his command for the longest possible time, because he hungered for glory and
honor, each exerted every effort to pull down for himself the best assignments, to the detriment of his rivals,
and sometimes to the detriment of the general conduct
of operations.

For example: There was a roundup in the region of
Batna. A rebel band was cornered by two battalions of
parachutists. The commander responsible for closing
the trap preferred to let the rebels escape rather than
see them fall into the hands of his rival, who would
then have received all the glory from the operation.

Dreaming of stars, the colonels argued among themselves over the best sectors, the most obviously profitable ones, those where the rebel bands were. And they
neglected all the other sectors where, in fact, the situation was often much more alarming because there the
rebellion was more profoundly established.

A new transformation for war: the sound of the horn
and the ride to the hounds. The commander in chief is
the debonair hunt master, and all the guests lay claim
to the best post.

This commander in chief was yet another old acquaintance, General Salan. Salan the indecisive, the
subtle, the head of the O.A.S. He of whom it was said
that he understood everything but never did anything.

These rivalries made themselves widely felt, and
when war politicized herself in Algeria, when the
thirteenth of May came and the putsch of the generals,
and then when the O.A.S. made its moves, they played
their part again.

Outside of these boutique rivals, there were those officers who genuinely tried, by calling on their own past
experiences, to understand and to analyze this new war.
They'd had enough of defeats—1940, Indochina—and
they didn't want to lose again.

Now, there is only one way to go about contesting a
revolutionary war and that is to fight a revolutionary

war in return. You have to imagine yourself in a revolution you are at the same time opposed to.

Contradictions! Those officers began to read Mao Tsetung, who was relatively easy to grasp, and Tchakhotine, *Le Viol des foules,* [64] who was much more complicated.

Each one desired to be one of the people, as much at home there as a fish in water. But the outlaws, the rebels, the Fellaghas, the Moudjahédines, all enjoyed a considerable advantage over them. They really were in their own waters. The F.L.N.[65] took the lead and created its own kind of unity, by persuasion and terrorism, and because the word "independence" rings more loudly than "reforms," "social security," "family allowances," and even "integration."

Like all revolutionaries, the F.L.N. began by eliminating the competition, the M.N.A. *(Mouvement nationaliste algérien),* which had preceded the F.L.N. in the struggle for independence and whose pope had been the old Messali Hadj.

That was the reason for the massacre at Melouza, which struck terror into the hearts of all the "dissidents" and convinced some among them, like Younis, to rejoin our ranks. We learned of the massacre one morning. A rumor, some confused information, reached the governor general. No one could be really certain of exactly what had happened in that little village perched high on its mountaintop in Kabylia, and of just who the assailant was.

A group of journalists tried to go by car from Algiers to Melouza. By a lucky stroke I was able to get aboard a helicopter which landed me on the spot, the first to arrive. Three hundred men, women, and children massacred. Their blood spattered the walls. A stale odor of a slaughterhouse, of butchery, hung in the air. The French garrison located two kilometers away had

64. *The Rape of the People.* (Translator's note.)
65. *Front de libération nationale.* (Translator's note.)

heard nothing. Because they were so near and in
order not to give the alarm, the F.L.N. killers had
used the knife. As men slit the throats of a herd of
sheep, they brought their victims out one by one. Two
held the man, the woman, or the child, pulling the
head back from behind, and the third performed the
deed, a single cut of the knife, opening the throat
without the victim ever having been able to utter a
cry.

Edward Behr, then a Reuter correspondent, joined
me. He'd just come out of the village where the butchery had taken place, and he was extremely pale. He
found me seated on a wall, peaceably eating a hunk of
bread and a can of sardines, the whole washed down
with a bottle of wine.

I couldn't resist my inclination to provocation, and I
said to him, "Three hundred fresh cadavers whet my
appetite."

He blanched, turned away, and vomited. He hadn't
understood, taking my reaction for that of a cynical
and hardened mercenary, of a racist whom the massacre of a number of Arabs by their like had left completely indifferent.

You were wrong, Edward; I was as frozen with horror as you were. I, too, had just glimpsed war behind
her vilest, most ignoble face as she came from the
massacre of innocents, of old people, of women, of children. Her lips smeared with blood, she breathed con-
tentment, finally surfeited. Like the mythical beast
that had devastated my country in Géraudan.

Simply in order not to be overcome by panic in front
of her, not to succumb to total despair, not to doubt
mankind forever afterwards, it was imperative that I
force myself to make a few familiar gestures to return
me to a supportable universe—chew bread, drink wine,
blink at the sunlight.

War pursued its course. The French ran down the Fellaghas, and once again there was the routine roundup,
lockup, and cleanup. But while the army cleaned

out the Jebel mountains, the F.L.N. implanted itself in the cities and ruined Algiers.

Then there was the unsuccessful Suez operation, a military victory that became a political debacle. The Russians joined the Americans in threatening the French and the English with grave sanctions if they continued their advance on Cairo. After that, what was to stop the massacre of the Hungarian insurgents who'd believed in the promises of "The Voice of America"?

I was in Poland. I'd believed that since the revolt had begun at Potsdam, it would be further pursued at Warsaw. It had been necessary to bring Gomulka out of his prison, while at the same time the Red Army tanks prepared to leave their cantonments in the countryside and were already warming up their engines to launch an attack on the cities. All resistance would be crushed, as had been done in Hungary.

The revolt was a near thing. Already at Warsaw the agents of the U.B., the regime's secret police controlled by the Soviet K.G.B., had been making their descent in the open street. And pairs of homeless students killed them, searched their bodies and went through their papers to find their addresses, and hurried to occupy their apartments. They believed their time had come.

In a Cracow coal cellar, by candlelight, I was in on the birth of an underground journal begun by *beaux-arts* students at the very time when all hope of escaping Soviet guardianship had at last vanished.

It went under a sign that the world most merited, that of a starved dog, Laika, the little dog that went round and round the earth in the first Sputnik. The emblem was a mixture of both despair and cruel irony.

I returned to Algeria, where the situation had abruptly deteriorated. We'd lost Algiers.

An order had come from Paris to the Tenth Parachute Division to return to Algeria from the Suez—where victory was almost in their hands—to restore order at all costs and by any means. The government was Socialist. Guy Mollet was counsel president, and

Lacoste the resident minister. He also belonged to the
S.F.I.O.[66]

The "leopards" of Bigeard, of Godard, and of Jean-
Pierre had "done what they had to," but not
wholeheartedly. Under the remote control of Massu,
and the still more remote control of Salan, they'd dis-
mantled the F.L.N. networks one after the other. And
there'd been only one way to go about it: to capture a
suspect and to force him under torture to confess everything he knew, to give names and addresses. Small
squads of men with radios were waiting in jeeps ready
to descend immediately on indicated locations. Nothing
would have been achieved by promising the suspect
barley sugar for turning in his friends. Methods that
would bring the desired results had to be employed.

One morning very early, one of my old war buddies—
from a war we'd fought properly and had won—
knocked on the door to my room. He was a one-time
schoolmaster who'd finally elected to go into the army,
into a parachute unit. He'd fought in the Resistance, a
boy full of principles, and one of those who'd approved
of the action of "Saint John the Baptist." You remember? In the Vosges, with the German prisoners?

I lived then at the Hotel Aletti. My friend was hag-
gard, his face anguished.

"Get up," he said to me. "Let's go out."

As we climbed toward the *Grande Poste*, he showed
me his hands and confessed to me, "For the first time
in my life I've tortured a man. We knew he'd placed
a dozen or so bombs in the city and that they were
set to go off about eight o'clock in the morning, just
when all the streets would be full of people on their
way to work. He had to tell us where they were, and
tell us in time for us to defuse the bombs. We were
running out of time. Dawn came. He told us what we
wanted to know. The bombs didn't go off. I was the

66. *Section française de l'Internationale ouvrière:* The French Branch
of the Worker's International. (Translator's note.)

one who tortured him. I'd wanted nothing so much as to be left out, that one of my lieutenants or captains dirty his hands. I was too cowardly, as cowardly as the politicians who'd given us the order . . . and who never want to know how their orders are carried out. I felt like shooting myself. So then I came to find you, one who'd been with me in the good war. What are we to do?"

"Let's have some coffee. The bistros are beginning to open. Then we can take a walk to Zéralda, along the beach. In January it's still too cold to swim. Too bad."

As I had at Melouza for myself, now for him I wanted to perform the simple, familiar acts, to escape for a time from the spell of war and all its horror.

These officers had three options open to them: to fight to win, and they could only do that by dirtying their hands; to do nothing, to see nothing, to hear nothing, like the three Chinese monkeys, one of whom hides his eyes, another his mouth, and another his ears, and wait for a promotion to a higher rank and an assignment back in France; or leave the army. I've regard only for the first and third categories.

All those who opted for revolutionary war soon discovered that they needed to find some justification for their actions. "Keep Algeria for France" was fine for those who were fighting in the Jebels. But it wasn't enough for those who had to demolish terrorist networks by any means and to do the work of the police, who'd shown themselves incapable of the task. Then higher reasons were needed. The Inquisitors had had God. The Communists had their hope that they could change the face of the world. The Fellaghas aspired to gain their independence and to write the history they never had. The new soldiers needed something too.

And they could never admit—these new soldiers of a much more dangerous war where one played more for one's soul than for one's life—that they'd tortured and that they'd lied to defend the wealthy colonists, who for the most part were already safe in France and who'd left their overseers to die in their place, or for the owners of big businesses, the Bugeauds, the Blachettes, the Germains, and others.

A few of those new soldiers even contemplated, on those nights when doubts tortured them, hanging some of those others from the general government's lampposts to demonstrate in the only way they could think of just how far apart they all were and how much they mistrusted them.

With every new minister in France, the government showed itself more incapable than it had been under the preceding minister to finish with the war in one way or another, either by negotiating or by going all out. Everyone believed we'd be successful when we called in the reservists, and again when we sent in the conscripts.

But we aren't going to refight here the Algerian war.

One trip on a train to Algiers and Djela, a simple train trip, made me understand that unless there was a miracle, unless the course of history was reversed, unless the entire country was turned upside down, we were not going to come out of that war victorious, that independence was inevitable with or without us.

In the train I looked and I listened. Nothing happened. The tracks weren't blown up, and we didn't fall into an ambush. It was just that all of a sudden I could feel that war had changed her tone, that she was playing another kind of music. I sensed it in the behavior of the civilians and of the soldiers who got on and off, in that of our little escort group, in the lassitude of one or another of the passengers, in the I-don't-give-a-damn attitude of the recruits, in the insouciance of the *Pieds-noirs,* in the general attitude of the Arabs who silently stood squeezed tightly together amid all their baskets in the end cars. What did they have in those baskets? Semolina or grenades? A sentence here, a word there, a gesture of defiance, a laugh that rang false. There was no doubt about it for me.

When I returned to Algiers, I tried to put that succession of fugitive impressions into some kind of order. I thought of them in connection with other events, other images. Such as the day when I was walking up the Bugeaud ramp and suddenly all the city's lampposts, mined by the F.L.N., exploded. All around me the shattered flying pieces of cast iron cut down the lines of people waiting for the bus.

For *Paris-Presse* I wrote a long paper which became a sort of panorama of the Algerian war. A day or two after its publication, Bigeard called me.

"I absolutely must see you," he said. "What you've written is exactly our feelings in the shock troops about this war. Nothing happens, and everything happens."

Bigeard invited me to dinner. I joined him at Zéralda near the beach. He was with several of his officers, one of whom, his executive officer, Lenoir, called him "old man." Seated on the terrace, we ate brochettes and admired the young *Pieds-noirs* who came to swim, the beautiful boys, athletic, muscular, foreheads a little low, in their skin-tight bathing trunks, and accompanied by splendid girls.

Bigeard followed them with his eyes, filling his pipe, as was his habit, with cigarettes from which he stripped the paper. Suddenly he said to me, "They're magnificent, those boys, aren't they? Solid, well built. But they never joined us, and they've no desire to die for Algeria. And what have we left to fight with? With metalworkers from the Parisian region or boys from the Southwest. But, my God, it's their war, too, those boys down there, and just because their fathers fought well from 1943 to 1945, they're not released from all responsibility. They've done nothing at all themselves."

If they had only been in a more favorable environment, they'd probably have proven themselves to be as courageous as their elders. But they'd have to have been torn away from this paradise of youth, of sun and sea. Youth is short in Algeria, and it is flamboyant. It hasn't room for reflection; just for the moment's pleasure, for the self alone. You have to take advantage of that moment, of youth, quickly before it fades.

The Algerian war was lost partly because of the obliviousness of all the young men and young women we watched as they passed by on the beach, chastely holding each other by the hand. Their romantic attachments were usually chaste. If they'd understood in time that the war demanded total commitment of all the people, especially of the youth, what followed would probably have been different. Algerian independence was inevitable, and any other notion is an illusion; but it could have been proclaimed under other conditions, need not have taken on the air of a debacle. We could have envisaged the existence of a *Pied-noir* state or province, a kind of Israel in Algeria. The Israelis were seven hundred thousand in 1948 when they proclaimed the state of Israel, the *Pieds-noirs* a million. The Israelis were surrounded by one hundred million hostile Arabs, the *Pieds-noirs* by fifteen or so million, counting all of Maghreb, and they were only opposed by resentment, rarely by hatred. Their cause was far from lost.

But Israel had been created in blood and tears, in pogroms and in concentration camps. And they weren't given any alternative between leaving and dying, between the coffin and victory. Life was too short in Algeria, France too close. Every year the *Pieds-noirs* could go there on vacation.

Then came the thirteenth of May and the putsch, which is history everyone knows, and all that followed.

I moved from one conspiracy to another, from the bistro in Ortiz where they fiercely supported the Committee of Public Safety and the army, without specifying which, to the villas and the Saint Rafael, where they supported Chaban and, as a secondary consideration, de Gaulle. For his own ends, Chaban freely used the antenna of the national defense, and the Commandant Pouget, and Delbecque, a militant member of the R.P.F.,[67] both men of charm and imposing appearance. He also used their easy entry into the best circles. I found Colonel Battesti in a sauna near the Forum, and he was for Michel Debré. The parachute captains were also looking hard for a "patron," someone to follow. They ended up, for lack of anyone better, by taking de Gaulle. What everyone *really* wanted was to find a word to set up against that of independence. They were given "integration."

It was Soustelle who found it. The word's magic, while it didn't ring quite as beautifully as independence, the sense of which remained a little vague, nevertheless stopped the war for several weeks. It even created a kind of fraternity between the Moslems and the *"français de souche"* during demonstrations in the Forum at that time, not *all* of which were staged.

Long afterwards in Mexico, Soustelle's one-time schoolmaster, Alfonso Caso, director of the *Institut indigéniste*, explained to me how his old pupil, caught unprepared in Algeria, had remembered how he'd tried in Mexico, with more or less success, to integrate the Indians into the national community. He remembered, too, the methods that had been used.

What did integration mean? To assimilate the Arabs into the French; to give them the same rights, the same advantages; to make them citizens, separate but equal (which they were not, even when they lived in the French departments); to educate them. Only fifteen percent of their young attended school, which was not compulsory for them.

Such integration was impossible, short of totally changing the face of France, of pulling her toward the Third World, away from the European family.

We were going to find ourselves burdened with ten

67. *Rassemblement du peuple français:* Rally of the French People. (Translator's note.)

million very prolific Moslems, endowed with innumerable families to whom we would have to grant all the same benefits the metropolitans had. And the metropolitans would have to foot the bill. The standard of living in Algeria was such that the good Mohammed who would receive family allowances for a dozen children had nothing but his two hands to do with. He couldn't have paid for anything. Then afterwards he'd have given thanks to Allah, may his holy name be blessed, for all his new benefits, no recognition whatever to France. Damn! The problems posed by Islam! How could a status comparable to that of a Frenchman be granted to a Moslem? He could never be moved from that submission to Islam he holds to so tenaciously and which is written in the Koran. Algeria was already essentially lost to us several months after we'd conquered it, when our military men, fascinated by certain alluring practices, played Mohammed off against Christ. That was how the Christ of Saint Augustine came to live again in the mountains of Kabylia.

But Christianize the Maghreb people? Increase the number of mixed marriages as the crusaders had done in the Frankish kingdom of Jerusalem? It serves nothing to try to remake history, but one can learn from it, as Israel had done, for instance.

De Gaulle wanted no part of integration at any price. His son-in-law, General de Boisseu, recounted the time when de Gaulle was shaving in front of a mirror, and, his face covered with foam, the old man grumbled, "To stick France with ten million more *clochards!*[68] It's idiotic!"

Another deeper sentiment impelled him to refuse that solution to the problem. He held the image of a Christian, occidental France wrought by generations of kings. To accept ten million Moslem Arabs to her bosom would change her nature. Hadn't Joan of Arc been entrusted with breaking the Berbers? She was

68. Bums, tramps, hobos. (Translator's note.)

his patron, and it was her cross of Lorraine he'd borrowed.

Carried away by their enthusiasm and generosity, wanting at any price a victory that wasn't just a military one, the centurions of Africa hadn't seen all the redoubtable consequences of their plan for integration.

I was there at the huge meeting in the Forum when de Gaulle, arms extended, deliriously proclaimed: *"Je vous ai compris!"*[69] A hand touched me on the shoulder, that of an American journalist—was it Joe or Stewart Alsop? I don't remember any more—who said to me, "Froggies,[70] you've found your king."

De Gaulle knew nothing at all of that new army which now mixed in politics, quoted Mao Tse-tung (often wrongly), was up to its neck in all sorts of Committees of Public Safety, and followed the orders of its chiefs badly, but which was remarkable in the field. He didn't understand it at all.

But de Gaulle needed power, authority. He'd fabricated his twenty years of legitimacy too late. He wanted, therefore, to meet that army, and one fine day he decided to go to see "Bigeard's circus" close up. Bigeard, applying characteristic methods not codified anywhere in military regulations, had just completely pacified a difficult sector in Oran.

Bigeard stood on a small platform beside de Gaulle, who was in full uniform. Bigeard was dressed in battle camouflage uniform, sleeves rolled up. The troops commenced to file past in easy step, eyes straight ahead: heads bare, faces bronzed, lean, shirts mostly opened over their muscular torsos. Not exactly classical, but impressive. De Gaulle was surprised and floundering on unfamiliar ground. To regain his bearings, he tried to catch the colonel out with what appeared to have been untoward behavior.

---

69. I understood you. (Translator's note.)
70. This is no translation. It is the author's word. (Translator's note.)

"Tell me, Bigeard, when a troop passes before a general, isn't eyes right the order?"

"Terminated! It's been abolished in regulations for two years."

He forgot that one might possibly address a general like that, never a king. He was to pay for it.

Bigeard had angered de Gaulle, who, however, sensed that this soldier of fortune, this adventurer from another school and of another stamp than his own, might one day prove to be useful. Providing he was removed from Algeria. To punish him, to humiliate him, to educate him, and to make him the kind of soldier de Gaulle thought he should be, Bigeard was sent to the war college.

I saw Bigeard often enough during that time. He raged at having to study completely outmoded methods of warfare, at not seeing his name in the newspapers any longer, at being forgotten. But he came through the test well, to the astonishment of de Gaulle who had to name him general. This after first having sent him to complete his penance at Camp de Bouare deep in Central Africa.

In June of 1956 one of my friends, Jean Rudin, a Nice bookseller, who had been called back as a captain on the Twenty–eighth Infantry Division, was flying a Piper Cub over the Moudakh wadi to the north of Aïn-Témouchent in Oran.

It was morning. A skirmish unrolled below him. An infantry company was located in the thalweg, hidden from its forward section, which had just taken possession of a hill. The radio was open and on the same channel as the infantry, and Rudin heard the exchange of orders and messages. He flew low enough to make out what was happening below.

From the hilltop the second lieutenant who headed the sector said, "I've just taken a prisoner. What should I do?"

"Bring him down," said the captain, who wanted to interrogate the prisoner.

The second lieutenant failed to understand, drew his revolver, and shot the prisoner down under the eyes of Rudin, who was flying only a few meters above and who could do nothing at all to prevent it.

War split her sides laughing. She adores that kind of joke.

In 1959 I wrote *Les Centurions*.

In the book I blended all my memories and my reflections with my twenty years' experience of wars won and lost, those in which I'd fought as an officer and those I'd followed as a correspondent.

Under my pen was born a book I hadn't really expected, the picture of a new kind of soldier who had very little in common with the traditional military man. The centurion was for the most part born of the Resistance. His origin and his social class were of little significance. Refusing the defeat thrust upon him because it went against the grain, he'd come to know death camps, Spanish prisons, and the underground. He could have been from a noble family, as Glatigny was; belonged to the university intelligentsia, as Esclavier did; been of Franco-Chinese mixture, as Boisfeuras was; come from the F.T.P., as Pinières did; been a Basque shepherd and smuggler, like their chief, Colonel Raspéguy was; been an Arab, like Mahmoudi, drawn at one and the same time by the call of the rebellion and by the friendship of the men of his sect; or been born on the shores of the Senegal, like the doctor Dia, a kind of beneficent black sorcerer.

In the Vietminh prison camps, they'd undergone a kind of reeducation. However much they'd rejected it, it had still marked them, made them think as they'd never done before of the problems posed the soldier at the end of the twentieth century in his pursuit of a colonial war. A war without right aim or reason and fought with the traditional methods of the old army. A war that could only lead to defeat.

They'd gone to Indochina to reestablish "order" and

to reinstall with all their one-time privileges old political hierarchies, administrators, and financiers who
were defunct, who'd gone bankrupt. The new soldiers
had quickly become aware of all this. Those who'd
fought for liberation under the German occupation
in their own land found that, in the face of a Vietminh
who also fought for liberation, their spirits grew more
and more confused.

They defended themselves against this confusion and
hid themselves behind obedience to the orders they received. But in so doing they had to disobey the precepts
of their old and traditional leaders, Pétain and the generals of the Army of the Armistice, who'd taken part
with them in their only victory, either at the side of
the Allies or in the underground which threw itself
into all the liberation movements.

They couldn't stop dreaming of a new, more just
order, more rigorous, fresher, a whole new army better
adapted to our times, capable of holding its own
against a revolutionary war. The underlying thought
was that this new army was also capable of revolution
in its own way.

At the same time—and here was their contradic-
tion—they refuted revolution in the name of their
past, of their traditions, and because they believed
that all that was best in their occidental civilization
could be preserved, especially liberty. They wanted no
part of the Marxist oversimplification of the world, of
its Manichaeism, of its catechism. For by having tried
too hard to convert them, the Viets had at the same
time vaccinated them against communism.

They no longer knew very well just where they were.

And then there they were back in Algeria, plunged
once again into a war of liberation. The traditional
army had failed because it had refused indefinitely to
conquer the Riff[71] and to pursue the tribe of Abd-el-

71. A mountainous coastal region in North Morocco. (Translator's
note.)

Kader. The new soldiers wanted to fight their adversary's kind of war, to fight to win, and to do so they
had to dirty their hands. The time had come when no
one could ever again fight a proper war.

Far from Rome they'd defended Rome, and back in
Rome the people had covered themselves with filth to
the point where the soldiers felt closer to those they
fought than to those for whom they killed.

That was the theme of *Les Centurions*.

One day they understood that they'd fought for nothing, that their comrades had died for nothing, and that
after having won the war in the Jebels, they'd lost
Paris.

Some of them were even prosecuted for having used
methods common to every subversive war—"forced
interrogation," or, to put it more bluntly, torture.
Also for the liquidation outside of all judicial procedure of enemy prisoners who'd escaped from prison.
They were slapped on the wrists for a principle, but
once free they would be especially careful never again
to be caught for the same errors, and they soon returned to combat.

Their chiefs, from whom they'd received the order to
"win, no matter what the price," played Pontius Pilate
and washed their hands of them. They also had no real
government at home. It changed every three months.

They revolted. They were pushed into it. They were
naïve and they hadn't a shred of political culture. They
had nothing to go on but their resentments and their
sense of right and wrong. Not knowing what to do with
the power they'd possessed themselves of with such disconcerting facility, they entrusted it to de Gaulle,
whom they believed was behind them.

And he, in the manner of all emperors elected by the
legions, thought only of how to get rid of them.

That was the theme of the *Prétorians*.

The title *Les Centurions* came to me one day when I
was at Massada, a tiny oasis in the Saharan Atlas,

where I'd joined Serge Groussard, who'd been recalled
as a captain.

A battalion of the Foreign Legion occupied the site of
an ancient Roman camp. It dominated a great ochre-
colored plain marked here and there by the dark
splotches of the oases. The white Képis[72] now held the
same lookout posts as the old Legionnaires of Cornelius
Balbus. Nothing had changed, just the black snout of
the machine guns and a 105 cannon taking the place of
the ballista[73] and the scorpion.

Seated on the overturned shaft of an old column,
Serge and I dreamed of those forgotten Roman defenders who'd watched the distant maneuvers of the squadrons of Numidian cavaliers. When night fell, the cavaliers, who knew the weakness of the Legionnaires,
would attack, and the Romans would have to defend
themselves alone, without hope of help. Meanwhile in
Rome the senate had become a marketplace where everyone was bought and sold, and politics had become a
rat race where everything was permitted.

The similarity of the Fourth Republic to that Rome
was there for everyone to see.

I ran my hand over the surface of the column. I'm
fond of ruins, and I love to caress old stones. Soon I felt
an inscription beneath my fingers. There were two, in
fact, and I set myself to deciphering them. The oldest
one, half eroded by sand and wind, was "Titus Caius
Germanicus, centurion of the Xth Legion." The other,
recently inscribed, read: "Friedrich Germanicus, of the
1st R.E.P." (*Régiment étranger de parachutistes*).

I had the title of my book: *Les Centurions*. The characters? I'd lived with them for twenty years. All I
needed was a publisher, someone who would advance
me enough money to last me four months, while I took
a leave from *Paris-Presse*.

---

72. The peaked caps of the Legion. (Translator's note.)
73. An ancient military engine for throwing stones. (Translator's
note.)

I made the round of publishers who'd already published books of mine. Gallimard offered me one hundred thousand old francs. Julliard wasn't interested. *La Ville étranglée,* which he'd published, hadn't done very well, despite its Albert London prize. Albin Michel *(Les Ames errantes, Les Baladins*[74] *de la Margeride, Les Clefs*[75] *de l'Afrique)* made an effort. He went to three hundred thousand. A few small publishers who've since disappeared offered me promises. Then Georges' Roditi introduced me to Nelson of *Presses de la Cité,* and without fuss or bother Nelson offered me the necessary sum. Georges Roditi loaned me his house in Saint-Cezaire, "La Porte romaine,"[76] and I began to write.

I invented the character Boisfeuras. I wanted him to be the extreme spokesman for my ideas, someone who would go directly to the heart of things and who would be lost because of his logical mind.

It was with this entirely imaginary character that most officers would later identify.

I sat myself in front of a window opposite a mistral-tossed cypress which stood out against a brilliantly lavender sky. It was March and it rained often, the heavy spring odors rising up to me from the gardens afterwards. Women came by to see me, but I didn't let them stay around. My characters began to take life, and already they were demanding. They wanted to be alone with me.

Jean Pouget, whom I'd met in Algeria at the time of the May thirteenth putsch, gave me precious information on Camp #1 in North Vietnam and on the long march of the survivors of Dien Bien Phu. That was the reason for the letter of the centurion Marcus Flavinius of the Augusta Legion which I used to open my book and which ends with that prophetic sentence: "Let people beware the wrath of the Legions!"

74. Fools, buffoons. (Translator's note.)
75. Keys. (Translator's note.)
76. The Roman door or gate. (Translator's note.)

There was only one thing wrong with the information I received from Pouget, though I didn't know it at the time. It had been fabricated by Roger Frey in the hope it would arouse the anger of the Algerian legions enough that they would chase a weak government from Paris, one incapable of solving Algeria's problems, and name an emperor. That it did.

Bigeard gave me some accounts of military operations accompanied by plans and photographs. Ducourneau, who'd become the military advisor to the minister resident, informed me about the reigning atmosphere of the government and of the general staff. Colonel Ruyssen, another old acquaintance of the commandos and currently a spokesman for the Arabs, clarified for me what went on in the opposite camp. But in hints. He was a discreet man, and his function required him to be just that.

I made my character Bigeard-Ducourneau-Raspéguy come from Saint-Etienne-de-Baigorry, because Bigeard was from Toul and Ducourneau from Pau, and because the Basque country and its people had always fascinated me.

In fact, a little before the thirteenth of May, with Pierre Schoendorffer as director, Raoul Coutard as chief photographer, and Mijanou Bardot heading the bill, we made a film there. *Ramuntcho,* alas!

For Esclavier I was inspired by Captain Barrés, grandson of the writer, veteran of Korea, killed in Tunisia in the course of an incursion of our troops—and by a few other people I'd met and glimpsed.

Glatigny was inspired by Captain Pierre Fresnay in *La Grande Illusion,* but recast more in the modern style, confronted by the problems of revolutionary war—as well as by Jean Pouget and a few others.

Then I turned my manuscript in. There was nothing left of the advance the publisher had given me, and I even had some debts.

"Interesting," Roditi said to me, after reading it. "With luck we'll make twenty-five thousand."

I returned to *Paris-Presse* and left on assignments. By small stages I reached the Far East, stopping at Beirut, where the American marines had landed to put an end to the civil war between Christians supported by the United States and Moslems and Druses supported by Syria and Russia. Chamoun versus Kamal Joumblatt.

At Teheran, Reza Chah married little Dibah, whose family I knew well. One of her uncles managed the Park Hotel where I'd stayed; the other was a veteran master sergeant of the Foreign Legion. We were only too happy to be together again, glass in hand, at P'tit Louis.

In South Vietnam the Vietcong had been making their appearance. In Saigon I rejoined the parachutists who'd just taken part in a *coup d'état* against Diem and who'd failed. I only had time to make it to Cambodia by way of the plantations. There was another neutralist *coup* in Laos, perpetrated by a little captain with whom I became friends, Kong Le. I stayed there several months, and it was there I got the idea for *Tambours de bronze*.

When I returned home, my book had been out for some time. To my astonishment I learned that *Les Centurions* had sold more than 50,000 copies.

Not only was my advance reimbursed, but I still had several million old francs to collect. Because of the temper of the times, the book had taken off like a whirlwind without publicity. Up to now it has sold 1,200,000 copies in France alone and has been translated into a dozen languages, including Hebrew, Yugoslavian, and Japanese.

By designating a certain kind of soldier the "centurion" I'd created a myth and regiven life to a word that was passing from our language.

My book ran away from me. It took on a life of its own apart from me, often unleashing passions and causing people to attribute political stances to me that were actually foreign to me.

Reactions to it were astonishing. For a long while the Communists hesitated to make a statement. Then *La Marseillaise* published an entire page of the book, praising not just the book but the revolutionary army, whose epic it recounted and who had understood that its way lay among the people.

After mature reflection, *L'Humanité* corrected its range and called the book fascist, saying that its author was better known as a mercenary than as a journalist. Hadn't he fought in Korea?

General de Gaulle, to whom I sent a copy, wrote me that he didn't think it was of much value.

Several years afterwards—when Salazar was again being oppressive with his people—I went to Lisbon and my publisher organized an autograph party there. I didn't expect the large crowd that came. Especially the simple soldiers, carrying for their lieutenants or their captains copies of my book to be signed, as though the officers feared to be seen there. I later learned the names of all of them. All afternoon I signed copies of *Os Centuriones* without even being able to lift my nose from the job.

A clandestine movement had been born into the country's army, among those who fought in Mozambique, in Angola, and in Guinea-Bissau. It went under the name *Os Centuriones*. It was to become the "Movement of the Armed Forces" to overturn the dictatorship of Salazar and Caetano, an excellent decision. But the movement nearly replaced that dictatorship with another, a Stalinist one, which would have been worse. The Portuguese centurions were improvising hastily, were immature, were politically untutored, didn't know where they were going. All of which Alvaro Cunbal knew only too well.

When Rome's centurions ceased to believe in the caesars and in the empire, they became Christians. The Portuguese couldn't do without religion, but Christ was no longer enough for them: his church had compromised with an antiquated and paternalistic regime of old and somnambulistic professors of Coimbre who wanted to preserve what was left of the heritage of Henry the Navigator.[77] The Portuguese centurions knew the empire was lost after several years of subversive war achieved no real objective, despite all their efforts and the fact that part of the population supported them, the people of mixed blood and the colonists.

Like our centurions in Algeria, they were hampered in their struggle by the quest for a miracle prescription, a cure-all. Communism was suggested to them. It was a simple-enough theory which offered at once a principle and a well-matched system of a catechism and a manual of revolutionary war that had stood the test of time.

They were so troubled, were so in need of direction, that they latched onto Lartéguy, who was, according to J. F. Revel, a Marxist on the banks of the Tagus.

I never really believed they'd swing all the way over to communism. When you are a defender of a particular occidental civilization, when you are still impregnated with Christianity and drunk on a barely recovered liberty, you don't easily give yourself over to an atheistic, totalitarian, sad, and economically disastrous system, even if you feel very strongly the need to communicate with the people, to be approved by them daily. Moreover, the Portuguese people were not Communist.

Our centurions in Algeria, after having first been tempted by a kind of Titoism (the "Country and Progress" movement), all but embarked on a course of neofascism. I'm speaking only of those "lost soldiers" who went into the O.A.S., courageous officers, honorable men, who preferred the dishonor of lost causes to the honors and prebends de Gaulle contemptuously distributed to those who remained faithful "to his person."

77. 1394–1460. Patron of voyagers and explorers, he established a school of navigation and an observatory; made no voyages himself, but spent his life directing voyages of discovery along the African coast; collected accounts of journeys to Africa and Asia; improved the compass and shipbuilding. The voyages he sponsored led to circumnavigation of Africa and establishment of the Portuguese colonial empire. (Translator's note.)

But the myths of Susini and consorts[78] were intolerable to men like Colonel Goadard, who as a lieutenant
had commanded the underground of the Glières, or the
commander of Saint-Marc, who at sixteen had been
sent to Buchenwald. Or for Salan, who belonged to the
old liberal tradition of southern socialism.

The O.A.S. ran aground. Apart from its being full of
contradictions, the movement was completely infiltrated by unofficial police and by the intelligence
services. Its excesses only hastened its downfall.

For France to hold onto Algeria, which would in any
case have become independent, there would have to
have been forced upon France the Celtic Cross of the
Occidental Movement. It would have been a mad venture. Or a Third World-style military regime which the
metropolitan French would never have tolerated—nor
I, especially not I.

For that reason and not for any sympathy for de
Gaulle and his regime, and to save the centurions from
the temptation to totalitarianism, I refused to have any
contact whatever with the O.A.S. I advised all my
comrades not to join the O.A.S., because they were
bound to lose, because they'd be obliged to divest themselves of honorable uniforms, and because an army
without them would be no better than a few squadrons
of riot police.

The result was a plastic explosive attack on rue de la
Montagne-Sainte-Geneviève where I lived.

In time I came to understand better the doubts and
the problems of the American centurions in Indochina.
Particularly among the Green Berets, who were
charged with a great many crimes, though at least My
Lai was not among them, nor the bombing of villages
by B-56s plugged into computers. The Green Berets
played out their roles in the jungles and the rice fields.

All the centurions face the same dilemma: to try to
carry the field in today's kind of total warfare—which

78. Presumably of the O.A.S. (Translator's note.)

is a mixture of everything: classical combat, psychological warfare, indoctrination, guerrilla warfare, conditioning of the populace—the soldier must always feel secure about the rear. Hence he must have a measure of control over it. Hence he must assume power for himself. To take this step in good faith requires that he question the very nature of even the political and social systems he claims to defend. The reason is this: A revolutionary war can now only be won by a totalitarian government, because only such a government dares to employ certain methods. Today, apart from atomic wars, *all* wars are revolutionary wars, but these certain methods are prohibited by democracies for all sorts of reasons, such as an easily stirred up public opinion, the belief in the old maxim that the civil arm should always take precedence over the military arm even in times of war, the refusal to accept necessary sacrifices or discomforts, and finally the preservation of a good conscience, which makes the digestion easier.

How do you explain that to save liberty, liberty must first be suppressed? And in that rests the weakness of democratic regimes, a weakness that is at the same time a credit to them, an honor.

The American centurions gave way beneath the burden. Many quit the army, like the colonel who came to find me in my room at the Continental to tell me, "We Americans have an army of computers and civil servants. And we've given the same kind of army to the South Vietnamese, with all the corruption into the bargain. . . . Our army has become an army of lies. . . . We've been more than ready to dispense money and material, but not the total commitment of the men, not their fatigue, which wins wars of this kind. . . . We're going to leave here despairing, going to let Vietnam be devastated."

And he finished by raising his glass. "I drink to your heroes, Monsieur, to your centurions who understood in Indochina the kind of war they'd have to fight in

Algeria and who were unable to do so. Every day we feel closer and closer to them, and we fear the same fate."

Colonel, neither you nor the centurions of Algeria would be able to fight that kind of war without changing the whole planet, without changing a democratic system of government with all its weaknesses and its erring methods and procedures for another that would be pure and hard but under which there'd be no liberty. Liberty you'd then have to impose by force.

For the want of liberty, men like me, out of favor with these democracies, fight and die. But if they weren't defended by soldiers like me, they'd risk losing their liberty.

Insoluble as usual.

Had war trapped me this time? Had I served her cause by making millions of men dream? Had she insidiously pushed me into giving her a seductive, romantic image?

I've just re-read *Les Centurions*. I hadn't opened it in fifteen years. My books are my lost children whom I never try to rediscover.

I will not repudiate my book. I sought only to describe men of goodwill at grips with contradictions, suffering and dying for them. At no moment did I celebrate war. They only fought the war because it was thrust upon them, never out of a taste for it, and they made every effort to limit its ravages—by being victorious.

I must recall for you here that in *Les Centurions* I never wanted to describe the French army, only a handful of men exceptional for their history and their behavior, men whom I made heroes of a novel but whom people then wanted to make a rightist sect in France, a leftist one in Portugal.

Once again, in 1967, I packed my suitcase to go see firsthand what appeared to be an affair of the Latin-

American guerrillas that people were making a big thing of, but which was really an affair of Fidel Castro and the revolution he wanted to extend to an entire continent. And of Ernesto "Che" Guevara, whom Fidel had given, or who had taken for himself, the mission of making the whole South American continent an immense Vietnam.

This time I took television equipment with me. It was time to familiarize myself with the technique that, to my regret, seemed likely to monopolize all the big news soon.

On the way, I went from Los Angeles to Mexico. It was a beautiful excursion, but the used car I bought turned out to be a dud. It ended up in a ditch north of Panama.

On to Havana. They photographed you when you boarded the plane, and on your passport they stamped your destination in large letters: CUBA. The hostess offered you one of those light green cigars, which an "instructor" taught you how to smoke, and a daiquiri, which had apparently become the official drink of all of Cuba's government hosts.

There still hung in the air of Havana whiffs of youth, of enthusiasm, of madness. Fidel hadn't yet completely sold his soul to the devil and his country to the U.S.S.R. But already the concentration camps were filling up with *gusanos*[79] and "earthworms," the enemies of the regime, some of whom had been Castro's companions in the Sierra.

Cuba was still revered among the intellectuals on the shores of the Seine. To express the least reserve about its regime was to commit a sacrilege. Castro, however, couldn't stand these "parasites," whatever country they came from, even the Communist poets like Pablo Neruda, even if they were Cuban, preferring sportsmen and technicians to any intellectuals. He soon began to launch into a spate of sarcasms against them, espe-

---

79. Grubs, maggots. (Translator's note.)

cially when they didn't lavish flattery and soft soap upon him with sufficient enthusiasm.

Being a writer myself and little endowed with the talent for showering anyone with flattery, and being catalogued as a reactionary, I hardly had a chance to see Castro.

After having inquired of me how much time I planned to spend in Cuba and received the response "ten days," they let me know that the *comandante* would not be able to receive me for a month. He was too busy with his sugar cane harvest. He was always occupied with something: zafra;[80] the cultivation of tomatoes in the Orient; his pilot farms where he went every day to taste the milk and the cheeses; the artificial insemination of cattle; the raising of rabbits, of goats, of crocodiles; his guerrilla training camps. Wasn't he President of the Council, Supreme Chief of the Army, Secretary General of the Communist party, Minister of Agrarian Reform, leader *maximo* and *orientador* of the armed revolution of all the Latin-American continent?[81]

Plus a few more sonorous titles I've forgotten.

I saw him from afar in the course of a great parade, at the end of which he gave an interminable speech.

With the exception of his beard, his size, his accouterments such as his cap, his olive green uniform, his outsized pistol fastened at his belt, he reminded me of Sihanouk. The same pathologically incoherent and repetitious speech, the same shrill little voice, the same oratorical procedures, the speech that became a dialogue, even megalomaniacal. Like the little Samdech, he wanted to be first everywhere and in everything, and he couldn't bear the least criticism. A critic was soon classified as a CIA agent, as was the case for the French agronomist Dumont, who found Castro's conception of agriculture utter nonsense and

80. The making of sugar. (Translator's note.)
81. *Les Guérilleros* (Presses de la Cité.)

dared tell him so. (I voted for him in our presidential elections.)

But there was nevertheless a great difference between the two men.

Sihanouk feared war. Castro loved it and considered that nothing good or worthwhile could be accomplished without it. Every struggle that wasn't armed rebellion was, according to him, necessarily doomed to defeat. And for him there could be no question of fighting a revolution in any fashion different from his, or of doing anything else in a fashion different from his.

He gave me the impression of being a big Galician peasant, rapacious, sly, vain, who'd studied a little. The entire island had become his private property, his *finca*.[82] He did everything himself, having no confidence in his majordomos (the ministers), his employees (the civil servants), or his laborers (the good Cuban people, who had been carried away, in his opinion, by rum, indolence, and girls, and who had to be kept firmly in hand). Fidel was a pure product of the education of the good fathers. He'd learned from his masters the taste for humiliating others and that need to know everything about those who surrounded him. His spies infiltrated everywhere, he had hotels and villas riddled with microphones, and he demanded the complete submission of everyone "for the greater glory of Fidel Castro and of his great works."

He was always searching for heresies to extirpate, devils to exorcise.

When I arrived in Cuba, they'd just adopted the *ley de vagos*.[83] The offenders risked forced labor. Later the workers, enrolled in the workers' brigades and encadred by officers, were obliged to don a uniform. No one protested, either in France or elsewhere. Fidel was sure of his coup. He'd known how to muzzle international opinion.

82. Land or estate. (Translator's note.)
83. Literally, law "against the idlers." It included not only those who refused to work in the areas designated them, but also those who refused to give up jobs they held to go cut sugar cane.

A worker who didn't work, or who practiced "absenteeism," in the Marxist jargon, was just a bad subject one could only reprimand, however rigorously, or fine. Dressed in a uniform he became a deserter, a spy, a saboteur. If he merely went to grab a snooze in the cover of a stack of sugar cane, he'd abandoned his post in the face of the enemy. There rose up the specters of the military tribunal and the execution post.

A South American historian, Aleides Alguedas, classified tyrants as follows: the barbarian tyrants, the lettered tyrants, the romantic tyrants, the insane tyrants. He forgot one category: the socialist tyrants, of which Castro became the tropical embodiment.

Malignant, sly, Fidel Castro had quickly understood that with a good secret police, with the alliance of the U.S.S.R. (he couldn't have survived without her), and with Communist ceremonials, he could allow himself to do what none of his colleagues of Haiti, of Santo Domingo, or of Paraguay had tried to do, and do it without raising international opinion against him.

He became the absolute king no legitimate sovereign would dare to be, bending the country to his fantasies and deliriums.

When I was in Havana, he'd taken it into his head to raise rabbits to offset the meat shortage. Everyone had to raise rabbits, to eat rabbits in every kind of recipe and with all kinds of sauces, in order to please the king. Everywhere restaurants were opening where only rabbit was served, and all the officials I met took me to eat Fidel's *conejos*.

Before that it had been goats, up until the day when Fidel noticed that the untethered goats destroyed trees and cultivated land. The goats were shot for sabotage at great expense to I'm not sure whom.

I'd used the services of a Cuban cameraman to film a demonstration. I asked of the *compañero* (there everyone used the familiar and everyone was called *compañero*), "What do I need?"

"A Rollex watch for underwater diving."

"Why a Rollex and not another?"

"Because Fidel has a Rollex, and if you want to be well thought of you must have a Rollex."

Fidel and his followers used only jeeps or Alfa-Romeos. For a courtier the supreme recognition was to obtain an Alfa-Romeo; it was a sign that he was close to God. This is what happened to Régis Debray,[84] whose head was completely turned by the attention he received. Nothing is more fragile than an intellectual who has fallen into the hands of a socialist tyrant who was raised by the Jesuits, is more seductive than a courtesan, and, moreover, is all the rage in Paris.

One day I was peacefully sitting in a ministry in Havana leafing through some documentation—the name given to propaganda in Cuba—with a large photo of Fidel on every page, when all of a sudden sirens began to blast. It was a general alert! The Americans, they said, had landed without warning on their shores. Everyone took on a fierce air, rose, seized his gun, and threw himself at his combat post.

I fell into step with a *compañero* whose fat rear was crammed into an olive green uniform. Seated behind some sacks of sand, we waited for the attack of the *gusanos* and their Yankee allies. I looked at his gun. It was badly kept and it had no breech.

The craftiness of Fidel: let his subjects play at being little soldiers, confident with weapons they can't fire, and mobilize them several times a week against imaginary perils.

A revolution where the people are armed with wooden rifles because the leader is afraid of the people.

If you were to ask me for a criterion of liberty, I'd give you this: you are free in a country where you may have a hunting gun and cartridges in your home.

84. French intellectual, writer, chronicler of Fidel, Che, Latin-American revolution, among other subjects. (Translator's note.)

Remember the Occupation[85] and the way hunting
rifles had to be stored in the town halls? In any Communist country, if you're not part of the machinery of
government, you have no right to own a hunting gun.
The day they begin to want to register, then collect,
hunting guns, watch out. Your liberty is about to be
taken from you.

Fidel had to make some of the intellectuals of his
stable confess to imaginary faults, require them to
make degrading admissions to being the homosexuals
he'd accused them of being (as in the case of the poet
Padilla), had to appear to be miserly, to see that the in-
vitations to the great fêtes at the Hall of the Congress
of the Americas became rare, before the Parisian intellectuals finally became aroused and saw the light.

Fortunately there was Chile and Allende. People
rushed there.

If you remember, Castro, president of the students'
union, had wanted to seize the barracks of Moncada,
had gone to jail, and had then rallied with friends in
Mexico. He'd returned to Cuba on a leaky old tub, the
Gamma, with eighty-two companions, including an Ar-
gentinian doctor collected along the way—Ernesto
"Che" Guevara.

The landing went badly. Fidel and his men came
upon Batista's troops, who were waiting for them. Soon
he had only a dozen men left. But they reached the Sierra Maestra. A magnificent adventure!

Twelve badly armed men along with the volunteers
they'd picked up along the way were going to rout an
army of several thousand men equipped with ultramodern material.

The dice were loaded in their favor.

Batista's army, despite its material, wasn't worth a
tinker's dam. They'd indulged in all sorts of extortion
schemes and had become unpopular. The Castroists
had at their command the support of the population,

85. Of France. (Translator's note.)

both the country people and the students in the cities, the small and great bourgeoisie, from which Castro had come. They'd all had enough of Batista, that coarse and primitive individual who'd sprung from the people, and of his corrupt regime.

He'd let his country out to the Mafia, and the island had become an immense brothel and gambling den. Castro and his men could count on the benevolent neutrality of the United States and on certain complicities of foreign ambassadors. No, you're going to be wrong—not the ambassador of the U.S.S.R. or of the Eastern countries, but of Spain, for one. Franco's Falangists were squarely behind him before he was touched by Marxist grace and his brother Raûl taught him the catechism.

Fidel, now in power and under the influence of Che Guevara, began to dream. Fidel the realist, Fidel the common man. He would be the new Bolivar who would free Latin America of its chains and of the imperialism of the dollar. All by the only means he understood: armed conflict.

One of his first errors was to believe that the tactics he'd employed in conquering his island could be utilized in the Latin-American countries. Born of necessity, those tactics had consisted of the formation of small groups which infiltrated the population outside the cities; then the creation of *focos,* centers of guerrilla activities into which were integrated valid local elements; and finally a superior stage, the development of a veritable army composed of mobile columns capable of seizing the principal urban centers.

Cuban-style guerrillas outside of Cuba met defeat everywhere for having wanted to follow the Castroist plan too closely, for having ignored national peculiarities and run slap at traditional Communist parties.

In Latin America these latter were rather conservative. Our Communists see themselves taking power with a certain strict Marxist legality. The Latin Americans already spoke yesterday as Marchais does today and didn't hesitate to ally themselves with bourgeois parties. They were ahead even of the Italians with their tastes for comfort and full bank accounts.

When I asked that Castro's military theories be explained to me, that someone also explain to me the new face he wanted to give to revolutionary war, I was advised to read the book *Révolution dans la révolution,* which he'd just published under the signature of Régis Debray, a young French intellectual whom they called brilliant, but who'd done no more than ghost-write for Castro.

I was led to understand that Che had been given the task of applying that doctrine in the field and that the revolution was on the march. Fidel, after having been Napoleon in the Sierra Maestra, had now become Clausewitz and had taken on a little Sorbonnard as his secretary.

I'm not going to give a résumé of that extremely confusing book, in which some passages smack more of the lucubrations of Sapeur Camember than of subversive or revolutionary tactics. The Vietnam War, to give an example, is very badly analyzed, even more badly understood. Finally, the Latin-American temperament is completely neglected, and the adversary, the Yankee, underestimated.

After Che's guerrilla-warfare defeat, Fidel let Debray go and said that the Frenchman was the sole author of the book and that he'd failed to understand his lessons.

The countries of Latin America seem always to have been dedicated to social injustice, and their political regimes to disgusting you with humanity itself: Nicaragua's Somoza, Santo Domingo's Trujillo, Haiti's Papa Doc. Then periodically a Don Quixote comes along who decides to clean out these stables, to restore to the most disinherited individuals, to the poor peons, the Indians, a certain human dignity and enough food to fill their bellies. This Don Quixote never comes from the people, but always from the oligarchy, those great families who've gathered between their hands all the power and all the culture of their countries.

Everything happens, every revolutionary experience takes place, every stance is held, within the circle of the same families, both guerrilla movements and counter-guerrilla movements. Cousins are to be found on both sides of the barricades. A young man can let his rifle or his machine gun fall to go dance with a pretty cousin beneath the bright lights of an old Spanish palace.

At Caracas one of these young men of the oligarchy gave a huge reception for everyone who counted in the city, to celebrate his departure—to the underground.

These sons of the oligarchy don't want for either temperament or courage. They may even have too much. They will say anything at all, do anything at all. They are forever changing their ideas, and they go from the heat of passion to indolence, from enthusiasm to despair, all very quickly—too quickly. They adore fine speeches, are capable of giving up everything for love, of risking everything out of bravado. They still have those qualities now lost in Europe—a species of savagery and of violence, mixed with wild romanticism and a profound authenticity.

They are the opposite of our French intellectuals, who are dry and peremptory, but don't know the least thing about a rifle drill manual. Below the Río Bravo one is born with a pistol in his cradle. When Régis Debray involved himself in Bolivia's guerrilla war, it was a catastrophe. He understood none of it. To discover how little he understood, one has only to read the journal of Che Guevara, who was so fed up with that parrot that he gently begged him to leave and to go to Paris to form a support committee for the revolution.

Unhappily these young revolutionaries age quickly, and in a few years Don Quixotes become Sancho Panzas and open-numbered bank accounts in Switzerland.

You meet an extraordinary young man, an authentic revolutionary, generous, disinterested, sincere, who honestly wants to bring about that which is good for the people, wants to break up the feudal structures

that hinder the country's progress. Three years later
you find him at the head of the country, having become
more conservative than the predecessor he'd forced out
or replaced after elections with a program that claims
kinship with social justice, with progress, and with the
revolution, but that is far removed from them.

It was at Bogotá in Colombia, the country of violence . . . hold on; there comes to my mind another
face of war I'd almost forgotten about: a seven-year
civil war had pitted against each other two parties
that had held power consecutively, the conservatives
and the liberals, with programs so similar it was difficult to distinguish between them, and with leaders all
recruited from the same circles. This civil war sur-
passed in horror anything yet known, the two parties
confronting each other through the *bandoleros* each
engaged to do their dirty work. Kidnapping, assassination, rape, followed by evisceration, castration—all
were the stage settings for death. In one place, all the
passengers of a bus were decapitated and their heads
carefully placed on their knees. In another place, all
the men of the village had their throats opened and
their tongues drawn out through their throats. That
was called *"coupe cravate."* Then there was *"coupe
télévision,"* where a hole was cut in the chest with a
machete and the head forced into it. Another time all
the musicians of the conservatory, who were making a
trip by bus, were decapitated by the liberal *bandoleros.*
Belonging to the conservatory, the musicians could
only be conservative.

In Bogotá I was shown hundreds of photographs; it
was enough to make me vomit.

Contingents of the civil war, the *comisiones,* went out
from the capital and devastated the countryside.
Drunk, they pillaged and slaughtered for the simple
pleasure of it. They tortured. They raped young girls
and children. Merry policemen brandished freshly cut
heads. *Comisiones* rested complacently in front of lines
of cadavers whose throats had been cut. Heads were

lined up on the lip of a well. Old people who'd been hanged swayed from the branches of trees.

They killed children especially, crucifying them on barn doors. Sadism? Worse. Realism. Each party had decided to destroy the other down to the last seed. Then, when the liberals and the conservatives had finally decided to make peace with each other, the guerrillas succeeded them and rallied the *bandoleros* to them, while the first group now joined the ranks of the counterguerrillas.

And so it continued. The army, which had remained neutral, now stepped in. Country people were burned alive in their homes; prisoners were thrown from planes into the guerrilla-occupied zones; there were mass rapes after which the victims were disemboweled with bayonets.

Things were no better on one side than on the other, until finally even the Castroists and the Communists were slaughtering one another.

And the origin of that insane mass fit was a stupid story of cuckoldry. A certain Roa accused his mistress of deceiving him with the mail carrier. And when it became apparent to him that the public thought him to be *sin cojones*[86] on her account, he had to prove that he did indeed have balls. For no other reason than to demonstrate his virility, his machismo, he shot the man of the day, the man most spoken of in the country, the liberal leader Gaïten.

Five thousand deaths in Bogotá in three days. Three hundred thousand in the combined countries from 1948 to 1966, and sixty thousand houses burned or otherwise destroyed.

But to return to Bogotá and what I wanted to say: One night I was at the home of Lopez Michelson, head of the opposition, of whom it was said that he'd allied the Communists and the guerrillas.

He'd asked me to stay with him. He thought that a

86. Without testicles. (Translator's note.)

move was going to be made against him and that the presence of a foreign journalist would keep death at bay.

We got drunk on cognac. Every five minutes the phone rang, announcing the arrest of this person, or the flight of another, or the liquidation pure and simple of another.

Dawn came and Lopez Michelson breathed a long sigh. He had one more day to live.

Just the other day I opened a newspaper and read that Lopez Michelson had become president of the Republic of Colombia, elected by the conservatives.

Strange, these guerrillas! They all say that they're fighting for an idea, that they want to change man, to improve him, to raise him so that he may enjoy a happier life, may come to know peace, security, justice. And that these can only be obtained by war. I believe, though—alas!—that before anything else, they love war, the romantic image of war. The other, the true revolutionary war, the war of the Vietminh they ceaselessly refer to, claim to be emulating, they don't really want any part of. She demands too much application, too much seriousness.

I followed Che Guevara all over Latin America, everywhere he indicated to me that he might be, but I failed to meet up with him. I'd barely arrived at La Paz in Bolivia when I contacted the representatives of seven or eight of the shades of the Bolivian Communist party. One evening some of them came to find me at my hotel. After we'd changed cars three or four times and climbed up and down all over the city, we finally arrived at a little house in a remote quarter. They served me very bad alcohol while a voluble and agitated man who neither introduced himself nor was introduced to me began a one-sided discussion with me on the subject of the revolution of 1798, the commune, Jean-Jacques Rousseau, and all the great principles of revolution. It was deadly dull, and I wanted to fall asleep through it. He talked and talked until I finally made my escape.

Later I learned that I'd been in the company of one of the brothers Peredo, one of Che's adjutants. After that information mission of his to La Paz in which he was to contact occidental journalists, I being one of them, he'd left to rejoin Che.

Instead of that show of erudition, he could just as well have said to me, "Come with me to Nancahuazu, to the Camirini *finca*, where you'll find the one you're looking for."

I tried to understand that woolly-headed, exciting, passionate, garrulous side of the Latin-American guerrillas which could lead to a Don Quixote, to deaths like that of Che Guevara, or to the gross Sancho Panzas, such as Fidel Castro, who run their countries like private estates where they exercise absolute power. Who also can't pay their debts and sell their soldiers to Russia as mercenaries.

Don Quixote is often sick and nervous, while Sancho Panza is always hearty. Che was afflicted with a chronic illness, a severe asthmatic condition which had often threatened his life as a child and which had made it necessary for his parents to abandon Buenos Aires in order to move to the foot of the mountains of Alta Gracia. He'd always had to fight his illness, and he hated being different from others.

One of his friends told me that as a young man he'd played soccer, not recommended for an asthmatic. He ran behind the ball while his friend remained out of the game, keeping at hand a kind of pump, an inhalator. As soon as Guevara began to wheeze, the friend went quickly to his side to administer two or three bursts of air from the pump, thus allowing Guevara to continue the game. At seventeen Guevara made a bicycle trip through Argentina, his inhalator always in his pocket.

When he became a doctor, he specialized in allergies, always hoping he'd find a way to cure them. But asthma, as we know, is a psychosomatic disease.

Something of his background: Through his mother

Celia, known by the surname "*La Rabalda,*" he was descended from the last Spanish Viceroy of Peru. Through his father he was half Irish, Guevara-Lynch. And before his parents went through their fortune, they'd taken courses from ballet dancers, singers, and musicians.

Ernesto Guevara suffered from being from a great family and at the same time not being able to continue in his station among the greats. It gave him a sharp taste for provocation. At the finest hotels in Buenos Aires, for example, he would arrive in dungarees or rags, with varicolored espadrilles on his feet.

His grand plan, when he came to power in Cuba and was named director of the National Bank by Castro, was to abolish money, a plan that had, at the very least, astonishing results. In *Socialism and the Cuban Man,* he wrote, "There can be no question of the profit motive nor of material profit." He signed his notes with his pseudonym, Che, and refused to put his name to International Monetary Funds, which had rendered Cuban money valueless to the foreigner.

Miguel-Angel Asturias told me that he'd once visited the National Bank and that in the middle of a vehement speech against money, Che had been overcome by an asthma attack, had fallen to the floor, and had lain stretched out, arms extended in the form of a cross, on the marble of the great hall.

"Crucified on the marble of a bank," Asturias repeated.

That hard and difficult man who didn't hesitate to preside at the execution of numerous partisans and officers of Batista[87] felt the need to be protected by women older than he. He always had a very deep love

---

87. At Cabona, Che watched the executions from a balcony. The commandant they'd just shot was taking his time about dying, so one of the soldiers of the firing squad asked Che, "Should we give him the *coup de grâce*?"

Dr. Ernesto Guevara answered, "No, the *pobrecito* [poor little thing] has lost enough blood."

And they let the man writhe in pain for a long time, refusing to put him out of his agony.

for his mother, "*La Rabalda.*" And when he married for the first time, he married a nurse who could care for him during his asthmatic attacks. He was obsessed with the possibility of those attacks, which could overtake him at any time.

I don't think he was politically a good Marxist. The trip he'd taken to the U.S.S.R. had cured him. He'd submitted himself to Castro's enterprise at the same time that he'd revolted against him. I imagine he had as much of Don Quixote in him as of Sancho Panza. Castro always remained the upstart in his eyes, with his gross cigars, his boasting, his self-conceit, his ambition to own the earth.

Castro wanted everything. Guevara wanted nothing. And Che was a pessimist forced to face the probability that his Bolivian guerrilla war, conceived contrary to all common sense and having drawn him away from his own land, Argentina, was an escapade of the Knight of the Sorrowful Countenance who'd attacked the windmills one too many times.

Money had already crucified him on the floor of the bank. The misunderstood revolution would finish him off in the Valle Grande washhouse, which served as a morgue in the Hospital of the Knights of Malta.

That death of Che, who'd been abandoned by everyone, made me reflect:

> In the course of the whole of the war in Indochina, in our seven years, it had been impossible for the French army to capture a single leader of the Viet zone. They were, however, neither causes nor symbols in themselves, but good regional executants.
>
> But in Latin America they'd let a sick man like Che act as infantry advance man in an underground made up of men of every kind who could not get along with each other because they hadn't the same ideologies and didn't pursue the same goal.[88]

88. *Les Guérilleros* (Presses de la Cité).

Latin-American guerrilla wars, the insouciance and the madness of those who directed them, their lack of military or political culture, however much they lay claim to both, have no relationship whatever to the teachings of Marx, of Mao Tse-tung, or of Giap.

They're all offspring of Bolivar, of Sucre, of the great Spanish authors—of Cervantes and of Miguel de Unamuno, who wrote:

> What kind of collective madness, what delirium, do we inculcate in these poor multitudes? We're going to be guilty of an outrage, going to launch ourselves into a new and holy crusade to go and reconquer the tomb of Don Quixote who, as everyone knows, never really existed.

The quest for an empty tomb.

Here is another disconcerting face of war in Latin America:

It is the young aristocratic or upper-middle-class guerrillas whose generous blood, surging with noble thoughts and revolutionary ideas, goes to their heads and impels them to strive to bring to the disinherited of their countries a certain dignity. The disinherited can think only of stuffing their bellies because they are starving to death; they can't understand what's being done for them, because they can neither read nor write.

Then if the young *guérilleros* aren't killed by an uncle or a cousin who commands an army or the police, they settle down, return to their old stations in life, and profit, with all the excess natural to these extravagant people, from anything and everything that will bring them power and wealth—until their sons revolt against them in their turn and make for their Sierra.

Guerrilla warfare there sometimes takes on an aspect of a gigantic farce, one in which the actors kill.

At the University of Caracas in Venezuela, I met the principal leaders of the guerrilla war, or those who made themselves out to be the leaders. All carried the rank of *comandante* to emulate Fidel. They were all jealous of one another, denounced one another, accused one another of all the sins of "ism." The police easily found out all they needed to know about them. They merely had to plant an informer in a corner bistro— what do I mean, informer?—even a simple policeman in uniform would do the trick.

One day the army had had enough and penetrated the sacrosanct precincts of the university. There were protests in the name of all the great principles against this violation of an ancient privilege, but protest was all anyone could do, even when the army brought out eight truckloads of weapons, among which was a heavy antiaircraft machine gun of Czech make weighing at least a ton. What was such a weapon doing there?

All these weapons belonged in the underground, but the Maquis were bored to death in the Sierra. The peasants and the Indians were too thick-headed to be educated, and while the Maquis might be willing to die, they were not willing to die of boredom.

There was, I'm trying to say, nothing whatever to be seen of the chill organization of the Vietminh, where the individual is strictly encadred, where he is only a cogwheel in an enormous machine designed to leave nothing at all to improvisation. Romanticism—even supposing it could begin to exist—is quickly stifled by a pitiless bureaucracy.

In Latin America there is no bureaucracy, except in Cuba. And yet even there the only organization that functions correctly is that of "Barbarossa," Commander Pineiro, who heads the political police and personally concerns himself with spontaneous confessions.

Everything else, everywhere else, is an immense disorder that drives the Soviet experts crazy.

I'm going to speak to you now of the soldier who is the most remarkable of all of war's servants, superior even to the Viet, and who at the same time detests war the most—the Israeli soldier. He greets you with the

word *"Shalom!"* which means "peace" in Hebrew, but
has undergone and won four wars in twenty-five years.
They were real wars, with thousands of tanks facing
each other in the sands of the Sinai or on the rocky
heights of Golan, with machine gun–equipped super-
sonic jets over the Mediterranean. The cause of these
wars was a city called "holy," Jerusalem, which to me
is accursed. People have fought for her for twenty centuries, and those who have lost her never stop dreaming of winning her back.

> Jerusalem, if I should forget you,
> May my right hand disappear . . .
> May my tongue stick in my throat,
> If I should not think well of you . . .

For twenty centuries the Jews of the Diaspora in-
toned this psalm in their synagogues. And the young
Sabras of the kibbutzes of Galilee now chant:

> If I should forget you, Jerusalem,
>   Jerusalem of pure gold,
> May your name burn my lips like a kiss
>   of the Angel of Fire
> Jerusalem of gold, of copper, of light.

Listen to her story. Her origins are Egyptian and
Canaanian, and that was her most peaceful period. Her
inhabitants were largely involved in commerce, she
being at the crossroads of the great caravan routes.
They worshipped the gods of the Nile and of Phoenicia.
Their priestesses were the sacred prostitutes who
enriched and set off the treasures of each sanctuary as
they sold themselves to the passing foreigners. And the
city was like them, a saint and a whore at one and the
same time.

Ten centuries before our era David seized Jerusalem,
made her his capital, and took the Ark of the Covenant
there. His God Jehovah, the one and jealous god, god of

the armies, clung determinedly to his title, given him when Solomon had built him the Temple after the design of the sanctuary of Baal. He proceeded against all who roused his anger, and any who refused to acknowledge him were put to the sword. Jerusalem was retaken by the Egyptians, razed by the Assyrians and Nebuchadnezzar, rebuilt upon the orders of Cyrus, taken by Alexander the Great. Greek was then spoken in Jerusalem; Greek characters were written, even in the sacred books. The court of the Temple was transformed into a gymnasium, and the statue of Zeus rose up. Jehovah agonized. He was returned to power in the orthodoxy of the Maccabee brothers, and the athletes were dispersed, the priests brought back. The Romans seized Jerusalem and gave it to Herod Antipas, who mistrusted all gods and honored them all. He rebuilt the Temple and raised the walls of the city.

Then was born the Christ who would die upon the cross, condemned to death by his own people while Rome's representative washed his hands, inaugurating a tradition all administrations would follow. A new religion was born which would spread throughout the entire world. Already the holy city of the Jews, Jerusalem became the holy city of the Christians.

In the year 70 of our era, the Jews revolted and massacred the Roman garrison. After a seemingly interminable siege, Titus's Legionnaires completely razed the city, massacring or selling as slaves all its inhabitants. They even changed the city's name, dedicating her to Jupiter.

Then Constantine was converted to Christianity and reconstructed the city, making her a Christian Jerusalem, which a Sassanian king then seized. Then the Byzantines. Then the Arabs. The Caliph Omar built a mosque on the site of the Temple, made Jerusalem one of the three holy cities of Islam, and baptized her "venerable sanctuary."

In the eleventh century the crusaders seized her. The narrow streets ran with the blood of Jews and Moslems.

The crusaders remained there a hundred years, after
which Saladin overcame them. Then the crusaders were
once more victorious, then the Arabs, then the Mon-
gol hordes, then the Turks.

Suleiman the Magnificent fell in love with her and
gave her a chain of walls made of beautiful bronze-col-
ored stone. Once more there followed revolts drowned
in blood and massacres, added to by the unrelenting
hatred between the priests and the faithful of three religions, all of whom worshipped the same God.

In 1917 the English succeeded the Turks, and the
Jews of the Diaspora hastened back. It was the return
to the Promised Land.

In 1948 the Jewish homeland, Palestine, became the
state of Israel. Jews and Jordanians fought violently
over Jerusalem, and again blood flowed. The Jordanians kept the old city, the Jews the new, which they'd
partly built. But hundreds of thousands of Palestinians
were chased from their homes, themselves now to know
exile and dispersion.

1967: Moshe Dayan's parachutists conquered the old
city. Jerusalem was entirely annexed, which pleased
the Jews but displeased the Christians and the Moslems.

1972: The war began again, that of Yom Kippur.
Throughout the centuries thousands and thousands of
men have died for that city, for an empty sepulchre,
for what remained of a temple, of a wall, for a bit of
rock from which Mohammed and his horse mounted to
heaven, and on which a blue mosque was built.

If I were to have to name a capital city for war, it
would be Jerusalem.

Not very long ago I walked around that fascinating
and frightening city, where within the space of a few
weeks a liberal Jew can be transformed into a fanatic
nationalist, a Bethlehem Christian into a terrorist, and
agnostics like myself can feel the reflexes of a crusader.
I could read on all the faces I saw that anguish, that
fear, that hatred. Arabs were always ready to leap at

the throats of the Jews and to throw their bombs. The Jews lay in wait and blew up houses all over the swarming places sacred to them for their saints and their tombs, the houses of whole quarters of the city where another kind of excavation was being made to recover the whitened bones of their past.

When the Six Day War broke out, I was in Mexico visiting the Tarahumaras Indians, peyote eaters and indefatigable runners. They live in the mountains of Mexico north of Chihuahua, completely isolated, without radios or electricity, with not a single tie to the rest of the world.

The Six Day War began and ended without my having known anything about it. I missed the defeat of three Arab armies, the capture of Jerusalem, of the Sinai, of Golan, of Cisjordan. All in six days. And this by an unknown army made up of men who, by tradition, were unfit for combat, endowed only with talents for intellectual speculation and for business.

Had war perhaps rejected me because I'd become skeptical about her? Because I'd come to believe she settles nothing, solves no problems?

No, she'd only made me wait a little. I was asked to write a book about the Israeli army: *Tsahal.* In Israel the army has a name and seems to have an autonomous existence: *Tsahal* said, *Tsahal* did this or that, *Tsahal* thinks, *Tsahal* decides.

I agreed to write the book.

I arrived in Jerusalem on May 2, 1968, for the commemoration of the twentieth anniversary of the state of Israel and for the solemn marriage of *Tsahal* with Jerusalem.

I attended an immense march, where I made my first acquaintance with the army. It couldn't march well, it had many women in it, and it was largely equipped with patched-together equipment. The soldiers wore their hair long or short according to their whims, they looked down at-the-heel, and they advanced too quickly. No one wore any decorations, and they all looked as

though they wanted to give the impression of being incurable civilians.

Ben Gurion, the creator and father of that army, had
declined to sit in the official stands, and his head shone
out two tiers below me. An Israeli diplomat said to me,
"I'm afraid the nuptials of Jerusalem with our army
will be bloody nuptials. Some of us in my ministry en-
tertain the hope that we can give the holy city an international status, make her the capital of world peace.
But it's difficult to refuse so fine a marriage, even if it
means we lose by it. We've loved and desired Jerusalem so much. The problem is that, sadly, we're not the
only ones who've loved her, who still love her.

"Beyond Solomon's walls live sixty thousand Arabs
who've determined, come what may, never to abandon
'their city.' "

A few days later I was at Golan Heights with a parachute unit whose lives and dangers I shared.

May 1968, and I knew nothing of what was happening apart from some sketchy news I overheard over the
bad transistor radio of a soldier who preferred rock and
who soon interrupted the news program. Fortunately,
what was apparently happening was a farce in which
urchins and old men were enjoying themselves. None
of them being interesting, war let them alone. There
were no deaths, merely a few skirmishes with the police and the C.R.S., bringing out a generation of combatants, those of a war or of a revolution the youths
hadn't yet seen. It required all their imagination to believe the old ones.

It wasn't easy to penetrate the secrets of *Tsahal*. I
was a stranger and I wasn't a Jew. Nevertheless I
enjoyed a certain presumption in my favor, thanks to
Les Centurions, some pages of which were read in the
parachutists' instruction centers.

"I have commanded," Raspéguy said, "the Thais, the
Vietnamese, the Chinese, Spanish refugees, Courbevoie
laborers, and Landes peasants. I could as well command the Jews if I were asked. I would give them a

yellow star for their insignia. The Nazis made it a mark of shame. I would make it a flag. We'd cover it with so much glory that even the Arabs and the blacks would be proud to fight beneath it. But first I'd make my Jews undergo two hours a day of physical culture, to make them as proud of their bodies as they can be of their courage. . . ."

It took me several weeks to realize fully that there didn't exist a regular army in permanent cadres in Israel, that all of Israel was one vast army and one fortified camp.

Ben Gurion, the "old lion," who'd also been baptized the "armed prophet" and who in 1916 had been the worst corporal in the British army, had created *Tsahal* with two aims in view: to defend Israel, and to make the army a sort of melting pot where all the non–Hebrew-speaking emigrants of over twenty countries could mix and find their places. The army was both a school and a training center out of which came a particular kind of person: the Israeli, very different from the ghetto Jew.

I interviewed all the generals of the armored divisions, the parachutists, and the air force who'd won that Six Day War: Moshe Dayan, the one-eyed man they called cynical; Rabin, who they claimed was fragile; Ezer Weizmann, who was hotheaded; Mordechai Hod, who asked me for fighter bombers; Yariv, who was gray and peaceable, but commanded the secret services; Ariel Sharon, who'd have liked the entire army to be parachutists. Also the armored division colonel who at El Kuneitra on the Golan Heights told me he could take Damas in seven hours. And General Chaike Gavish, who was the only one to tell me (at Gaza) he liked war. And General Tol, who said through thin lips, "The destiny of a people fashions its conduct, as destiny has made us a nation of warriors." All the generals were very young. The age limit for a commander in chief was forty-five.

As my research progressed, I perceived that Israel, a democratic country where everyone could think and speak as he pleased, cohabited with another country, *Tsahal*, where everything was secret and subject to captious, even absurd censorship. There was the state of Israel with its president, a figurehead; its president of the council; its ministers; and the parliament, the Knesset, which apparently possessed all the powers of the government. And alongside this was *Tsahal*, the army, which also had its government and its ministers. The one seated in Jerusalem, the other in Tel-Aviv.

Golda Meir reunited her cabinet to the council presidency, the cabinet seated in her kitchen, where everything was decided. While she stirred her pots, she clarified and perfected her small schemes and grand plans. Then the Minister of Defense, Moshe Dayan, jumped into his car and drove to Tel-Aviv and military headquarters, where another get-together was held. Dayan made his report before the "committee" of generals and the old chiefs of the general staff. They studied the repercussions the measures taken in Jerusalem might have on the army. And taking the view that what was good for *Tsahal* was good for Israel, they asked for, sometimes demanded, certain modifications, when they didn't abrogate some of the measures outright.

Today it appears that the two governments have blended. The council president is an old chief of staff of the general staff, General Rabin. His assistant is General Sharon, and his vice-president is another old chief of staff, General Yigal Allon.

The Israeli army was born of the revolutionary ideas of Orde Wingate, mentioned earlier in this book, the father of the "Chindits" of the Far East whose training I followed. Wingate made my task [in Israel] easier by giving me some of the keys I needed to understand that army which clung to its secrecy.

Wingate was the first to say to the Jews that they can become excellent soldiers without having to confine themselves within the rigid codes of traditional armies. He teaches them how to fight by night, because Arabs fear the night. He requires them to know their country by night, because a country isn't the same in full daylight as it is in the darkness. He is creating, under the cover of training auxiliary Jewish police, midnight battalions, the first veritable regular units of the Haganah.[89]

After his departure the Haganah continued with his methods, particularly suited to a clandestine army with scanty means. The army kept its taste for darkness, for parallel hierarchies, even when she came out into the open after her sometimes dramatic demonstrations of unity (Irgoun and Stern against the Haganah, and within the Haganah conflicts between the regular units and the shock units, the Palmach). Until after the Six Day War, she remained a group of commandos as economical of her materials as of the life of her men, and by preference operating behind the enemy lines, using daring and surprise.

Reservists constitute the major part of the army—240,000 for the 60,000 regulars, a quarter of the reservists being women. The reservist keeps his own uniform, equipment, and individual weapons, as the Swiss do. He may be mobilized at any moment if there is a threat of a conflict, and also to participate in a limited operation, such as a raid on enemy territory, when he may be sent out for three days and then return, always with the greatest secrecy. He first serves for three years as an active soldier, and then goes into the reserves, where he may serve up to three months a year and undergo rigorous and intensive training. He must never forget that since its creation, Israel has always been in a state of war. Should he forget it, as at Yom Kippur, he'll regret it.

A radio signal, a note in cipher, a sentence in code, a telephone call—and our reservist can, in a matter of minutes, equip and ready himself and then, in a matter

89. *Les Murailles* (walls) *d'Israël* (Press Pocket).

of hours, by hitchhiking or by taking his own car or that of a friend, report to his base. The base is generally underground, and here is where is found the heavy equipment—the cannons, the tanks, vehicles of every kind. A whole division will exit from out of the sand. The major bases are often hidden in the Negev desert or next to kibbutzes that are responsible for them.

Less than twenty-four hours may elapse between the moment when a reservist of an armored brigade is called and that when he is engaged with his tank on the battlefield.

Tsahal has a conception of discipline totally different from ours, much less strict, much more profound.

The soldier addresses his chief in the familiar; calls him, even if he's a general, by his first name; lives just as he does; and eats the same food. The simple soldier knows very nearly as much as his section chief about tactics and armaments and could replace him at any moment. Behind the lines he may debate indefinitely with his chief, but in combat he obeys instantly, because his chief has earned his rank, has stood the tests and proved himself. The soldier has confidence in him and admires him. An officer who isn't supported by his men is quickly recalled. Israel is the only country where, at no matter what echelon, a chief, be he captain or general or commander of a division, may be relieved of his command even in the middle of a battle. Without damages! His adjutant, or the adjutant of that adjutant, must always be ready to replace him at a moment's notice. In that army there's no such order as "Forward!" The officer—the chief—always goes before his men and has replaced that order with "Follow me!" Hence the large number of losses in the higher ranks, though this is less serious than in any other army, because an officer can be made instantly from a simple soldier. Nothing is codified; everything is tacit. The state of Israel has no constitution and her army no regulations.

An army such as that, with no need for exterior

signs of respect, where standing at attention is unknown, must be remarkably trained just in order to
maintain its cohesion. More than that, it must be remarkably motivated.

An Israeli goes into the army at fourteen, joining a
paramilitary unit for youths called Gadna. Here is
shaped a spirit and a common behavior. Boys and girls
undergo the same regime, and the girls are often in
command of the boys. Gadna is dependent upon the
army, and the mandatory courses of instruction are
spread out over four years, after which time the young
men and women go into a regular army unit, where
military service, properly speaking, will last three
years. Training is pushed to the limit, but is always
based on the principle inculcated in the midnight battalions created by Wingate, a principle that perfectly
suits the Jewish temperament: the individual with all
his qualities and his initiatives, instead of being ground
down by idiotic discipline, is exalted, confirmed in his
qualities and his faults. Confidence is placed in him,
and he is expected to get along in combat with the
means given him, even should they not be sufficient.
He's told the general direction of an operation in which
he's involved, and he must be capable, even if he loses
all his chiefs, even if there is no one left to give him orders, to pull himself through alone.

For a long time people have sought to explain the
failure of the Palestinian resistance in occupied territories by the refusal of the population to support the
Fedayin infiltrators. The Fedayin thus had to move
through deserted zones where they were soon spotted
by radar and the air force. The real reason isn't that.
The Fedayin found himself face-to-face with an army
that wasn't classical, that instead was made up of
small, autonomous, well-trained, fast-moving groups,
capable of acting independently, without the need to
refer to anyone else at all.

Their motivation is evident. The Israelis have no
choice. They must fight and win, win without ceasing,

or they will disappear. They know no one is going to
give them anything. Their backs to the Wall of Lamen-
tations, they've been dropped by most of the countries
they counted on. France was the first. They fear the
United States will follow. And they are so few in number. Hardly three million facing one hundred million
Arabs. The Haiku I used as an introduction to my book
Le Sang sur les collines applies to them.

> Nighttime
> Facing an immense army
> Two men
> In their hole.

I witnessed the Yom Kippur War—or rather I
glimpsed it—from the Arab side. In Syria, in the port of
Latakia, cargo ships flying Russian and East German
flags unloaded missiles, tanks, MiGs, rockets, but I didn't
pay them much attention. On the way from the mountain post of Faraya I'd seen a battle between Syrian
MiGs and Israeli Mirages that had ended in defeat for
the Syrians. What was there to fear?

Later, after war had been declared, from the terrace
of an inn at the foot of Mount Hermon, as I drank raki
and ate *"mezzés,"* I saw another sky battle. I was a
privileged spectator at one of death's great circus
shows. The fight was between a Syrian SAM, a rocket-
propelled aircraft, and an Israeli Phantom. The SAM
was the hawk and the Phantom the lark. In the hawk
was an electronic brain, and in the Phantom was a
sweating, anxious pilot. The Phantom tried to escape
and dove, climbed, and veered across the skies. The
hawk, more rapid, more flexible, pursued him. Then
the hawk struck and the Phantom exploded. A blind
rocket had defeated one of Israeli's magnificently
trained young pilots, one of the best in the world. But
on the ground, in what will perhaps be his last victory,
that long-haired Israeli boy who lounges in the bars of
Tel-Aviv will win over the machines. Thanks to the

very particular character of that army, the least disciplined and the most disciplined of the world, the battles that unfolded during the Yom Kippur War didn't mean the same kind of catastrophe for the Israelis that they might have meant for someone else. A classical army such as ours, or that of the United States, even Giap's, finding itself in a similar situation, would have been swept away.

On the eve of the Yom Kippur War, Israel was caught up in a paroxysm of triumphalism. Everywhere Dayan spoke of the ten years of tranquility they'd had. For the first time in her history Israel commanded safe borders, and her principal centers were all protected from surprise attack.

She celebrated Yom Kippur with joy and with total unconcern about her security. Any mistrust of her neighbors slept. Israel finally knew peace, could luxuriate in it and in idleness, in becoming a society of conspicuous consumers. Her politicians subtly disputed with one another in learned discourse, arguing like rabbis over the meaning of a word. And everyone accepted the principle of returning the occupied territories, where necessary creating in them military colonies and kibbutzes, "Nachals." Israel was in grave danger of peace.

Everyone was on vacation in the Negev, in the occupied territories, in the Sinai, in Jordan.

Israel's positions on the Suez Canal appeared to be so secure that they were held only by small units of reservists, the greater part of the army being on leave.

Hadn't they, after all, constructed a veritable fortified line facing the Egyptians? It was the Bar Lev line,[90] a kind of Maginot line crammed with tricks to

90. The Bar Lev, or Barlev, line was named after Israel's chief of staff and was built to hold the waterline against the Egyptians. Mobile patrols were to protect the line between the strongholds, and mobile armored troops were prepared to move to any point on the line that appeared to be in danger. This was referred to as the

catch the enemy: along the full length of the line ran pipes which could at a signal spill out streams of oil, turning the putrid waters of the Nile into flaming barrages. At great cost they'd also erected a huge, impassable polygon of sand which cut off advances by enemy tanks, and behind it concrete blockhouses. The Israeli had ceased to be a commando. They'd transformed him into a sand crab. The intelligence services, the Massad, Modiin, Shin Beth, whom everyone believed in, who were supposed to be infallible, let themselves become intoxicated with what appeared to them to be the direction of the danger. Obsessed by the struggle against Palestinian terrorism, they forgot military intelligence. And the *whole* time it was possible to see, by means of binoculars, that there across the canal the Egyptians were making preparations.

The officers and soldiers of the ramparts who watched the enemy's preparations from their blockhouses continued to warn Israel of the danger. No one listened. The general staff said it was only maneuvers they saw. Sadat didn't want war. He wasn't even capable of making war. He was bluffing.

When war broke out simultaneously on two fronts, that of Syria and that of Egypt, the members of the general staff revealed themselves to be the ones incapable, incapable of handling the situation that suddenly confronted them. They conducted themselves hardly better than our own general staff in 1940, obstinately refusing to recognize their errors.

When Ben Gurion created *Tsahal*, he intended it to be apolitical. At Sde Boker, in the Negev kibbutz where

---

"shield and sword" effect. In 1970 Israel expended over one hundred million dollars to redo the entire line to resist any possible artillery attacks, with the first line of strongholds backed up by a second line six miles farther inland. The defense plan in part was that if tanks were strategically placed on firing ramps between the fortifications, they could repel an attack of fifteen hundred enemy tanks. When the Egyptians attacked, however, on October 6, 1973, the major part of the armored divisions was not in position between the strongholds, and the enemy bypassed and isolated the strongholds. (Translator's note.)

he'd withdrawn among the roses, he said to me, "Insofar as we are Jews, we are greatly given to endless discussions and Byzantinism. In our country, which is permanently menaced by her neighbors, we have to have a force that is above all parties."

Israel had forgotten that elementary principle.

After the Six Day War, the general staff politicized itself under the influence of Dayan and Golda Meir. Generals were no longer chosen according to their abilities, but according to whether they belonged to the party in power. They became sluggish in the comfort of their hierarchies, no longer living and working in tents, but in air-conditioned houses and offices. Thus it was that Sharon's division was isolated and that Bar Lev, who hadn't the requisite qualities for the job, became, alongside Dayan, the one responsible for the army. Dayan spread himself too thin and let those victories he attributed to himself, or that were attributed to him, go to his head. His downfall was only going to be that much crueler.

The Israeli army had ceased to be a manageable grouping of commandos and had become instead a cumbersome machine equipped with sophisticated weaponry furnished by the Americans, upon whom Israel had grown closely dependent.

Take for example the Phantoms delivered to Israel by the United States. When the pilots of *Tsahal* found the Syrian and Egyptian SAM rockets coming upon them like flocks of pigeons, they suddenly realized that their planes were missing the electronic gadget that would have permitted them to deflect the ground-to-air rockets.

The Americans were happy enough to supply Israel with the planes, but intended to control the unfolding of the war and the advance of Sharon's troops, which encircled an Egyptian army and menaced Cairo. The United States did not want a third Israeli victory.

The Syrians on the Golan Heights and the Egyptians in the Sinai, having nothing to oppose them but a screen of troops and equipped with ultramodern weapons, could in no time at all have swept aside the Israelis. Dayan and Bar Lev, who didn't believe the war could happen, demonstrated their inability to improvise a riposte. The high command was no better. It was then that Israeli soldiers, a sergeant, a lieutenant, a colonel here, a general of the reserves there, took it upon themselves without orders to decide upon certain maneuvers—very nervy ones. For example, to cross the Suez Canal, which was for all practical purposes fully at the disposition of the Egyptians, who'd already installed themselves the full length of the Israeli banks. Or equally, despite month-old orders to the contrary by a command that hadn't foreseen an attack by the Syrians, to abandon certain threatened support points, to fall back almost to the peaks dominating the great kibbutzes of Galilee, in order to let the Syrians attenuate their lines before counterattacking them with very inferior forces. Also to concentrate themselves on given points, where they could divide the enemy's armored brigades before annihilating them one after the other.

Amid all this confrontation of tanks on the ground and high-speed battle in the skies, the MiGs, the Mirages, and the Phantoms spitting fire and pursued by SAM rockets, in all this delirium of machine and electronics, individual merit and fighting qualities were going to win out over both technology and numbers— perhaps, as I've said, for the last time.

By his own initiative the *Tsahal* soldier restored a desperate situation. He was able to do so because his intelligence hadn't been obscured by discipline, by perpetual submission, because his reflexes were quick, because he didn't have to lose any time ceaselessly appealing to higher authorities, which he'd had to do without finally in any case.

Meanwhile Dayan, after his pitiful press conference, avoided all journalists, he who knew so well how to make use of them; and in her kitchen old Golda wandered helplessly among her overturned casseroles.

Israel is another Sparta. Each casualty is a dramatic loss. Each victory costs her more and more dearly. Whereas the Arabs don't need to count their dead and can renew their assaults indefinitely, even leaving their dead by the thousands to mummify in the sands of the deserts.

And the Arabs have the arms. Oil has given them more money in one year than the Jews have received since the founding of Israel: in 1974 the revenue from Arab oil was forty billion dollars, while the Jews have received twelve billion dollars since they became a nation.

In such a situation as that, of what import is it that the intelligence quotient of the Egyptian or Syrian soldier is way below that of the Israeli soldier and that his training is mediocre? He was motivated too. He wanted to wash away the shame of the Six Day War, and this time he was determined not to be dishonored.

After the Yom Kippur War, Israel went from triumphalism to despondency and rancor. As they did under the Nazis, they began to see themselves wearing the yellow star. They were condemned at the United Nations as colonialists, imperialists, and racists, and they were excluded from UNESCO.

Their crime: they were unlucky in their timing. Arriving in Palestine in the wake of the English, it was their misfortune to come too late upon the scene.[91] And after Yom Kippur they weren't strong enough, numerous enough, weren't sufficiently supported from outside by satellite parties to be able, like Russia, to defy international opinion.

The U.S.S.R. occupies a part of Poland, of Germany, of the Baltic countries: Latvia, Lithuania, Estonia. She directly controls the governments of East Germany,

91. The fifty-or-so-year-old Zionist movement was beginning to be questioned internationally when the first Zionists reached Palestine. By then, too, another nationalist movement, that of the Arabs, was ready to oppose them. (Translator's note.)

Bulgaria, Czechoslovakia, Hungary, and Poland, indi-
rectly that of Finland.

No one says anything. The Jews annexed Jerusalem,
and the entire world rose up against her. Her people
were victims of an epoch, of the cowardice of the Occident, who had let the Jews embark on their adventure
and had not backed them up. They are also victims of
their own contradictions. At least twenty-four percent
of the Israelis do not believe in Jehovah, but remain
subject to the dictates of their rabbis. They may marry
only among Jews and must have a religious ceremony,
may eat only kosher foods (nearly inedible, except for
breakfast), and must abide by certain anachronistic in-
terdictions. All of this makes for a particularly painful
kind of intolerance in a land which in everything else
is authentically democratic, the only democracy in the
Near East except for Libya, which is going to die.

The Islamic countries are foreign to us. They seem to
be another kind of civilization, and for that reason you
can come to tolerate the forbidding of alcohol and of
pork. While in Israel, a country not at all exotic, where
you feel at home, where you sense an occidental solidarity, such conduct, such intolerance, is a shock. An
example of Rabbinical stupidity made of me, for the
week it took me to calm my resentment, a convinced
anti-Zionist:

Two years ago my wife and I were in Israel's Lod
Airport waiting for a plane to Paris. Since it was Pass-
over and there wasn't a restaurant open anywhere, my
wife had carried along two sandwiches purchased the
day before in an Arab city. She took one out and bit
into it. Such general indignation! We had dared, in a
public place, during Yom Kippur, to eat something
unkosher. We protested to no avail whatever that we
were not Jews. Suddenly we understood the Biblical
stoning of the adulterous woman. If there'd been a
heap of stones in the waiting room, we'd have been
likewise punished. With each step I took in Israel, I,
who recognized no church, felt myself to be more and

more a Christian; for this is a country that makes you feel the need to take up again all the old beliefs you thought you'd jettisoned.

Once we were at the bar at the Hilton, again during holy week, and I asked for a Scotch. I was told, "Impossible. Scotch isn't kosher."

"Then we can't have anything to drink?"

"Yes, Israeli gin or Israeli whiskey."

Both of which are undrinkable—but kosher.

The real reason for this fierce attachment to a dead God seems to me to be evident. The only right the Jews, so many of whom are not Semites, have to claim Israel as uniquely their country is that it remains for them their "Promised Land."

Who promised it to them? God. If he doesn't exist, their claim is based on nothing.

According to a recent thesis, the Palestinians, those of the country, the land, are the only authentic descendants of the Hebrews. Had they remained where they were, they'd have converted to Christianity or to Islam in order to keep their lands. If this thesis is correct, you arrive at this paradox: the Jews, who are largely not Semites, make use of that promise of a God in whom they no longer believe to install themselves in Palestine and to chase authentic descendants of the Hebrews from lands they never left.[92]

In the creation of Israel and the annexation of Jerusalem may be found the germ of all possible wars: holy, racial, political, economic, social, civil, international—tomorrow perhaps atomic. Because of Israel there rose

92. According to P. Alem (*Jews and Arabs, 2,000 years of History*, Grasset), there has never been a Jewish race; the myth was created by anti-Semites and by the Nazis.

The Ashkenazim are originally from Europe and are a mixture of Khazars, Touranians, Anatolians, Slavs, and Teutons. The Sephardim are a mixture of Palestinians (Hebrews, Canaanites, Edomites), Phoenicians, Arabs, and Berbers. The Palestinians are a mixture of races, but the Hebrew element is the most important. The last Hebrews of the Israeli religion disappeared from the Holy Land after the crusades and the Tartar raids.

up one more time from out of the depths of the mysterious, obscure, and bloody history of the Middle East sects like that of the Haschischins, who were put to use by the Syrian and the Russian secret services.

As I told you, the Fedayin never did succeed in creating a Maquis in the territories occupied by Israel, or in Jordan, or in Gaza. As large as their divisions were, they were never able to form a government in exile recognized by all the resistance movements, let alone the United Nations, which is ready to recognize anyone. Then, too, the Palestinian organizations were turning in the direction of another form of action—terrorism—that contagious disease which is spreading over the entire world.

Our word assassin comes from the Haschischins, the eaters of haschisch. The sect is officially Moslem, though that no longer appears to be significant to the present members. Its founder was the Persian Hassan Sabah, childhood friend of Omar Khayam. He set himself up in an impregnable castle at Kasvin, from where he planned to rule the world by crime and political assassination. Under the influence of haschisch or opium, his faithful followers, his Fedayin, believed they'd glimpsed paradise in the magnificent gardens of the fortress, and to be able to return there they killed all those designated by their master.

Throughout several centuries, the Haschischins led reigns of terror in Persia, Syria, Libya, and even among the crusaders. The modern assassins aren't drugged on hash anymore, but are conditioned by incessant political propaganda, by an intensive program whose leitmotiv is "revolution." The precise sense of the word is carefully guarded for them, as are the goals of the revolution, in order to preserve all the magic of that word in their minds.

There are other drugs: despair, hatred, inaction, and tedium are prevalent in the Palestinian refugee camps. I visited several of them in Libya and in Jordan. One is ready to do anything at all to get out of them, especially if one is young.

The Haschischins form an immense international organization with the Baader group in Germany, the Red Army in Japan, the Italian anarchists, the French leftists, the Dutch provos, the members of the provisional I.R.A. in Ulster. And everywhere they indulge in violence, murder, the taking of hostages, the hijacking of planes. At Lod it was the Japanese who massacred the innocent Puerto Rican pilgrims. At the Olympic games it was the Palestinians who killed the Israeli athletes. And at Paris it was Venezuelan or Cuban "diplomats."

They have enormous funds at their disposal. They are often formally trained in Libyan or Syrian camps, in Cuba, and behind the iron curtain. But they're all dedicated to the Palestinian resistance.

In reality, they are concerned with much more than Palestine. Gorged on propaganda, they want a worldwide revolution and the end of a civilization. While in the upper echelons they no longer dream of anarchy, but of order, of power, of influence, and of preparing the way for those who could become the masters of a new and great occidental empire: the sons of Peter the Great and of Joseph Stalin. Just as the Syrian assassins of old dreamed and waited for leaders among the Templers, who on their part dreamed of becoming the world's masters through money.

Thanks to the immunities they enjoy and to the innumerable complicities at their disposal, the Palestinian terrorists and their allies have instituted a new kind of war. It's a fully metastasized worldwide cancer. You know the symptoms by now: taking hostages (often children), kidnapping, murders, bombs exploding planes in mid-flight. Innocent people have become fair game because of the color of their skins, because of their religions, the political systems to which they belong.

You remember when the Palestinians burned three large jets of different airlines, American and European, in the Jordanian desert. The planes were the symbol of the high technology of the Occident, of its science, its wealth, and at the same time its weakness. They made an *auto da fé*. They were burning us and our civilization in those costly effigies.

George Habache, one of the foremost leaders of the new sect of assassins, a doctor like Che and as sick as Che was, a Christian before he discovered Marxism, was preparing to blow up the Hotel Jordan and with it all the journalists inside it. To everyone who wished to dissuade him from his project, such as the French ambassador, to all those who told him that what he proposed was worse than a crime, but a grave error in judgment, because some of those journalists approved his actions, he never ceased to repeat, "God will recognize his own." He is like Simon de Montfort, who roasted the entire population of a city without ascertaining whether they were Christians or Albigensians.

That was to be a black September in Jordan. King Hussein's tanks fired on the wretched huts of the Palestinian refugees. Beirut, heedless and charming capital of the commercial ports of the Levant, so proud of its palaces, its banks, its buildings, its nightclubs, but which allowed miserable refugee camps to be built at its gates, collapsed in flames. The sect had decided it was expendable.

I was there again yesterday. Beirut—amused and confounded by all the mundanities of that other time, the receptions one could attend every evening, first here and then there, always with the same astonishment and the same pleasure. The petrodollars of the shieks and the emirs poured through the nightclubs and the casinos. And the girls came from the four corners of the world and adorned themselves with their spoils. Today when you cross a barricade, you must show your identity card, on which is inscribed your religion. You are Christian and I am Moslem, so I kill you. You are Moslem and I am a Christian Falangist, and with a burst of fire I dispatch you to the paradise of your Allah. They tell the following story:

An automobile driver was stopped at one of the barricades held by the Moslems. He was asked to show his identity card. Fearfully he drew it out. His religion: Protestant.

"What do we do with this one?" asked the militia-man of his chief. "What's a Protestant?"

The chief thought, then said, "Let him go. He's one of our allies. The Protestants are those who are killing the Maronites in Ireland."

Adieu, Beirut. How I loved the bar of the Saint Georges, the small seafood restaurants on the shore, the decadent charm of those gatherings where the women all closely watched one another and came to whisper in an ear, "That dress isn't Dior. She had an Armenian dressmaker run up a copy." Interminable card parties and backgammon parties. Georges Chehade, hardly having received his royalties, played blackjack in the shining gaming temple which was the casino; and when he'd lost everything, he contemplated the sea and composed a new and very beautiful poem which he recited to me as we stood facing the sea.

The Syrians of Assad and the Palestinians of Arafat are going to take the city, carrying with them their fanaticism and their *tristesse*. Beneath the ruins of the great hotels, corpses rot.

We've taken several turns about the dance floor with war, to the sound of different musics and in many different countries. I've tried to show you the danger there is in her ability always to renew herself, in her vivid imagination. Once Clausewitz wrote of her: "She is a chameleon."

I especially wanted to show you how not to be taken in by her, how not to fall into her trap of distinguishing between just wars one is allowed to wage and unjust wars one must condemn. War is war!

You might well say that vis-à-vis war, I've adopted a simplistic attitude myself. But I was necessarily confined in my books and in my articles to speak of those who had to undergo war, had to wage war, without concerning myself with whether their cause was good or bad. Besides, what is good and what is bad changes so!

When you live with an army, as I've done, when you accompany into combat, up to death, those individuals who show themselves to you without masks, men more or less courageous, men who waver and who hope, men who dream as anyone might of an F4 or of a shanty in Normandy, but who are going to pay with their blood, with their fatigue, men who feel isolated, lost, who need your sympathy, you can only sympathize with them and be their friend—even if you do not espouse their cause. And more often than not, they don't have a cause. They just obey.

I loved those soldiers who fought in Italy, in France, in Indochina, in Algeria, and so I was taken to be a Fascist. To speak of war as I do, to uncover her secrets and her methods, is to be a Fascist. What am I, really? Like many another person, I'm changeable and varied: a man of order who provokes disorder, a misogynist who can't do without women, an anarchist who knows that anarchy is impossible. But my travels, my wars, my prisons have taught me that the only thing that counts in this world is freedom. Even before justice. If in certain circles in France I'm thought to be a rightist, in Portugal I'm considered Marxist for having written *Les Centurions,* and in the United States I'm called a liberal because of *Tambours de bronze.* May I not be just a free being?

Am I a racist? I prefer certain peoples to others. I've a weakness for Asiatics because of the way they behave, the way they reason. And they're atheists. If they practice religions, they're religions without God, as Buddhism is. They've never waged religious wars of extermination as people do under Christianity and Islam.

Could humanity survive a single day in a universe where war was excluded? War has enabled me to earn a living through some of my books and articles, but I don't like war. War bores me. It disturbs me. It disgusts me. It's a piece of rank stupidity, and those who make war, whose profession it is to prepare for war and to wage war, those who know it best, also know its rank stupidity—more than anyone else they know it.

I frown on attempts to conjure war away by some magic formula: "Abracadabra, by Christ and by Karl Marx and by Buddha, there will never again be war."

Magic just won't work. To defend ourselves against it, to limit its proliferation, we must apply the same treatment to it that we'd apply to cancer, because war is a cancer. We should apply everything at our disposal: the surgeon, the physician, X rays, the cobalt bomb, chemistry, psychosomatics. We should work to cure it without ever letting up, and even should peace appear to be established. Behind every peace, a war is being prepared. War remains an abscess that must come to a head at the surface of the globe.

Be modest; tell yourself you can't suppress war forever, because it is too horrible, too absurd. With care we can only prolong peace as much as possible, as we can, with care, prolong life.

Think back. When were wars the least bloody? During the time of fortified castles with their crenelated walls and ironclad knights. Compare our fine era of social progress with those centuries of the Dark Ages. Those were the centuries of peace. Compare the inquisition of craftsmen with our great scientific extermination enterprises, such as the Gulags of Stalin and the death camps of Hitler.

Such peace as those ages knew was possible thanks to the Holy Church. It was forbidden to fight from Sunday to Monday (the truce of God) and during certain great festivals—Christmas, Easter, the Assumption—both during the period of their celebration and for a prescribed number of days afterwards. It was also forbidden to fight during Lent.

It was forbidden to involve women, children, clergymen, artisans, peasants, anyone who was not immediately involved in the conflict, anyone not profes-

sionally engaged to bear arms. Before a man was
knighted he had to swear on his sword to protect the
widow and the orphan, to be faithful in combat, not to
lie or deceive. If his enemy asked for quarter, it was a
crime to kill him. The prisoner had to be well treated,
even invited to the table if he could play a good game
of chess or play agreeably upon the viol d'amore. The
Pope had gone so far as to prohibit small private wars
between petty nobles where their peasants would pay
the heaviest price, because such wars often began with
the burning of the enemy's crops. But there the Pope
was not fully successful, wanting to go too far, too fast.

To calm the overgenerous blood of the men of that
time, to keep them busy—because boredom has always
been a breeding ground for war—tournaments were
invented and the hunt was codified. Tracking the running stag and hunting the hare with the falcon became
complicated and intricate. One had to know to perfection all the rituals of the hunt, had to learn its precise
language. Especially if one had the leisure time in
which he might otherwise have waged war.

There were no mass confrontations, no carnages. Verdun had to wait for a later day when war became a big
business, when it was no longer necessary for the soldier to furnish his own armor and steed, when the state
took it upon herself to furnish all the material of war.
Go back a little in the history of mankind, and it was
the Chinese who first simulated war in order to avoid
having to wage it. Confucius said, "A good general is a
general who hates war."

Said Sun Tzu, who lived two thousand years before
Clausewitz and was his master, "War should be waged
to inflict the least possible pain and with the least possible cost to humanity. It should inflict upon the enemy
the fewest possible casualties. . . . Military action
should not have as its objective the annihilation of the
enemy's army or the destruction of its cities and lands.
. . . Weapons should be resorted to only if there exists
no other solution."

Chinese generals of the *Haute Epoque* disposed their troops about the terrain like pieces on a vast chessboard. Then they called them all together, each leader giving an account of the position of his battalions, of their number, of their value, and of their armaments.

Each in turn had to describe the maneuver he considered to be the most effective, describe how he would employ his archers and his cavalry, detail his overall tactics and how he'd respond to particular initiatives of the adversary. Then the judges decided which party was the victor. The vanquished retired from the field and the victors occupied it, without one drop of blood having been spilled. Out of that highly civilized conception were born the great games: chess, go, even checkers.

Konrad Lorenz describes for us how wild geese avoid fighting. They've developed a ritual of combat that involves striking certain attitudes, using certain gestures, certain aggressive positions, without ever going too far. We have become worse than the dumb beasts. Even the wolves are more civilized than we. Do you know what happens when two wolves fight? As soon as it becomes apparent to one that he is the weaker, that he will lose, he extends his throat to the other as a sign of submission. The victor understands and never kills the other, who turns away, tail down, but alive. Among men we move immediately into mortal combat, to the extermination of the vanquished, civilians, women, and children included. Even if their only crime is that they're found on the side of the losers.

Do you want an example? Shall I tell you what's happening today in Cambodia?[93] I read to you from *Le Monde,* a newspaper kindly disposed to all those in the Third World who want revolution. Listen well to the program of the Khmers *rouges:*

93. "Cambodia, Nine Months Later," Francois Pouchard (*Le Monde,* February 18, 1976).

A democratic Cambodia must be constructed upon a wholly new foundation . . . to rebuild the new Cambodia a million men are sufficient. There is no more need for the prisoners of war (the population deported in 1975) which have been left entirely at the absolute discretion of the local chiefs.

Before war reached her, Cambodia counted 7,540,000 inhabitants. Six hundred thousand were killed in the war, and eight hundred thousand during the deportation of the population afterwards. There remain then five million people to liquidate to build the new Cambodia. "This is a terrible assertion," continues the journalist, "everyone would prefer to believe is exaggerated. But for anyone who has carefully followed the course of the Khmer revolution, it is not, alas! unbelievable."

An important part of the gross national product of all the world is actually in the manufacture or the planning of new arms. Wars of the distant past needed only small budgets. An entire regiment dressed in fine suits decorated with gilt and with matching plumed hats cost less to outfit than a Mirage, MiG, or a Phantom, with all the requisite ground infrastructure. And a party of knights dressed in coats of mail and equipped with armor cost less than a T.56 tank with its infrared sighting instruments.

And today's costly material is quickly outdated. Cannons are no longer used. Armies want only tanks with teleguided missiles. The electronic sight? Take it away. There is now the laser.

The poor idiot black king or Arab sheik who hasn't the very latest weapons of war feels himself to be seedy, second-rate. He'll bleed his country to death to have the most recent model of an A.M.X., an S.S. 11, or a Mirage fresh out of the factory. He'll let his people go without essential food to be up to date in modes of war.

War monopolizes all scientific budgets. Medicine, science, technology all take second place to war.

The greatest discoveries of our century are linked to war. Without war, would sufficient sums have been raised to discover how to split the atom? Would the rockets that can put man on the moon have been invented? Certainly not. War hasn't only her retinue of poets going back to Homer; she fascinates and attracts all the greatest minds of the world, those who view her not only as a calamity but as a source of progress. Humanity will continue to progress from war to war.

Joseph de Maistre:

> Mankind is charged with slaughtering mankind. The entire blood-steeped earth is an altar where everything that lives must be endlessly immolated, without measure, until all evil is exterminated, until the death of death.

Or Victor Cousin:

> War is nothing but a bloody exchange of ideas, and a battle won is nothing but the victory of today's truth over tomorrow's. When the idea of a people has run its span, those people disappear, and it's well that they do disappear. But they don't give up their place without resistance. Out of that resistance comes war.

War fascinated even Kant:

> A long peace makes predominant the spirit of profit, of cowardice, of effeminacy. War on the other hand is something exalting in itself. As dangers grow greater and courage becomes more necessary, she raises a people's spirit enough to more than meet the need.

And Hegel:

> It's in war that the state attains its highest accomplishment.

And Proudhon, father of humanist socialism:

Wolves and lions, no more than do sheep and beavers, do not make war among themselves. For a long time people have used that observation to denigrate our own species. How is it we haven't seen that on the contrary precisely there is the sign of our grandeur? That we haven't wondered whether it isn't possible nature has especially made man alone an industrious and warlike animal, without which qualities we'd immediately sink to the level of the beasts? Salute to war! It is through her that mankind lifted himself a little up out of the mud which was his womb, and she that calls forth his majesty and bravery. The streams of blood, the fratricidal carnages horrify our philanthropists, but I'm afraid their flabbiness can only bring about the freezing of our very virtue.

The struggle against war demands a slow, difficult labor and much humility. I doubt that intellectuals with their fragility and their conceit can bring it off. They try to conjure war away in the fashion of priests by the use of formulas and then are trapped by her because they understand her so little, don't realize she's like Proteus and can even take on the appearance of peace.

Utopians will tell you that we must begin by forbidding war, by making it against the law. Why not forbid as well old age, disease, death? With as much effect. We had thought to create an international force that would intervene in all conflicts and by war prohibit war. It sent some of us to Korea to fight under the blue flag of the United Nations, and we were looked on as representatives of peace in the world. I no longer know who proposed that before declaring war, every government must allow the entire population to decide on that war in a national referendum. It seems quite normal and just that those who are going to have to live through a war should be the ones to decide on it. Alas! That suggestion didn't make allowances for one of the great mutations of our time: the importance of the hold the mass media have on our daily lives, their influence on all our actions. Television and radio allow any government that controls them cleverly to, so to speak, rape the people—to condition an entire nation, to make the people accept, even demand, a war.

Listen to the Moroccan radio or the Algerian radio.

Wouldn't it be possible for us to limit, as they did in the Middle Ages, the ravages of war, to codify it, to clip its wings? But who's going to do it? There isn't a real church anymore, and the Congress of Peace operates exclusively for the other side of the iron curtain, where they actively prepare for war, the good war, that which will bring peace. Prohibit war films, war books, destroy the history manuals of Mallet and Isaac, all those which deal with war? That would only make it all the more fascinating.

Apparently the only positive way to limit war is through terror. The fear of the atomic bomb alone has hindered nuclear wars. War doesn't dare blow up our planet. Where would she go to live?

I see only one acceptable remedy: that we do not any longer deceive ourselves about war, that we tell as much as we have come to know of her as eyewitnesses, without glossing anything over.

We've all seen how easy it is to deceive ourselves about the past, how we sweep under the rug, as a bad housekeeper does the dust, the memory of our disappointments, of checkmates of our best endeavors, of all our mistakes, in order to recall our successes. The same thing happens with the memories of war. You only remember the moments of friendship, of great pub crawls, of drinking sprees, of cities taken, and of willing girls. But you sweep under the carpet the wounded who howl their lives away with gaping belly wounds, the fatigue, the exhausting marches, the idiotic orders, the even more stupid counterorders, the disorder, the mess, the lost time, the wasted energy. And the despair you carry with you everywhere as you contemplate the immense stupidity that is war and that resolves nothing.

Remember your fear, your panic. Have you forgotten

them? You're stretched out with your head on a stone, badly protected from the rain by your poncho. You know that in three hours you have to attack and that you haven't much of a chance of coming through with a whole skin. Your stomach is knotted, you're sweating, you feel like pissing forever. Your body wants no more of the agony and abuse you've inflicted on it. It has only one desire: to let you fall and to lie curled up in a hole somewhere. It hates you. You try to overcome the weakness you're ashamed of. And, indeed, you manage to do it, because you're in the grip of the system, caught up in its toils, and honor is forced on you by your fear of the gendarmes. But you still can't get rid of the bitter taste in your mouth, and your stomach continues to heave, to the point where, though you're dying of hunger, you can't so much as swallow.

And the other fear, the worse one, that of the spirit. Do you remember that? When you say to yourself, "In just a few hours I'll perhaps slide off the edge of life into a great void." You've nothing to which you can cling. You lost your faith a long time ago, faith in God and faith in mankind. You're going to disappear, and with you that little bit of a universe you've clumsily and with great hardship scrabbled together to your measure and according to your changing tastes. You're twenty years old, thirty years old, you have a crazy desire for beaches, for mountains, for girls, for friendships; you have your own little idea of how to re-make the world and how to reorganize your future. But there's no more time. The last grains of sand in the hourglass have just run through. You're going to place your entire welfare, your life, in the hands of chance, to go and fight with grenades and machine guns with individuals like yourself who are generally your own age, who experience the same fears, who have undergone the same suffering. Then you reach the place where you say to yourself, "Shit, after all! Advance!"

Forget the crowds that acclaimed you as a victor in Alsace, the old farmer who embraced you because you'd liberated his few acres of land. Remember instead those moments before dawn and the beginning of the attack. It is four o'clock in the morning and you lie hidden, waiting for the thrush to finish his song. It is the hour when once you returned from your grand rounds of the bars where, by the magic of alcohol, you gathered up all those marvelous acquaintances, like the many fish out of the miraculous one fish. Or the hour when you left a girl you'd loved for the first time and in whom you believed you'd found the true, eternal, moving face of love.

Many memories crowd in on you at that moment, more than you can grasp, and they are always images of peace. But all of a sudden war takes you brutally by the shoulder. Forward, poor fool! The night is disappearing, but the day hasn't yet come. Everything is blurred; you're confused. The shadows move. The bushes are the enemy creeping up on you. Danger is everywhere. It's the hour at which they awaken those men in their cells who are condemned to death. And you are one of them. You don't spring gallantly to advance or leap to the charge to the sound of the trumpet, as they do in the picture books.

You proceed slowly, heavily, after having thrown away your last cigarette. You move first through a zone defended by friendly troops. Everything is fine so far. But all of a sudden the enemy artillery begins to pound. You're on the alert, ready to seek shelter, to jump into the nearest ditch. You reach the mortar zone, first the 80s, then the 60s, which make a particular characteristic sound, a whistling as they pass through the air and then a horrible noise of breaking dishes as they pass directly over your head. You're now within reach of the infantry weapons, and you fall flat wherever you can; you slip from cover to cover until you reach the point of "contact." You pack yourself into a hole in the ground, a protective hole from which you must nevertheless tear yourself away to expose yourself to the bullets and the grenades of the other side. And the others, whom you suddenly begin to detest, are only silhouettes you can hardly see at all. You see just the brief gleam of light off an automatic weapon, a sight that glues you to the ground, or off the grenade that speeds to seek you out. When it is over and you have either won or lost the battle, when you take stock of the fact that you are neither dead nor wounded, when you feel that exaltation such a moment brings of having pulled it off, whatever it was you had to do, when you believe like the old Aztec warriors that by all that spilled blood you've helped the sun to be reborn, when you recover your reason and become a man again, you suddenly understand just how much you've been had! This is what you must remember of war. This *is* war.

Do you want another story? I didn't experience it, but Pierre Schoendorffer told me about it. He even filmed it. Unfortunately you'll never see it on film, though. It's buried at the back of a bunker at Fort d'Ivry, where, carefully hidden, are all those things that might give us the true picture of war. He was a cameraman in Indochina for the army's cinematographic service. He followed an infantry unit on an operation into the brush in Thailand, among the deep grass and the elephants. Suddenly the Viets let loose phosphorous incendiary shells upon their rear. The grass blazed and the soldiers began to go up in flames like torches. Schoendorffer, who'd been filming the advance of the front of the column just a few minutes earlier, returned to the rear. He had the burning soldiers in his camera sight. He rolled the film, hardly realizing the full horror of the situation until one of the burning lads found the strength and the courage to raise his hand and give a small sign of farewell.

And again war is the glazed eyes of that young girl of fifteen whom two filthy beasts had just raped. It was in the Black Forest in Germany. I came upon her after the act. She didn't even cry. She was like a bound animal waiting to be slaughtered.

Do you know where war is happy, where she dreams her best dreams? In the military burial vaults, in the long uniform lines of wooden crosses, in the charnel houses, in the monuments to the dead which disfigure the least of our villages.

War is that beautiful sergeant of twenty with a bullet in the vertebral column who, at Val-de-Grâce, was tied to a star-shaped steel apparatus which could be turned in circles. Every two hours he was turned, one time head in the air, the next time head at the bottom, in order that his flesh not rot, his limbs not die, while he still lived. Until that day when he'd had enough and asked to be allowed to die all at once. It was of me that he begged to be permitted to die.

If you want, let's speak of something other than war. Do you want me to tell you how beautiful autumn is in the Aigonal, when the mushrooms push up through the moss and the forests take on all the colors from purple to old gold, when you listen for the first trills of the thrushes? Or of springtime in Provence, when spring is still new and fragile and the almond and peach trees are beginning to blossom? All of a sudden there winds through the air the powerful odor of sap, which changes the laughter of young girls. They linger along the terraces of the cafés, where the boys are playing cards and exchanging curses as they remember that Beziers defeated Montferrand at rugby. You'd like that I speak to you of the pleasure and the peace you experience while you wait for the break of day at your ease alone at the helm of a sailing ship, propped between the mast and the wheel, above you the planet Venus by which you steer your course, the first star to appear and the last to disappear, in your ears no sound but the whispering of the wind in the lines, behind you nothing but the long gray waves that seem to be following you?

And if we begin to forget war? Is it possible the same thing will happen as happened with the ancient gods, who simply ceased to exist when men no longer wished to believe in them, to worship them?